Praise for *Carrie Kills A Man*

"This was…quite a read. HIGHLY recommend. Moving & funny!"
– **Patton Oswalt**

"*Carrie Kills a Man* is a funny, insightful and highly relatable account of navigating the choppy waters of starting again when you thought you knew who you were. Carrie not only takes us through the intricacies of coming out as trans, but also invites us to see where our experiences align with hers, deftly puncturing the divisive rhetoric that often dominates this topic. Charming, warm and thoughtful in equal measure."
– **Heather Parry, author of *Orpheus Builds A Girl***

"Carrie Marshall invites us into her world and does not hold back. This memoir is humorous, harrowing, heartfelt and ultimately healing. Carrie powerfully reflects on both what one can lose by choosing to honour their truest self, but more importantly what she has gained. This book is an act of love and defiance against all the noise and bigotry clouding stories centred in power, love and truth. Long may such lives flourish!"
– **Andrés N. Ordorica, author of *At Least This I Know***

Published by 404 Ink
www.404Ink.com
@404Ink

All rights reserved © Carrie Marshall, 2022.

The right of Carrie Marshall to be identified as the Author of this Work has been asserted by her in accordance with the Copyright, Designs and Patent Act 1988.

No part of this publication may be reproduced, distributed, or transmitted, in any form or by any means, electronic, mechanical, photocopying, recording, or otherwise, without first obtaining the written permission of the copyright owner, except for the use of brief quotations in reviews.

Please note: All references within endnotes were accessible and accurate as of May 2022 but may experience link rot from there on in. 404 Ink is not responsible for the content within linked third parties.

Editing: Kirstyn Smith
Proofreading: Heather McDaid
Cover design: Wolf Murphy-Merrydew
Typesetting: Laura Jones
Co-founders and publishers of 404 Ink:
Heather McDaid & Laura Jones

Print ISBN: 9781912489558
Ebook ISBN: 9781912489565

Printed and bound in Great Britain by Clays Ltd, Elcograf S.p.A.

404 Ink acknowledges and is thankful for support from Creative Scotland in the publication of this title.

CARRIE KILLS A MAN

A MEMOIR

CARRIE MARSHALL

Introduction: Do you want to know a secret?   1

Part One: Smalltown Boy

Life is a minestrone	7
Goody two shoes	9
Sharp dressed man	19
Been caught stealing	25
We float	33
Girl afraid	39
Transgender dysphoria blues	47
We exist	51
Girls on film	59
Sexy and you know it	63
Crash	67
Love changes everything	71

Part Two: Black Holes and Revelations

Numb	81
Playing video games	85
Nowhere to run	89
Things will never be the same again	93
The act we act	95
I've got the power	101
We are family	107
Cherry Lips	115

Part Three: We Sink

Fa Fa Fa Fa Fashion	125
Shout, shout, let it all out	131

Part Four: Rip It Up and Start Again

Wrecking ball	139
Love and Pride	141
Sexy! No no no	147

Shame shame shame	153
Wildest dreams	157
What's the story?	163
That's not my name	169
Say my name	175
Flip your wig	179
Shake it off	187
Lose yourself	193
Merry Christmas everyone	197

Part Five: What It Feels Like For A Girl

Call me	203
It's just history repeating	207
True Colours	211
Everybody hurts	215
High voltage	219
One day like this	223
The queerest of the queer	225
It's different for girls	231
Suspicious minds	237

Part Six: New Rules

Music makes the people come together	245
Swim till you can't see land	249
Yesterday, when I was mad	253
We live in a political world	261
Burn the witch	267
A nice day to start again	277
That joke isn't funny any more	285
It's the end of the world as we know it	291
Skin feeling	299
We walk with steel in our spines	303
Epilogue	*311*
Acknowledgements	*315*
Endnotes	*317*

CONTENT NOTE

As comes with the territory of writing about being trans, please be aware that transphobia, homophobia, violence and suicidal ideation is discussed throughout *Carrie Kills A Man*, in many ways and levels of detail, across the entire book.

INTRODUCTION

Do you want to know a secret?

Some secrets are butterflies, gossamer-light with translucent wings. If they escape there's barely a flutter; the most they'll disturb is a few motes of dust. But some other secrets are barrels packed with plastic explosive, so unstable and so dangerous that you have to bury them deep and cover them in concrete. If you don't, they'll erupt with so much force that they'll make the dinosaurs' meeting with a meteorite look like a suburban dinner party.

I knew that my secret wasn't a butterfly.

Some boys want to be Batman when they grow up.

I wanted to be Velma from *Scooby-Doo*.

Velma was super-smart, super-serious and sometimes sarcastic. I adored her. In her big glasses, oversized jumper and orange socks, she was irresistibly odd, bookishly beautiful and completely compelling. Daphne may have got all the boys' attention, but Velma was the one who solved the mysteries.

I didn't know that Velma was a lesbian icon back then. I didn't really know what a lesbian was either. All I knew was that there was only one cartoon character I wanted to be, and it wasn't Batman, He-Man or Captain Caveman.

I also knew that I needed to keep that very, very quiet.

In 2016, I had what appeared to be the perfect life. I was married to a beautiful woman. We had two beautiful children. We were living the suburban dream with all that suggests: the black Labrador, the Saab estate, the Jamie Oliver cookbooks in the kitchen and the Oyster Bay in the wine rack.

My secret threw a hand grenade into all of it.

PART ONE

SMALLTOWN BOY

Life is a minestrone

Have you ever made minestrone? It's really simple: some veg, some oil, some stock, a few cloves of garlic, some broken bits of pasta and some beans. As they simmer, the garlic and the veg and the tomatoes fill the air with flavours you can almost taste on your tongue: it's a happy, homely aroma that brings to mind red and white checked tablecloths, bottles of Chianti in wicker baskets and a Gaggia coffee maker spitting steam in the corner. But no matter how many cookbooks I consult, no matter how many overlong online recipes I pore over, no matter how carefully I chop or cook or sauté or simmer, the minestrone I make doesn't taste like the minestrone from the café round the corner or from the little Italian where everything is just like mama used to make.

That's because minestrone is just a simple label for something incredibly complicated, a multi-layered mix of interactions between lots of different things. Even the most delicate deviation can have an enormous effect: a slight change in the ingredients, in the recipe or in the cooking method can completely transform what you end up with.

Conceiving a child is very much like making minestrone.

Not literally. Unless something is very wrong, sex should be considerably more fun and less likely to involve the use of cabbage or kale. But even the most complex recipe is nothing compared to the recipe for people, and as a result there are almost infinite variations in every aspect of our brains and bodies.

Even when people are genetically identical there can be profound differences. We come from the same genetic stock but my brother has dark hair, a strong build and normal feet; I have reddish hair, longer limbs and hammer toes.

Those things make me a beautiful and unique snowflake. Globally, 98% of people don't have red hair. 97% don't have hammer toes.

And, as far as we know, 99% of people aren't transgender.

Transgender is when the gender you know you are, such as man or woman, doesn't match the one you were assigned at birth when the doctor slapped your backside and proclaimed "it's a boy!" or "it's a girl!" Most people are cisgender, which means the doctor's initial impression was correct. But doctors don't always get it right. With my brother and I, they only had a 50% success rate. He's cisgender, or cis for short. I'm not.

I don't know why my recipe was subtly different to my brother's. Maybe it's genetic; maybe it's hormonal; maybe it's chromosomal; maybe it's more than one of those things or something else entirely. Maybe something didn't kick in when it was supposed to kick in, or maybe it didn't kick as hard as it should, or maybe I was more kick-resistant than most.

Whatever the explanation, I ended up with a body that didn't quite match who I am, a biological soup that wasn't quite what I ordered. And because I'm British, I didn't complain and I was too scared to send it back.

Hi. I'm Carrie.

Goody two shoes

I wasn't born in the wrong body. I was born on the wrong planet.

Where other kids at my school obsessed over football, I was more interested in far-flung galaxies, space travel and sci-fi stories. I spent a lot of time daydreaming about them or staring in awe at the fantastic worlds and skyscraper-sized spaceships on the cover of sci-fi books. There was absolutely no doubt in my mind: I was going to be an astronaut.

Astronauts care little for earthly things, so instead of the on-trend Adidas satchels my classmates proudly wore I'd rock up to primary school with one of my dad's old plastic briefcases full of model space rockets – a look that attracted the odd bit of negative attention and quite a lot of bemusement. I was regarded with some suspicion because I hated sport, talking about sport and being around people who talked about sport, and I couldn't understand why I had to hang around with the boys instead of the girls, who seemed much more interested and interesting.

As if that wasn't enough to make me stand out, I spoke with a different accent, I was new in town and I was younger than my classmates. That was because of my dad's job: he worked for a construction company who moved us down the east coast of Scotland before cutting across to Ayrshire on the west. I'd started off in Inverness and moved down to West Lothian, where I was mocked for having an accent that was too posh; I changed it just in time to move to a different part of Scotland where my accent was now deemed too rough. One of the people who told me this was my next door neighbour, an older boy who wasn't very nice to me but who grew up to be a very nice man. He's my accountant now, but I have a long memory and I never pay his invoices on time.

I wasn't bullied much, though. I'd have the odd parka-pulled-over-the-head encounter with some tiny fists trying to pummel my torso, but they were more like dancing than fighting. I didn't experience anything particularly traumatic: I'd be called "poof" from time to time by people hoping to get a rise out of me, but even then I knew I was very bad at fighting so I didn't rise to the bait. And I quickly found a protector in the form of Davy, a gruff, gentle giant of a boy who befriended me in much the same way you'd rescue a stray dog and who seemed to enjoy my company and my daft jokes. I didn't quite cower behind his legs when I was threatened, but the other boys seemed to understand that if they messed with me, Davy would mess with them. Our friendship wasn't based on that protection — it was more about debating which Madness song was best, swapping comic books and seeing who had the worst jokes; Davy was and is a funny guy — but I don't doubt that if it weren't for Davy I'd have had a much rougher time. If I were from another planet then Davy was the Elliott to my E.T., the friend who helped me navigate a world I didn't understand.

I liked primary school. I came home with consistently glowing school reports, although my teachers despaired at my tendency to talk all the time. One of them, at her wits' end after yet another barrage of questions, locked me in the stationery cupboard to stop me talking. My friends, I'm sure, have frequently felt like doing the same.

Primary school was also where I fell in love with books. I didn't so much read books as inhale them, and according to my teachers, my reading age was double my actual one. Once I left primary school I began borrowing books not just with my own library card, but with my mum and dad's cards too.

I was drawn to horror – Stephen King's *Carrie*, *Christine* and *Salem's Lot*; James Herbert's *The Rats* and *The Fog*; William Peter Blatty's *The Exorcist* – and SF, especially the bleak stuff such as Nevile Shute's *On The Beach* and Ray Bradbury's *Fahrenheit 451*. I also adored wry, funny SF by the likes of Kurt Vonnegut and Douglas Adams, both of whom had a huge influence on my sense of humour and on my writing style too. And I devoured endless crime novels ranging from the Scottish police procedurals of William McIvanney, and later, Ian Rankin, to the often repellent noir of James Ellroy and the macho mafiosi of Mario Puzo's *The Godfather*. I'd take out ten books and finish them inside a week. To this day, I get really uneasy if I don't have at least one unread book at home; I often accumulate vertiginous towers of to-read titles that I can topple in case of emergency.

Books were everything to me. An education – I often mispronounce words because I've never heard them spoken aloud; an adventure, taking me to the faraway galaxies I knew by now I wasn't actually going to visit or showing me horrors that I hoped only existed in the authors' imaginations; and more than anything, an escape. Books were a portal to other worlds, enabling me to escape not just from the outside world but from the cacophony inside my skull.

I can't tell you exactly when I first tried on my mum's heels or a skirt but it was definitely before I went to the big school, so it was several years before puberty. I remember a summer between primary school terms when I saw the family a few doors down playing in their front garden. The girls were a little older than me, and they'd persuaded, forced or bribed their little brother to dress in their clothes for their amusement. I recall seeing him and immediately going red from a mix of envy, embarrassment and confusion.

At home, I'd become fascinated by the women in the Littlewoods catalogue, the late-'70s equivalent of online shopping (and for older boys, the late '70s equivalent of PornHub thanks to its pages of women in bras; the internet wouldn't arrive for many more years). When nobody was around I'd stare at the girl-next-door models and the clothes they were modelling. I remember a very strong feeling of yearning, almost like when you have a huge crush on someone: there was a pull, a feeling that if I could just somehow enter the picture everything would be okay. I wanted to be as elegant and as beautiful as the women in the photographs. I wanted to be as beautiful as my mum, a tall, head-turning blonde who'd turned down the advances of footballer George Best at the height of his fame.

Had I been a cisgender girl, that wouldn't have been a problem: we've all seen the trope of the young girl dressing up in her mum's lipstick, pearls and heels a million times. It's considered cute, because of course it *is* cute, and it can be a beautiful moment for mother and daughter. But it's not considered cute or beautiful when boys want to do it.

I didn't know much at that age, but I knew what the word sissy meant and that it was not something boys should be. But I couldn't stop myself from wanting to see a very different me in the mirror, to feel more like the me I wanted to be. It felt right in a way I couldn't articulate back then: the shiny polyester of an underskirt felt like a shiver against my legs, a sensation unlike anything I'd ever experienced from the clothes I'd worn as a boy, and as I layered up with a work skirt, American tan tights, M&S bra and pants and a plain but fitted blouse the different fabrics would move across each other in subtle, whispering ways. I'd try to keep my balance in too-big shoes, attempting to walk but only managing a stiff shuffle, but if I posed just right I could see my reflection in the mirrored wardrobe and see how the heels made my already long legs even longer. Dressed in everyday workwear I looked and felt like a business class Bambi: cute, unsteady and likely to fall on my arse any second.

Have you ever done the thing where you try something that's above your pay grade – the really expensive facial scrub, the Egyptian cotton bedding with an incredibly high thread count, the birthday money bottle of wine or those huge fluffy bath sheets that you want to live inside and only ever come out of to scavenge for chocolate? That's what female clothes felt like to me: satin sheets after sleeping beneath a scratchy, smelly old blanket.

It made me happy, if just for a short time. And it was always a short time, because I knew that if I got caught it would be the end of the world. I'd dress, totter around the room a bit while looking in the mirror and then carefully put everything back again. The happiness I felt faded fast and was replaced by much stronger, longer-lasting feelings I would become very used to: sadness, self-disgust and shame.

At night, I'd send secret prayers to God. I wanted him to kill me – painlessly in my sleep, because I'm a coward – and bring me back as a girl. He must have been on the other line because despite my best efforts for a very long time, he never did.

I hatched a plan. If God wasn't willing to do it, I'd do it for him. So I decided I'd strangle myself. I'm very glad this was in the pre-internet era, because if it wasn't I'd have googled the best way to kill myself properly – something I have done as an adult. But back then I was young, naive and completely unaware that you can't strangle yourself with your own hands. I gave it a good go, but the best I could manage was to give myself a sore neck and have a bit of a cry.

I remember a school trip to see a pantomime - oh yes I do - and being utterly fascinated by the principal boy, a young woman playing a male character in tights and boots. But my only other memory of gender weirdness from that time is from when my family and I were in Belfast for our annual trip to see our extended family. During one of the many, many house calls we made – I come from a big family – I got to hang out with my favourite cousin, a smart, funny and pretty girl the same age as me. Photos were taken, and when they were finally developed months later I was struck by how similar she and I looked: it's not an exaggeration to say that in that particular photo we looked like identical twins with our round freckled faces and bowl-cut bangs. I remember being fascinated by that photo and dearly wishing I actually was the girl I looked so much like.

I loved doing creative things at school, particularly telling stories, using language and trying to make music. Escapism was a big part of it – I spent most of my days daydreaming. Creative writing and plonking around on instruments I couldn't play were really just opportunities for me to daydream out loud without being yelled at by a teacher – but I also loved being able to express myself without fear of being mocked by the boys. Like many people who don't fit in, I was also quick to learn the power of being funny as a way of being seen without also being slapped.

I liked and I think I was liked by all my teachers bar one, my music teacher, who took an instant dislike to me and told me flatly that I didn't have a musical bone in my body. A few decades later a different adult would tell me that I didn't have a feminine one either. They were both wrong.

My main musical memory was of a day when we were allowed to bring records from home. I don't remember the reason – it was probably an end of term thing, or maybe our teacher fancied himself as one of the cool teachers and saw an opportunity to ingratiate himself with us. Whatever the reason, I persuaded my dad to let me borrow one of his Reader's Digest music compilations, a thick vinyl record in a vivid red sleeve. This was 1980, and one of the discs was a compilation of new wave and post-punk music. My choice of song, XTC's 'Making Plans For Nigel', was played in class and made me cool in the eyes of the other boys for a whole day: they were all into bands like Madness, and the XTC song fitted really well with that. I remember the glow of approval, of feeling like I belonged, of being the person who brought along something cool that the others hadn't discovered yet. My adult friends know that side of me very well: I'm always thrusting books and music links and longreads at the people I love because I want them to be as excited or as happy or as fascinated by those things as I am. Experiencing something is just the beginning for me: it's the sharing of it, especially the sharing of joy, that makes me feel useful and alive and part of the world rather than just a passenger on it.

My love of music continued into secondary school and adulthood; I'm as in love with pop music now as I was back then. My timing was great. The early '80s were a golden era for pop music and for magazines about pop music, which was going through an imperial phase of experimentation and innovation.

The '80s were particularly good if you liked music by artists who messed with gender. I was fascinated by Adam Ant's androgyny, Suzi Quatro's leather, Boy George's femininity, Annie Lennox's masculinity and Phil Oakey's lipstick and asymmetrical haircut. For a few years it seemed that bands couldn't get on TV if the men didn't wear makeup and don tea towels as headwear. I remember being fascinated by Culture Club's debut album *Kissing to Be Clever*, which was in my house because my parents had bought it as a Christmas present for an older cousin. Before it was posted I'd stare intently at the cover, because while I knew Boy George was a man he certainly didn't look like one in the cover photo. He looked fabulous.

There's a trans joke I find bleakly funny: "At school I was bullied for being gay and being a girl. Turns out they were right." I was, and they were. But I didn't realise it at the time.

I started secondary school in the early '80s when I was just ten. I remember it like it were a Ready Brek advert, the orange lining of our dark blue, dark green and black parkas like shards of light through endless shades of grey. In my memories the Ayrshire skies were always the same shade of grey Girvan sea, barely distinguishable from the roughcast council houses below them. I remember really noticing the West of Scotland architecture as Stranraer hove into view on our return ferries from family trips to Belfast, the red bricks of Northern Ireland replaced by roughcast grey, the streets' cascades of cookie-cutter terraces replaced by symmetrical rows of semi-detacheds. On the bus to school in the mornings I'd wipe the condensation off the window using the sleeve of my parka so I could see the rain better, waiting for the giant monochrome and mustard blocks of Garnock Academy to loom out of the murk and announce the dawning of another dull day.

It couldn't have rained all the time, I know. I remember heatwaves when the girls would come into school with the fronts of their legs painfully scarlet, the result of afternoons spent no-SPF sunbathing in lawn chairs when the words "skin cancer" weren't widely spoken. And my memories of being outside school are all very sunny. But the West of Scotland is infamous for its inclement weather and the early '80s were pretty gloomy too, so I'm sure that's coloured my memories: instead of rose-tinted glasses, I see the past through Joy Division ones.

I was moving into secondary school while the valley around me was undergoing its own kind of transition. The car plant in Linwood where some of my friends' dads worked shut down in 1981, the year before I went to secondary school, and the steelworks that employed so many local people and kept everything from the Co-op to the Chinese restaurant in business was in the managed decline that would see it close its doors and suck the life out of the valley in 1985. I remember the year before, when I was twelve, playing on a large patch of green land next to the bypass as Yuill and Dodds trucks with metal grates over their windscreens and heavily scuffed Scania logos thundered past at frightening speeds. They were en route to the Hunterston ore terminal in Largs, a regular convoy set up to try and destroy the miners' strike by bringing in "scab" coal from South Africa and South America. I remember seeing the violent scenes of massed policemen cracking heads on the TV news, shocked that it was happening just ten miles from my house.

★

Starting secondary school at ten is unusually young. Most kids start at 11 or even 12, but I'd completed primary school a year early. That was a hangover from when my family moved about a lot during my earliest school years. When we landed in Ayrshire my parents were given the choice of sending me to a very small school with just a handful of pupils, or to have me skip a year and move into Primary Four in the town's main primary school. They chose the latter, and because my birthday falls just before Christmas I was also in the younger half of the pupil intake when I went to the big school. As if that wasn't enough, God or Strathclyde Regional Council decided to put me in a class with a disproportionate number of unusually big and strong boys, many of whom were two years older and considerably more physically developed than me.

The difference between 10 and 12 may not sound much, but it's enormous. At 10 or 11 you're still a child, and then your body hits the big red button marked puberty and suddenly your voice can't decide which key it's in and all your limbs hurt. And of course, bits of you get bigger and/or grow hairy. That was very much in the future for me, but for many of the other boys it seemed it was already in the past.

I hated and feared them. I particularly hated them during P.E., which was little more than regular humiliation by the older, stronger kids. It was a diet of football, rugby and other outdoor unpleasantness occasionally leavened with a bit of gymnastics or country dancing. The indoor stuff wasn't exactly fun but it was the outdoors I quickly learned to hate. That was where I'd stand in the freezing rain waiting to be the last one picked; where I'd be shoulder-charged and pushed into puddles; where I'd fall on the red blaes pitch and end up pulling red ash chips from my tattered knees.

By the time I'd started secondary school I'd started to cross-dress secretly and frequently at home. I desperately wished to be like the girls in my classes. I remember being in my first year, watching the girls playing hockey and netball and feeling 50% in love with all of the girls and 50% wishing I could wear the same skirts that they did – something I'd have been willing to endure actual sports for.

I got the sports but not the skirts. An awkward, skinny kid with glasses and biscuit-tin feet that couldn't kick straight and who thought sports were a waste of valuable reading and listening to music time, I was a liability to any team. And after forty minutes of humiliation and horizontal rain, my reward for surviving was to shower with the other boys. It gave me – or perhaps just uncovered – a fear of communal showers and changing rooms that I've had all my life. It didn't help that my body at the time was so different from the older kids'. To my ten-year-old eyes they weren't boys, they were men. I was – and still am – terrified of men.

I was never attacked in the showers or anything like that. I didn't fancy boys and at this point nobody assumed I did, so I wasn't singled out for any of the homophobic abuse that some of the other boys would get. Or at least, I wasn't for the first couple of years. I wasn't mocked for my lack of muscles or body hair any more than any other awkward skinny kid, and I never suffered the indignity of the unwanted erection, something that got at least one of my peers a mild kicking. But there was something about the older kids' aggressive nakedness that I found really intimidating, a shoulder-rolling, towel-snapping, dick-swinging swagger that I couldn't imagine ever being able or wanting to do.

I felt like a lamb in a tiger cage. As an adult, I'd feel the same in gym changing rooms and swimming pool showers. Trans women are routinely demonised as predators, but I've only ever felt like prey.

Sharp dressed man

When I was eleven, I found something that I knew would change my life. It would earn me the admiration of my peers, the adoration of the girls and the respect of the boys.

It got me thrown into a bin.

What I wanted to wear to school was a white blouse, a grey cardigan and a grey lined knee-length skirt, like the girls I adored wore. But I wasn't going to tell that to anybody for, ooh, *decades*. So what I asked my parents to let me wear was the same as the other boys: casual clothes and whichever trainers were fashionable that term.

What my parents actually let me wear was a black blazer, a white shirt that somehow managed to be too tight at the neck no matter how big a size we bought, black trousers with a razor crease and a tie that felt like a noose. So with the same desperation that would later motivate me to wear a "zany" tie to my office job, I begged my parents to let me at least choose a pair of shoes.

And what a pair of shoes I chose.

These shoes couldn't have been more 1980s if forty years later they'd reformed and gone on tour to pay their tax bill. They were black patent leather brogues – oh yes! –with glossy red piping where the upper met the sole. Think Dr Martens without the height, the yellow threads replaced with lurid red. Were they comfortable? No, they were not. Were they practical? Not particularly. Were they the greatest shoes I had ever seen?

They absolutely were.

They were perfect. They looked like Lamborghini sports cars, like Playboy-logoed bed sets, like KITT from Knight Rider. What could be more masculine?

My parents bought them for me on the Saturday and I proudly wore them to school on the Monday. I strolled into school like John Travolta in Saturday Night Fever, ready for the admiration and adoration that was surely coming.

After a full day of being called "poof", of being shoved around and eventually thrown bodily into one of the bins, I put the shoes at the back of a cupboard and never wore them again.

I got the message. Don't stand out.

I tried really hard not to, but for years I'd do my best to dress like everybody else and somehow still discover that I'd screwed it up. And on the very rare occasions when I managed to get it right, to wear the same thing as everybody else and not the Puma instead of the Adidas or the boots with the wrong number of lace holes or whatever other detail I'd managed to miss, God would sabotage me. For example, after the disco shoes disaster was forgotten I somehow managed to persuade my folks to get me a pair of Docs. Not only were they the right colour – black, of course – but they had the right number of lace holes too. They got a puncture three days in and I clump-hissed my way around the corridors for months afterwards.

It was around this time that I started writing songs to express my deepest truths. The chorus of one of them, "I Hate This Town", was fairly typical.

I hate this town
I hate this town
I hate this town
I hate this town

My town and my school were in a former industrial powerhouse where the town centres were inhabited by more ghosts than shops. Like other industrial centres it had, and I think still has to some degree, a working class culture of strong, proud masculinity. Authors such as William McIlvanney (who grew up in Kilmarnock, just south of me) and Andrew O'Hagan (Kilwinning, a few miles to the west) capture it beautifully in novels such as McIlvanney's *The Big Man* and O'Hagan's *Our Fathers*: these were tough towns where tough men did tough jobs.

When the jobs disappeared, the culture around them remained.

I think it's fair to say that that culture did not exactly wave a rainbow flag.

From time to time I like to imagine what my life might have been like if I'd worked things out and come out as trans in my late teens or early twenties. Perhaps I'd have become a snake-hipped, androgynous rock superstar. More likely, I'd have had my pretty little head kicked in. The very few gay people I knew of back then faced extraordinary abuse, including physical attacks and bricks thrown through windows. In my town the word "poof" wasn't just a taunt but a trailer: it was the shout that told you trouble was coming.

At the time, nobody really bothered to make a distinction between gay men – "poofs" – gender non-conforming people – "poofs" – and trans women – also "poofs", because the newspapers didn't. I remember reading my mum and dad's *Daily Mail*s and *Sunday Times* and my grandparents' *Sun*s with their tales of a "gay mafia" or "gay lobby" pushing a "vile" and "perverted" campaign to push a "homosexual agenda" and "recruit children".

I remember seeing the Prime Minister, Margaret Thatcher, on the six o'clock news when I was 15. "Children... are being taught that they have an inalienable right to be gay," she said, to rapturous applause. "All of those children are being cheated of a sound start in life. Yes, cheated." Section 28 was introduced shortly afterwards, effectively banning any discussion of LGBT+ people's lives in schools.

In 1987, *The Sun* – which ran stories with headlines such as

"I'd shoot my son if he had AIDS, says vicar! He would pull trigger on rest of family too"[1] – printed an editorial: "*The Sun* has never been hostile to the gay community… we reject entirely the claim by SOME gays yesterday that *The Sun* and the *Daily Mail* have run a hate campaign against them." The same editorial urged its gay critics to leave the country on a one-way ticket and was headlined, "Fly away gays – and we will pay!"

This went on for many hateful years, and in Scotland it reached fever pitch in 2000 when the Keep The Clause campaign fought against the repeal of Section 28.

Keep The Clause was never a grassroots movement. The campaign was a collaboration between the millionaire Brian Souter, his PR consultant and the *Daily Record* newspaper with some help from Cardinal Winning, the *Scottish Daily Mail* and a handful of zealots. It was breathtakingly cynical, an attempt to reframe Section 28 not as blatant discrimination against LGBT+ people, but as a child safeguarding measure. It wasn't so much a dog whistle as a foghorn: the queers are coming for your kids.

Sound familiar?

Many of the bylines will be familiar too. Several stars of the current trans panic were part of the gay panic too. Tabloids including the *Mail on Sunday* characterised AIDS as a "gay virus plague"[2] while the *Sunday Times*, under editor Andrew Neil – who today chairs *The Spectator* – demonised gay men and printed despicable AIDS denialism while the disease was killing their loved ones.[3] Over at *The Sun*, Piers Morgan, who now rails against "the howling woke mob"[4] and gender fluidity and claims to identify as a penguin,[5] wrote about a soap opera kiss between "yuppie poofs" under the screaming headline SCRAP EASTBENDERS[6]. Morgan also wrote a "Poofs Of Pop" feature in which he and a colleague gave "our totally ill-informed verdict on whether endless male pop stars were gay or not, and telephoning their agents for a confession or furious denial."[7]

It's hardly surprising that Social Attitudes Surveys of the time saw anti-gay sentiment, already high, rise during this period: the percentage of people who believed same-sex activity was "always or mostly wrong" was nearly 80% in both the US and the UK.[8] Because most people didn't think they knew any gay or lesbian people – because who'd come out when the country thinks you're the Devil? – the press, in cahoots with religious groups, reactionary right-wingers, police chiefs and malevolent millionaires, were able to incite fear and hatred of some of the most vulnerable people in society.

Many people they demonised are dead. But some of the perpetrators and their proprietors are still very much alive, and still using their power to incite hate.

The newspapers weren't the only media demonising and mocking us. Films used queerness and crossdressing to evoke villainy in everything from Disney cartoons (well, hell-ooooo Scar! Hiya, Ursula!) to *Dressed To Kill* (one of Michael Caine's worst films, which is saying something), *Psycho*, *The Silence of The Lambs* and *The Rocky Horror Picture Show,* while sitcoms were full of mincing gay men and what seemed to me like constant transvestism. I'm sure I have a bit of confirmation bias, but until relatively recently there really was a lot of crossdressing in English TV comedy: from portly comedians doing old-lady drag and Cambridge Footlights alumni playing deliberately unconvincing female characters to sitcoms sticking male characters in lingerie for laughs, it seemed that crossdressing was second only to racism in its innate hilarity.

I remember two characters in particular: Kenny Everett's improbably breasted and bearded Cupid Stunt, a brassy, short-skirted socialite whose bawdy adventures were always done in "the best PAWWWSSIBLE taste", and Herr Flick, a Nazi officer in the truly terrible sitcom *'Allo 'Allo*. A running gag in the show was the sexual tension between the buttoned-up Flick and his subordinate, Helga, tension that would occasionally erupt; in one episode he and Helga both strip off to their underwear, with Flick behind a screen and Helga in the foreground. We then see Helga in a black and red corset, black stockings and suspenders before Flick provides the punchline: he emerges from behind his screen wearing identical underwear. This was something of a habit: in another episode, Flick is shown shackled in a dank dungeon while dressed in a different red corset and with a black bob wig. "Herr Flick, may I kiss you?" Helga says. "What? Kiss me, chained to the wall, dressed in the underwear of a woman?" Flick responds then pauses before continuing. "Of course."

I didn't find Cupid Stunt or Herr Flick hilarious, but they did make me feel funny.

Do you remember how it felt when you were watching TV with your folks and something slightly sexual happened on screen? The heat in your cheeks, the wanting to look but not wanting to be seen looking, the sudden awkwardness in the room? Take that memory and replace the tame on-screen action with the most lurid, outrageous, joyous depiction of whatever floats your sexual boat. Imagine the reaction as everybody in the room is shocked, horrified and scandalised.

Everyone except you.

You don't feel shocked. You feel shame, because you feel seen. You too would very much like to be kissed by a woman who doesn't care what clothes you're wearing or who thinks they look hot on you. But that frisson of excitement, of recognition, is drowned out by the pounding of your heart. There's ice in your stomach and fire in your cheeks because you know what you're seeing, what you want, is not normal.

And neither are you.

Been caught stealing

I remember it in flashes.

The mess of the room. The plain black skirt hanging above yellow tights in the open wardrobe (yes, yellow tights. It was the '80s). The Madonna poster on the wall, *True Blue*, an album I haven't been able to listen to since. The first sound I heard: a gasp in the doorway, followed by the sound of the sister charging downstairs and, then, the sound of heavier footsteps coming up. The feeling of my heart trying to hammer its way out of my chest as, panicking, I ran for the safety of the bathroom. The shake of my hands as I slid the lock closed. The thumps and shouts of the mother demanding I open the fucking door right now. The look of utter hatred on my friend's face.

What I'm going to describe now fills me with great shame. When I was twelve, I began sneakily crossdressing in the houses of my friends in clothes borrowed without permission from my friends' sisters or mothers, improbably long toilet breaks enabling me to briefly swap my boy clothes for girl ones. I am deeply ashamed of and deeply sorry for doing it, and I don't have any explanation or justification for it. As soon as the possibility of being able to crossdress entered my head it was like a loud car alarm going off. The only way to silence it was to try to look like a girl.

It wasn't primarily a sexual thing, although at this point I was a teenage boy going through puberty so sometimes it was a turn-on in the same way that at that age the vibration of a bus engine, the sight of the back of somebody's knee or just being awake was a turn-on. But mostly it was about imitation, not stimulation; emulation, not masturbation. I'd wear one of the incredibly frumpy grey pleated skirts the local school mandated and I'd try to see a different me in the mirror. I wanted to look like Jennifer, or Alison, or Gillian, or any other girl I was currently infatuated with and far too scared to talk to, let alone ask out.

I remember being torn between wanting to be with those girls and wanting to be like them; at the time I didn't realise that those things didn't necessarily have to be mutually exclusive.

In the language of the time, I was a transvestite. The term "trans" hadn't been popularised yet; transgender was first used in the 1960s before I was born, but the shortened "trans" didn't really become common until the mid-1990s. This is one reason it's difficult to work out which historical figures were or were not trans: many people who'd call themselves trans today called themselves other terms instead. For example, Marsha P Johnson of Stonewall fame variously described herself as gay, a transvestite and a (drag) queen.[1]

On the basis of the very limited information available to me, I believed that there were just two kinds of T-people. The first kind were transsexuals, which occasional documentaries showed as figures of pity in ill-fitting floral dresses. I knew transsexuals wanted to have sex changes, which I didn't, and to marry men, which I didn't want to do either. Until very recently I believed that most trans people were heterosexual; that is, trans women were attracted to men. The reality is that most trans people are not heterosexual at all. In the 2018 UK National LGBT Survey,[2] just 9.4% of trans people said they were straight; 71% were gay, lesbian, or pansexual and 5.4% asexual.

But I didn't know that back then. Whatever transsexuals were, the girl-fancying me couldn't have been one of them.

So that left transvestites. I discovered their existence in the lurid advertisements for a "He to SHE" dressing service in

London that I saw in my grandparents' copies of *The Sun*, in the problem pages of my mum's magazines and in salacious tabloid tales of what Eddie Izzard would later call "weirdo transvestites" as opposed to the "executive transvestite" she considered herself to be. As Izzard tells it, executive transvestites travel the world, appreciate the finer things in life and are generally groovy; weirdo transvestites are maniacs like J Edgar Hoover whose crossdressing is revealed after their death and people go "well, that explains *everything*!" or cave-dwelling, heavily armed, goose-murdering madmen who are later discovered to have a huge collection of suspiciously sticky women's shoes.

In the tabloids of the time, all transvestites were weirdo transvestites.

It was the same in the fiction I was devouring. Transvestites were considerably more common in the lurid crime and horror novels I enjoyed than they appeared to be in real life, and whenever they appeared in one of my library books they would either turn up dead or turn up to make everybody else dead. Transvestites were never the good guys, the kind, twinkly-eyed sheriff or the action man who saves the day. They were deranged, perverted killers or the sex workers those killers preyed upon.

I learned a new word from those books: tranny.

I hated that word. Still do. Some trans people have reclaimed it in much the same way some Black people have reclaimed the N-word, but for me the sound of it is the sound of somebody shouting it across the street or screaming down a telephone line late at night.

It was also the sound I heard in my own head. It's what I began to see myself as, what I feared the other kids finding out about me, what I knew they'd call me.

The word echoed around my head.

Tranny tranny.

I didn't want to be a tranny.

Trannies were dirty. Deviants. Disgusting. Everyone knew that.

And yet that's what I was.

I hated myself for it.

I hated the way the thought of crossdressing would pop into my head uninvited, the feeling of pressure building inside my skull until I couldn't concentrate, the heart-thudding fear of being caught and the brief moment of calm when I looked in the mirror and saw something close to the me I wanted so desperately to be.

I'd try copying the mannerisms of the girls I liked, imagining I was one of them before carefully putting the clothes back in the cupboards I'd taken them from – or if I thought I'd spent too long already to risk taking any longer, into the washing basket. I'd then vow never, ever to do it again. And I wouldn't, until the next time the thought came into my head and the pressure started to build.

Of course, crossdressing in other people's houses is not just a very stupid thing to do, but a very risky thing to do too. It was just a matter of time before I got caught.

It happened when I was 13. I was at a friend's house. We were watching Arnold Schwarzenegger's *Commando*, one of many violent or horrific VHS tapes rented from a video shop that couldn't care less about age ratings. It was pretty boring, and I excused myself to go to the toilet. The bathroom was upstairs, and the door to my friend's sister's room was adjacent. I hadn't gone upstairs to crossdress, but as soon as I saw the open door the familiar noise in my head started up.

That noise was always the loudest sound I'd ever heard, drowning out everything else. It wasn't a sexual thing, although it shared desire's ability to make the whole world disappear when you're in the moment. But desire is a want. This was a *need*, like a hunger or a thirst or a craving. The closest I've come to it in other circumstances was in a Parisian airport shortly after France banned smoking indoors; I was still going through three packs of Benson & Hedges a day and after several hours of delays I was so desperate for a smoke I'd have paid to suck the nicotine from another addict's yellowed fingers. In the end I sneaked a smoke in a toilet cubicle, standing with my feet on the seat so I could block the smoke detector above my head in the hope of keeping the armed cops at bay. It wasn't my finest moment.

Being locked in this bathroom wasn't exactly a highlight either.

I don't remember what happened after I locked myself in the toilet, beyond a lot of shouting. Somehow I got home and my parents went to apologise to my friend's parents, which I understand was a spectacularly unpleasant experience: I thought that my friend's mother was a deeply unlikeable woman at the best of times, and this was not the best of times. She was full of righteous fury that evening as she subjected my parents to a great deal of verbal abuse about their disgusting, perverted, sick fuck of a child.

After what seemed like an eternity, my parents returned home and we had an excruciatingly awkward conversation about whether I was gay and whether I was one of "those transvestites". My head said yes to the latter but my mouth said no, and I politely declined my mum's kind offer to buy me a bra and pants that I could wear in the privacy of my own room. I declined not just because I wanted the ground to open up and swallow me – the birds and bees chat is bad enough, but to have a conversation about how you're what the rest of the world sees as a filthy pervert is a whole different level of awfulness – but because right then I knew that I would never, ever crossdress again.

I wouldn't be allowed to forget that day either. My friend, now very much an ex-friend, teamed up with a small group of co-conspirators who would spend more than a decade shouting abuse outside my house. For my former friend I guess it was simple anger; for the others I think it was straightforward homophobia and transphobia (the two were interlinked for most people at the time); for one late addition to the group it was because I didn't want to fuck him.

That wasn't my imagination. He'd been trying to convert me into a fan of his favourite musician and on one particularly weird afternoon he suggested we bunk off school and hang out. When we got to the house it turned out that music wasn't the main thing on his mind; he said that he'd discovered his mum's stash of lingerie and suggested that it would be fun if we tried it on. Just for a laugh, of course. You know. Like manly male men do.

That sounded like a great idea to me.

Being the hyper-intelligent, sexually aware person I am, I didn't think his idea sounded in any way strange, that it might be a set-up or that there was a good chance I'd end up with my limbs turning up in multiple bin bags across multiple wheelie bins. So I didn't think he might have any motive in getting both of us into really scratchy and probably highly flammable pants. When he showed me his erect penis straining against the fabric of what looked more like dental floss than underwear, it became clear that, "What are you doing? No. No!" wasn't the answer he'd been anticipating. I made my excuses and left hurriedly, and he dedicated the rest of our time at school to being the loudest of my tormentors. He never did persuade me to like his favourite singer. It's hard to love music that immediately makes you think of someone else's erection.

The bullying changed my view of school from vague dislike to active hatred, and I abandoned my plans to go to Heriot-Watt University to study journalism. But as much as I wanted to, I couldn't leave school because I was still too young – I wouldn't turn 16 until I was in sixth year. So instead, I started distancing myself. I'm lucky to have the kind of brain that remembers just enough to pass exams and then forgets it all immediately, so I did the bare minimum I could get away with and spent the rest of the time "dogging it" – skipping school to drink vodka, smoke cigarettes and sing Five Star's greatest hits with my female friends.

My teenage male friendships centred on *stuff* – planning world domination for our as yet unformed rock bands, analysing the lyrics of po-faced prog rockers Marillion, smoking banana peels, Tetley tea bags and OXO cubes because someone's big brother said it totally got you high, watching shlocky horror such as *Reanimator*, *The Thing* and *The Evil Dead* – but my female friendships were much more open and more emotional. At house parties I'd often end up in a huddle, consoling an upset friend or planning great escapes with girlfriends while the boys dared each other to drink aftershave, hit each other with improvised weapons or accidentally knocked out the odd hallway window and tried to re-seat it with toothpaste instead of putty. I wasn't immune to the male silliness, though: until an unfortunate mistake involving methylated spirits, six snapped guitar strings and surprisingly hot arms made me reconsider, I'd occasionally pour lighter fluid over my leather jacket, play my guitar and set myself on fire.

We float

I think God invented hot baths and testicles on the same day. By making the perfect temperature for a soak exactly three degrees warmer than any scrotum can abide, He, She or They guaranteed themself a gut-busting giggle every time someone squats awkwardly in the tub, delicately dipping their dangly bits into the too-warm water like someone making the world's least tempting cup of tea.

As a teenager, I spent many hours escaping everything by taking to the water. I'd take a boom box with a cassette of my current musical obsession in with me and prop it up against the opposite wall, and once I'd finished my human teabag act I'd immerse myself completely in the water before bringing my head up just enough so that my ears were uncovered. I'd lie there and listen until the tape reached the end of side one, and then I'd quickly turn it over, top up the hot water and listen to side two.

Music was my safe space, and I felt safest when there was nothing but music. The bath made my body disappear and I could close my eyes and immerse my ears in the songs. I played Pet Shop Boys' *Disco*, U2's *Wide Awake In America* and Talk Talk's *The Colour of Spring* to death in there, trying to unpick what made them magical, and I still remember every single thing about them – the adorable little voice in the kids' choir during Talk Talk's *Happiness Is Easy* that's just slightly out of time, the guitar chime that is somehow the saddest sound in the world in U2's *Bad*, and Pet Shop Boy Chris Lowe's spoken litany of dislikes followed by "I don't like much, do I? But what I do like, I love *passionately*" in *Paninaro*, which I think describes my attitude perfectly too.

I didn't ever think I could make music: it seemed so magical, so unknowable. But when I was 13, a friend showed me how to play the bass line for Eddy Cochran's *C'Mon Everybody* on their electric guitar. If you don't know it, it's so simple a dog could play it. But for me it was an epiphany. Music is a thing I could do.

Badly, as it turned out.

Most bands are awful, and that includes many of the bands I've been in. They were tremendous fun, though, and with hindsight absolutely hilarious because we were so clueless and pompous. One band was mistakenly booked into a golf club for a '60s night because our name sounded like a country and western band; unaware of the mix-up, we debuted our new, very loud, very metal song "Suicide Eyes" through a massive PA to an audience of frankly terrified North Ayrshire pensioners before the owner cut the power and booted us out. The same band booked the school assembly hall for a hometown gig to silence the haters; once again we hired a massive PA system, this time with pyrotechnics. And when the smoke cleared after the first song's explosive introduction, we discovered that we were rocking out for the benefit of exactly two people.

I didn't like performing live, because while making an enormous noise is always thrilling things often went terribly wrong for us: singers forgetting how to sing, bassists in brand new blue suede shoes slipping and rocketing past me on stage like a runaway train, amplifiers that would interrupt my playing with interference from local taxi drivers, drummers announcing mid-song that they had contracted arthritis in their thumb and could no longer play. I also had severe stage fright. But I did love writing songs, and it didn't take long for that to become my main form of self-expression.

My lyrics weren't exactly brilliant, but they were better than my bandmates' – one of my singers' proudest moments was when he showed me his scathing takedown of Thatcherism: "She's as cold as ice / She's as welcome as lice" – and I found that I was able to put a lot of myself into them.

It turned out that there were two themes I kept coming back to. The first was unrequited love.

I wrote love songs long before I ever had a girlfriend. I was a late bloomer, partly because I was desperately shy and partly because I was terrified that my terrible secret made me unloveable. I was scared of being discovered, of trusting someone with a secret I knew they wouldn't be able to keep, let alone accept. And I was incredibly critical of my appearance and my personality too. I was too awkward, too talkative, too weedy, too unlike the other boys to be a suitable candidate for anything beyond a half-hearted, Merrydown-flavoured winch on someone else's sofa. I was the boy your mum didn't mind you bringing over, the one you invited into your room to talk about your boyfriend or to help you work out how to handle your overly strict dad. And as much as that was okay, as much as I love feeling useful and being able to help people, it was hard not to feel that my destiny was to always be the bridesmaid and never the bride.

When I did start dating I was hardly Casanova. Around the time I turned sixteen I briefly went out with a girl who taught me how to kiss, and then I briefly went out with another with whom I thought I lost my virginity, although I soon realised that I hadn't. I wasn't very worldly then or now. I'd be reminded of it as an adult when I became part of a family whose eldest dog, a grizzly-chinned, sad-eyed, rough-haired rescue with extreme anxiety and a head that'd flip up like a pedal bin when I scratched his neck, would occasionally try to have sex with ghosts. He'd hunker down in the garden, his erection like a lipstick, his hips thrusting vigorously into the air. He had the moves down pat but wasn't doing anyone any favours; he seemed rather confused about the whole thing but was giving it his best shot. The first time I saw him do it I laughed in recognition, muttering "you and me both" under my breath.

But despite my hopelessness I did end up going out with the most beautiful girl in the whole of Ayrshire with whom I'd been deeply, and I thought hopelessly, infatuated. We were together for about seven months, and after we broke up I didn't date again for thirteen years.

That wasn't a deliberate decision – I hadn't taken a vow of celibacy or anything like that – but I convinced myself that my terrible secret would be a deal-breaker for any girl who discovered it. Better not to date at all than to date and be dumped for being a deviant. And I didn't think I was worthy of dating anyway. If I didn't like me, how could I expect anybody else to?

Even if I hadn't started to think I was undateable, circumstances made meeting Miss Right difficult anyway. We tend to meet our boyfriends or girlfriends or partners in places such as school or work or in clubs, but I had quit education; my work colleagues were a computer, a vending machine and a mouthy misogynist; and the one time a friend and I went to the Metro nightclub in nearby Saltcoats in the hope of meeting girls – a plan I had to be talked into, because I get really claustrophobic and anxious in clubs. People thought we were the drug squad.

I was also starting to think that there was something else wrong with me. I knew I was attracted to women, but I was uncomfortable with intimacy. When my friends hit puberty they all became libidos on legs, and I didn't: on one musical road trip we all stopped at a motorway service station, my bandmates all bought pornography and I bought a magazine about trucks.

I'd like to clarify here that I am not sexually attracted to trucks.

There's a term I've only learnt recently: demisexual. I think it applies to me; like the gender stuff, I didn't know the term at the time but it makes a lot of sense when I look in the rear view mirror. So *that's* what it was!

Demisexuality is on the same spectrum as asexuality. Some sexual attraction is there but it's rare: you only feel it when there's a strong emotional bond. So you might be massively attracted to someone you care for deeply but not to anybody else.

That's me. A really beautiful human can take my breath away, and I have a long history of intense crushes on people I find incredibly beautiful and fascinating. But I don't want to be physically intimate with someone I'm not emotionally intimate with. I feel kinship with the woman whose Tumblr post made me laugh till I cried: when her boyfriend asked her to talk dirty in the bedroom, she told him that she had been a very naughty girl. When he asked what she had done, her mind went blank. After a pause, she finally came up with something. "I burned down a house!" she spluttered.

I turned my crushes into songs, where I could say the things I couldn't possibly say to the women I was infatuated with. And I started writing another kind of song too, to say the things I couldn't yet say to myself. Songs like this one:

She puts on her make-up
And her new party dress
Ties back her hair so it won't look a mess
She looks in the mirror
But she just sees herself
Just sees herself

Girl afraid

I have done all kinds of scary things. I have stood on stages where I was so terrified I could hardly play. I have walked through football crowds in a floaty floral dress. I have been to Bob Mould concerts without wearing earplugs. But I have never done anything as frightening as shopping for women's clothes while being obviously male.

When I started working, I was finally able to buy the clothes I longed to wear. But this was before homes had the internet, so there was no eBay, let alone New Look's online-only range for tall women. If you wanted girl clothes you had to go into a shop, buy them in person and hope to God they fit you because if they didn't, there was no way you were going to take them back.

I didn't buy much because it was an ordeal every time: of white-knuckled fear driving to the next town to avoid bumping into anybody, of deciding which single shop you'd go into before the panic sent you scurrying back to the car, of checking the aisles were clear before you tiptoed into the aisle of Things That Are Definitely Not For You, A Man.

I was like Tom Cruise dangling from wires in *Mission: Impossible*, trying not to get spotted for fear of the potentially fatal consequences.

I kept my head down, avoiding eye contact, and I'd pretend to be really interested in Stanley knives, LPs or hammers until the coast was clear. The trick was to never, ever enter the Girl

Things aisles if there was already someone there or if someone looked as if they might be thinking about going there.

If I made it to the Girl Things I'd grab the first piece of clothing I saw in what I thought might be close to my size: a stretchy skirt, perhaps, or a floral top. Trying them on just wasn't a possibility, even though the places usually had changing rooms: I hadn't the faintest idea what girls' changing rooms were actually like but I assumed they were packed with various transvestite detectors and anti-transvestite weaponry wielded by frightening, angry anti-transvestite attendants.

So I'd put whatever I'd grabbed in my basket and place something completely unrelated but reasonably manly on top of it. A car magazine, perhaps, or *Queen's Greatest Hits*. That would provide the cover story for when I went to the checkout.

If I managed to keep my nerve long enough – and sometimes I didn't; I'd decide that I couldn't do it, abandon my basket and race out of the shop close to tears and wanting to die – I'd clutch the right number of pound notes in my clammy hand and wait for a queue-free checkout to become available.

As she tapped in each item's price into the till, the woman on the checkout (and the checkout operators were *always* women) might fuck with me a little bit by asking if the skirt was for me. Mostly, though, there would be silence. But I knew what she was thinking. I knew that she had seen right through my impressively cool facade, that the skirt or the tights or the floral top was for me, that I was a *tranny*. By the time I'd paid and managed to exit the shop (always after pushing the pull door or vice-versa, because why should any of this be easy?) I'd been through such an emotional wringer that the tang of diesel fumes and leaded petrol smelled a lot like freedom.

I had to wait a long time for online shopping to be invented but I soon discovered the next best thing, the Next Directory. It was a clothing catalogue bound like a hardback book and featuring some of the most beautiful women in the world, women I immediately wanted to both marry and mimic. I spent a fortune buying things from it.

In the same way I wanted to dress like the girls I went to school with, now that I had a job I tried to discover how I could become like the women I worked with and commuted alongside. By now I had office jobs, so naturally enough my initial Next Directory purchases had a distinctly secretarial bent: straight black pencil skirts, fitted white blouses, shoes with low or no heels. My purchases were all very practical, or at least they would have been had I been a young woman.

But they weren't *always* practical. From time to time I'd see something so extraordinarily beautiful that I absolutely had to have it, like a spaghetti-strapped evening dress in the most gorgeous shade of deep green. I've no idea where I thought I'd be able to wear that one. I have similar impulse buys in my wardrobe now.

I'm quite sure my mum suspected transvestism-related tomfoolery when packages arrived and I refused to open them when anybody was in the house, and I'm quite sure she found the not-entirely-secret stash of women's clothes which I kept in a small filing cabinet in my bedroom. I had my own filing cabinet! Why was I still single?

But if she knew, she was kind enough not to embarrass me about it.

I dressed every chance I got. I became an expert at detecting the sound of a returning car or incoming courier, a sound that'd send me into a panic as I tried to get out of my clothes and back into my boy ones. I became the Harry Houdini of crossdressing, capable of changing my entire gender presentation in just a few seconds. The trick, if you'd like to try it yourself, is to concentrate on getting back into your jeans and t-shirt as quickly as you can and pull on a plaid shirt. You can swap the underwear around later.

Sometimes – if the folks were away, it was late at night and I'd found some much-needed courage – I'd dress fully female from head to toe and either go for a drive or walk around the estate, euphoric that I was outside in a skirt and terrified that somebody would spot me. If anybody did, and I'm sure they did, they clearly didn't care. I remember being really scared, but also feeling strangely calm.

And it was fun. Boy clothes weren't.

My patent leather shoe adventure put me off showing any signs of flamboyance, so I spent many years with the kind of wardrobe the late Steve Jobs would have approved of: black t-shirts, black leather jacket, black boots, blue jeans. At work I might express my incredible zaniness with a novelty tie. But in private, I had much more fun with my presentation. My male clothes were utilitarian. My female clothes were an adventure.

My girl clothes felt nothing like my boy clothes. The cottons were softer, the layers thinner, the knits finer. Male clothes are a lot more fun now than they used to be, but they're still largely functional. With women's clothes, you're more likely to get something odd glued to the backside than anything practical such as usable pockets.

I was fascinated by the differences, by the bits cut out for no apparent reason and the perfectly functional items – such as zips, buttons, ties – that were moved to places even a contortionist would find tricky to reach. I love fabrics that are embroidered or embellished, ordinary items given glittery thread, shirt sleeves that roll back to reveal a different and fun pattern underneath. I love all the little details, the little sparkles there for no reason other than to make you smile.

The difference wasn't just how they looked. It was how they felt too. Lined skirts felt nothing like Levi's. Tights compressed my legs and made them feel three degrees colder. Shoes shifted my centre of gravity, making me walk differently and stand differently.

And then there's makeup, another symphony for the senses. Nail polish transports me to childhood, its smell of Pear Drops evoking long, warm summers and carefree days and beautiful girls in floaty dresses. Clear coat chills the cuticles and makes my nails feel like they're shrinking. A fresh eyeshadow palette makes me see my eyelids as canvases. Lipstick tastes of stolen kisses and dangerous liaisons.

These things together, the sensations and the motion and the sound, made me feel conscious of my body and of its movements in a way I never felt in male mode. I may have looked terrible, but I didn't feel terrible. I felt confident and alive and in my head at least, maybe even pretty.

I feel slightly uncomfortable when I talk about clothes and how they make me feel, because I know that there are plenty of people who will seize upon the blandest statement and present it as a gotcha, evidence that trans women are just men playing dress-up for some sinister reason, that our identity is a mere performance that we can put on or take off. One anti-trans writer tried to persuade me that a trans woman posting "It's a shame skirts aren't really in fashion right now" was proof that trans women are fetishists.

But that's not how it works. I didn't decide I was trans because I wanted to wear women's clothes. I wanted to wear women's clothes because I'm trans. As Eddie Izzard put it: "They're not women's clothes. They're my clothes. I bought them."[1]

When you're out of the closet, being able to wear your own clothes is something you take for granted. As the joke goes, the difference between a crossdresser and a trans woman is that a crossdresser can't wait to get home and put a bra on; a trans woman can't wait to get home and take the bloody thing off. But when you're in the closet, it's one of the only ways in which you can be and see yourself, one of the only opportunities you have to express a part of you that you have to keep secret all of the time. And when you're out of the closet, the clothes you wear are important in a different way: they tell others how you want to be responded to, and sometimes they're a suit of armour to hide how scared you are.

★

No matter how cute the clothes I bought or how happy they made me feel, my purchases never lasted long. I got into a cycle, familiar to many closeted trans people, called purging: I'd accumulate a reasonable collection of clothes and then one day I would feel terrible shame and vow never to crossdress again. The clothes would be given to charity, or just thrown away. I shudder to think how much money I wasted.

Between purges, I bought some very beautiful and utterly impractical clothes, clothes that looked wonderful on the models but that wouldn't have worked quite so well in the Kilbirnie Co-op even if I were a cisgender girl who could safely wear them in public. I bought long skirts that barely allowed my ankles to move; elaborately patterned tights that made my calves feel like they were being grated; scratchy pants that were actually painful to wear for more than a few minutes; and countless pairs of heels that I couldn't balance in, let alone walk. I also learned the hard way that many cuts and lengths of dresses and skirts are designed to look good only on tall and willowy Eastern European models and nobody else. I remember one flared, pleated black skirt that was stunning in photographs but somehow managed to make me look like a cross between an umbrella and a Dalek.

I don't think there's a single sexy-lady stereotype I didn't at least attempt to copy. I wasn't dressing like I do now, for everyday comfort. I was trying to emulate what the wider culture told me was desirable because deep down, I wanted to feel that I could be desired too. In a highly sexualised culture like ours, that meant trying to be a sexy secretary, not a scene-of-the-crime officer, truck driver or dairy farmer. It meant trying to get the hang of pencil skirts and heels, not relaxing trousers and flats; enduring push-up bras and tight blouses, not big knickers and bobbly hoodies.

I'm writing this many years later, and if you were to ask me to describe my look I'd say it's just really ordinary. Although there's a big part of me that's irritatingly perky and drawn to big, bold fashion, there's also a considerably more grumpy and gothy me that keeps her in check and leans towards the all-black wardrobe. If I were younger and thinner I'd most likely let both mes out, but at the moment my wardrobe choices are much less entertaining.

That's partly because nowadays, I don't dress to try and *be* things. I dress to *do* things: school runs, dog walks, supermarket shops. On the school run I don't dress any differently from the other school run mums who aren't on their way to the office: it's skinny jeans and trainers with tunic tops or t-shirts, and if I'm really going for it I might wear a cardigan. I smarten up a little bit if I'm going to a work thing – I'll wear a tunic with leggings or a simple dress with black tights and ballet flats – and I had a brief period of passive-aggressively glamming it up on stage, but mostly I dress like I'm going to put the bins out or walk the dog, because that's usually what I'm going out to do. I'll glam up for a big night out but that's about it.

My days of trying to be sexy are long gone too. I'm probably more likely to wear a dress than the average woman of my age – I didn't wear a dress in public until I was 45, so I've got a lot of dress-wearing to do before the novelty wears off – but I covet warm jumper dresses and thick opaque tights, not silks and stockings; autumnal colours, not Ann Summers. The most exciting clothes I've bought lately are a three-pack of socks, a black jumper and some big pants.

Transgender dysphoria blues

There's a town in New South Wales, Australia called Yass, and when you look at it in a maps app it seems to be the happiest place in the world: there's Public School Yass, Yass Local Court, McDonald's Yass, KFC Yass, Yass Engineering...

That's what gender euphoria feels like: yass feeling happy in your own skin, yass looking in a mirror and not wanting to die, yass feeling that everything is in its right place.

Gender dysphoria is the distress you feel when your sense of who you are doesn't match the gender everybody tells you you are. And gender euphoria is how you feel when you get to feel like you. While many trans people experience dysphoria, not everybody does; of the people who do, some experience it very strongly and others don't. As far as I can tell, gender euphoria is much more common. I've experienced both.

It's very hard to describe gender dysphoria to someone who hasn't experienced it. For me it was a feeling of profound disconnection from pretty much everything. Not just from my body, but from the world more generally. I felt like a fictional character walking down streets that somebody else had written, my body a vehicle I had to drive around but wouldn't have chosen for myself.

Gender dysphoria is commonly compared to acting, the

stress of playing a role you haven't prepared for when you can't remember your lines and the costume doesn't fit. I've described it as being parachuted behind enemy lines where the slightest slip will summon enemy soldiers. Others describe it as looking in the mirror but not seeing yourself, wearing a Hallowe'en mask that everybody thinks is your real face, speaking a language that isn't your own, being stuck in shoes that are several sizes too small, a feeling that you're observing your life rather than living it, a constant feeling that something really important *just isn't right*.

For me, gender dysphoria felt like a version of impostor syndrome. That's the psychological phenomenon particularly common in women, especially successful ones, where instead of celebrating your achievements you're in constant fear that people will discover you're nothing but a fraud and throw you out of the building. Friends and family excepted, I disliked male company because I felt vulnerable around most men; I still do. I lived in fear that I'd fail at some simple man thing and the gender police would arrive with sirens blaring.

I felt trapped, but I've never felt "trapped in the wrong body" as the cliché puts it. Few trans people do. The phrase was never meant to reflect what it actually feels like to be trans; it was an attempt to simplify it in such a way that people who aren't trans could understand and empathise with us.

Gender euphoria is wonderful. I experience it in lots of ways now. Something as simple as buying a lipstick becomes a great euphoric adventure because when you buy a lipstick, you're not just buying a lipstick: you're buying a story, imagining the clothes you'll wear with it and the incredible night out you'll have and the incredible people you'll meet and the incredible compliments you'll get because, goddamn it, you are *hot*!

No wonder it takes so long to pick one: you're not dithering, you're trying to bring the future into focus.

If you're a man and thinking "how shallow", I bet you do

exactly the same thing when you read a car magazine or a sexy-tech one. Lipstick, laptops, Louboutins and Lamborghinis may be very different things, but they all represent escapism, adventures, possibilities and above all else, fun.

And being trans is a lot of fun.

My levels of gender dysphoria have ebbed and flowed through my life, but every time I got the opportunity to be me, my gender euphoria was always turned up to eleven. Getting to be me, even for a short time, was like having a holiday inside my own head.

Being yourself can be a joyous, glorious, exciting and fabulously fun thing to do, even when the results are rubbish. I discovered how varying combinations of materials would interact and how to discern the often tiny differences between styles and shapes; which shoes would make me look like an Amazon and which ones would turn my toes into mince; what kinda worked with what, and what really didn't work at all. I would see young women with particularly great looks on the train or on the street and mentally file the details for ordering from Next later and, when I felt I'd got the look more or less right, I felt a happiness I can't describe.

We exist

The internet hasn't always been a bin fire. The internet I discovered in my mid-twenties had no Facebook or YouTube to drive me into the arms of the alt-right, no Twitter enabling incel armies to abuse women with impunity, no messageboards radicalising vulnerable new mums. On my internet, "fake news" was The Onion and trolls were music fans winding up fans of other bands.

My internet also enabled me to inhabit a female persona. In some discussion forums I did just that, but I got bored quickly: to be female on the internet wasn't as fraught as it is now, but it still invited patronising bullshit from blowhards and lots of unwanted romantic attention. Luckily this was a text-based medium: the internet of the time wasn't fast enough for unsolicited dick pics, a technological limitation that I am very grateful for.

There might not have been dick pics in the days of dial-up, but the internet for women has always been very different to the internet for men. And it's not just the obvious creeps and trolls. Apparently nice guys often seemed to be problematic too.

There's a music criticism term I love: the truck driver's key change. It's the bit in the final choruses of a song where the whole thing suddenly jumps two semitones higher, for example by moving from a starting note of G to a starting note of A. Boy bands do it a lot, and they do it with all the subtlety and smoothness of a tired trucker trying to nudge a knackered

Scania into third on a steep hill somewhere near Sheffield. Hence the expression.

When your online persona is that of a young woman rather than a young man, you'll experience something very similar: the truck driver's subject change. One minute you're talking excitedly about The Edge's guitar pedals; the next you're suddenly and horribly aware that the other person has changed the subject and might not be typing with both hands.

The internet of the early 1990s felt friendly, tolerant, helpful. Clearly, it was going to make the world a better place. It's hard to believe in this era of social media trolling, online race hate and permanent outrage, but the internet used to be a safe space where weird people were welcome because *everybody* was weird.

I'm from Generation X, the last generation to be born without the internet all around us, the generation who had to get off the internet when their parents needed to use the phone. And I lived in a small town where people might not have pointed at aeroplanes, but if they did you wouldn't be surprised. It really felt to me that for me and my peers, going as far as Glasgow was pretty exotic. And here I was making friends with and/or fighting with people from places I couldn't pronounce or find on a map.

It was profoundly liberating. I had no idea what race or religion most people were, how old they were or even what their gender might be: my online friends were called things like Melon, Moonboot Phenomenon and Roars. We were friends long before we ever met up, something that's common now but felt really strange at the time. And we did meet up: I went to London – London! – to meet forum friends from Manhattan and Minneapolis and Belfast and Buckinghamshire to talk about pop music and to finally discover what all the fuss was about Starbucks coffee; and I acted as tour guide for forum friends from Boston and Florida, driving them around Scotland so they could see how expensive all our tourist traps and how small our cars are.

I knew in my heart that this global village would make our differences irrelevant. We'd see what we had in common, not what was different. This incredible technology would make the whole world smarter, better informed and so much more tolerant.

I got that wrong, didn't I?

But while the internet didn't change humanity for the better, it did change my life. I met my future wife there, and I found a career that I love. And I discovered the four most important words the internet can deliver: you are not alone.

The internet showed me that there were other people like me. CompuServe had forums for every conceivable subject, and one of those subjects was crossdressing. The people there would share personal stories and dressing tips, political opinions and silly jokes. I discovered that the USENET network, a pre-Facebook form of social media, had crossdressing groups too. Over time I'd discover other forums, such as URNotAlone, a photo sharing site, and the UK Angels, a support and discussion board. There were transsexual forums and sites too, and some of the crossdressing ones overlapped, but I tended to steer clear: the conversations comparing hormone regimes and discussing post-surgical complications in graphic detail were too much information for me.

On many forums I was a "lurker", someone who visits but doesn't join in the conversations. That's partly because in most online social spaces it takes time to work out what the vibe is, who the important people are and what kind of stuff gets you piled on, and partly because I was still very much in denial about being trans and scared of accidentally outing myself. But on some forums I didn't post because I didn't want to get to know or be associated with some of the people that posted there.

The thing about trans and gender non-conforming people is that they're people. And while most people are great, some people are awful. So some trans people are profoundly sexist, with deeply reactionary views of femininity. Some are clearly unhinged. Some are self-hating and profoundly destructive. Some shouldn't be allowed cutlery, let alone computers. But what I didn't understand then, but understand all too well now, is that it's easy to judge an entire community on the basis of a few of its worst members. I didn't want to be associated with the often older and very right-wing trans women I saw online performing a simpering, eyelash-fluttering, giggling, 1950s "I need a man to make me feel like a real woman" persona; what I didn't understand at the time was that most other trans women didn't either. The reason I wasn't hearing their voices was because they had better things to do and better places to go.

What I also saw online was attempts by some trans women – again, mainly right-wing and considerably older – to define who and who wasn't "trans enough" to deserve respect, rights and protection. By some strange coincidence, their criteria for inclusion always described people exactly like them, not people like me. But their gatekeeping of people like me and my irritation at people who are not like me were two cheeks of the same arse: the willingness, and in some cases the desire, to throw other people under the bus to save yourself.

When you're a member of a marginalised group you naturally want people to see you as one of "the good ones", not the embarrassing ones or the weird ones or the crazy ones. But trying to distance yourself from people you have absolutely no connection with other than a single characteristic is a trap. You're accepting the framing of the people who are hostile to people like you. To them, there are no "good ones"; they're asking when you stopped beating your wife and you're saying that someone else beats their wife more than you do.

The internet didn't "trans" me. I have always been trans, and I have not always had the internet. But the internet did help me make sense of it. And one of the ways it did that was by bringing me something that fascinated and still fascinates me: photos of other trans people. Crossdressers, trans and gender non-conforming people were taking and uploading endless selfies long before anybody invented the smartphone, let alone Instagram, and I spent hours scrolling through them.

Many of the pictures were hopeless. Even basic makeup is a skill that takes time to learn and longer still to master, and some of the photos were by people like me who hadn't learnt it, let alone mastered it. And in another mistake I also made, some people were dressing as the age they wanted to be rather than the age they actually were.

I'm better at it now, but my early attempts resembled some kind of tragic disaster at a fancy dress outfit factory. I'd never been able to summon the courage to use an in-shop tester for foundation or lipstick, so I hadn't the faintest idea what colours or shades I ought to get. For a long time I oscillated between looking like the killer clown from It or looking like an Oompa-Loompa, depending on how white or how orange my foundation was. I coloured in my brows until I looked like Groucho Marx's grandmother, channelled my inner ABBA in blue eye shadow and used so much blusher I appeared to be suffering from extreme hypertension. It took a lot of failed experiments before I stopped looking like I'd been drawn by a toddler.

And then there were the clothes. As much as I believe that the most appropriate clothes for a woman aged 20, 30, 40 or 70 are whatever she damn well wants to wear, I also know that what looks fantastic on a size 10 twentysomething will look very different on size 20 middle-aged me. Or at least, I know that now. I didn't at first, so I bought the clothes I'd like to wear rather than the ones I'd look okay in: too-short skirts, too-tight tops, dresses that hung badly or emphasised the bits I'd rather conceal. I still don't really know what I'm doing, so now when I see a trans woman roughly my age dressed like she's 14 in a shocking pink mini, sheer black tights with a huge ladder up one calf and enough eyeliner to sink a goth, I feel a stab of warmth and recognition: "Aaaaw! A baby tran!"

I skipped the photos of the newly hatched eggs and focused instead on the ones that really fascinated me: the ones where the crossdressers and trans people successfully "passed". That is, they didn't look like crossdressers or trans people. They looked like cisgender women.

Passing can be a matter of life or death for trans people. If you pass, i.e. don't appear to be a trans person, you attract less unwanted attention. Visibly trans or gender non-conforming people are much more likely to face verbal and physical abuse than cisgender people, or people who appear to be cisgender.

I knew I didn't pass and probably never would, but I was fascinated by the trans women who did. I looked at page after page of women, many of them around the same age as me, many of them looking how I'd like to look. And it struck me that they didn't look like monsters, or people who should be ashamed of anything. They were beautiful.

I desperately wanted to be one of those women, but my twentysomething body had other ideas: while nobody would have called me particularly masculine, there was nothing that seemed particularly feminine about the skin I walked around in either. I also lived in a place where men showing the slightest hint of effeminacy were guaranteed a trip to A&E. So I continued to dress in secret and feel miserable whenever I was unable to dress or to get on the internet.

From time to time I tried to change my body – not to make it more feminine, but to make it more masculine. I was skinny and angular then, and I think I thought that if I could become more muscular it might fix me in a "fake it 'till you make it" kind of way: if I looked more manly, maybe I'd feel it too and then all the cute girls would fancy me.

In my twenties, my attempts to become more manly were in gyms – places where, ironically enough, I couldn't have felt *less* manly. I'd look at the guys lifting massive weights like they were teabags while I strained and sweated on the Babybel-sized barbells; at the runners racking up the miles on their treadmills while lactic acid blazed through my legs after the first fifty metres; at the people who not only understood how all the equipment worked but seemed to enjoy using all of it. I'd go late, when it was quiet, because the only thing worse than a gym is a busy gym locker room. If other men were showering at the same time as me I'd stay longer in my cubicle until I was the last one there in the hope that they'd be dressed and gone by the time I got out. If I heard the tell-tale sounds of banter, I'd stay in my cubicle, shivering, waiting until it stopped.

My attempts to become more masculine started long before I set foot in a gym. I tried using my dad's Bullworker, a ridiculous resistance-based torture machine that looks like some bizarre fisting accessory. I'm looking at an old ad for it now. NOW YOU CAN LAUGH AT SKINNY WEAKLINGS, the headline says, with a picture of gleaming, muscular footballer Peter Shilton holding a giant aluminium piston with what appears to be one of The Hulk's fists on either end of it. Mr Shilton is standing in his underpants, appears to have been brushed with creosote and has a definite twinkle in his eye.

I saw the Bullworker in my comic books, where it was advertised with a cartoon showing a skinny wimp humiliated in front of his girlfriend by a beach bully. In another ad, bodybuilder Charles Atlas promised: I TRADE NEW BODIES FOR OLD.

Oh, Charles. If only.

Girls on film

In 2000, Kirsten Dunst starred in *Bring It On*, a lightweight, inconsequential comedy about rival cheerleaders. It's set in San Diego with a few good lines, one very good sight gag, some good choreography, a lot of very pretty young women and a thoroughly average and probably overly generous 63% rating from Rotten Tomatoes. I was a little bit obsessed with it. Not obsessed enough to buy any of the straight-to-DVD sequels, but obsessed nevertheless.

The appeal of *Bring It On* isn't hard to explain. It features a lot of impossibly good-looking young women bouncing around in cheerleader outfits for quite a lot of the time. As a person who's attracted to women, that works for me. But it also worked on a much deeper level, because while I wasn't deluded enough to think I could ever look like Kirsten Dunst, there was a really big part of me that *really wished I could*. I was back to the Littlewoods catalogues of my youth, torn between attraction and identification. I wanted to *see* Kirsten Dunst, and I wanted to *be* her.

I felt like that about a lot of imaginary people. With very few exceptions, the characters that fascinated me on TV were the women.

A huge part of the fascination, I'm sure, is that actors and comics are hugely talented and often very good looking. But so is Edward Norton, and I've never cried in front of a mirror wishing I could look like him. I'd lose track of an episode of

Braquo because I was just fascinated by the way Karole Rocher slouched, miss a gag in *Scrubs* because of the way Sarah Chalke stood, ignore a dubious joke in *The IT Crowd* (which I can longer watch because of its writer and his views on trans people) because I was wondering if Katharine Parkinson's suit would look even look even a tiny bit as good on me as it did on her.

I think I understand the difference now. Ed Norton, and all the other male actors I watched, were playing roles. But these amazing women were role *models*. In the absence of a big sister, they were the people I looked to for clues and to model myself on. I think I was trying to crack the code of what made them so compelling in the hope that if I knew it, it could work for me too – even if that was only in private.

Looking back on it now, that all seems so incredibly obvious – as was my strong identification with music and movies about wanting to be somebody else or live a different life. My second most favourite film, *Jacob's Ladder* (1990), is about a man suffering mental anguish because he's trying to deny the truth that will set him free. And my very favourite, 1993's *Fearless*, is about a man who has a near-miss with death and decides to live his life very differently. Novelist and screenwriter Rafael Yglesias was inspired to write the story after surviving a car accident that destroyed his car but, incredibly, left him unhurt.

There's a particular scene in *Fearless* that has me in floods of tears every time. Carla (Rosie Perez) and Max (Jeff Bridges) are plane crash survivors, drawn together because of their shared horrors and shared inability to return to the lives they had before. Carla is barely existing, grieving her child and convinced that his death was her fault: as the plane plummeted, the air crew told her to hold her baby as tightly as she could. Carla survived, but her baby didn't.

So Max tries to help her. He gets her to sit in his Volvo and hands her a toolbox, telling her to hold it as tightly as she can; whatever happens, he urges, she mustn't let go. And then, to a soundtrack of U2's propulsive "Where The Streets Have No

Name" and me sobbing on the sofa, he floors the accelerator and deliberately drives the Volvo at high speed into a wall.

Of course, Carla can't hold onto the toolbox any more than she could have held on to her child. The toolbox is torn from her grip, smashes through the windscreen and crashes, mangled, onto the crushed bonnet of the car.

Max's solution to Carla's grief is horrifying, extreme and of course, stupid and dangerous. But the lesson, that no matter how hard you try to hold onto something you can still lose it, is one I'd have to learn too.

My list also includes *The Shawshank Redemption* (escape, quite literally), *Fight Club* (living in quiet desperation and wishing you were a better you) and, er, Christopher Nolan's *Batman* films. The resonance of nihilistic, glowering, borderline-fascist thug Batman isn't immediately obvious, I know, but while his alter ego Bruce Wayne appears to have it all – money, social status, good looks and great health – he's deeply unhappy and can only find peace when he dresses up in an elaborate costume to become someone else. And when he reveals his true identity to the woman he loves (Rachel Dawes, played by Katie Holmes in *Batman Begins*), she rejects him: she loves him and wants them to be together, but she can't be with him if he can't stop being Batman.

Batman is a better detective than I could ever be: it took me years before I realised that the almost comic raspy voice Batman has in the films is because he doesn't want anybody to hear him and go, "Hey! I recognise that voice! That's Bruce Wayne!" I've tried to do that too, to make my voice sound different so that the bad guys hear me and not the person the world knew me as. So maybe I grew up to be a bit like Batman after all.

Sexy and you know it

In my twenties, Eddie Izzard turned my whole world upside down. She didn't identify as trans at the time, although she does now; she used he/him pronouns and was proud to call herself a transvestite. Not just any transvestite, though: an "Action Transvestite... running, jumping, climbing trees, putting on makeup when you're up there." Izzard was hilarious, and pretty hot too.

It's hard to overstate the importance of Eddie when the last reasonably well-known portrayal of trans people was a murderous psychopath in the Rocky Horror Picture Show. Seeing a "sweet transvestite" was undeniably thrilling, but once again it was the trans person as a dangerous trickster. The film is problematic for other reasons too: it's safe to say its sexual politics haven't aged well.

Positive representation – representation where you're not seeing people like you portrayed as wicked, as sinister, as The Other – matters. Knowing that you're not alone, that not only are there people like you but that there are *happy* people like you, makes a world of difference to your mental health.

To hear Izzard not just admit to being a transvestite but to do so proudly, to make jokes about it – "Shag everyone! Wear their clothes!" – to dress in whatever the hell she wanted *and have all the cool girls fancy her*... it was like suddenly seeing the world in colour.

I've asked straight, bi and pan women friends about Izzard's appeal and had lots of different answers, but I think a lot of it comes down to that evergreen combination of astonishing charisma and confidence (whether felt or faked) that all the best stars have. But I think there's also more to it than that. Izzard's surreal flights of fancy were hilarious, but there was an obvious softness and vulnerability there too: you got the impression that Izzard really felt things more than other people.

As paradoxical as it sounds, I think Izzard's femininity could also be read as a kind of non-toxic masculinity – the same kind of confident but unthreatening masculinity that Harry Styles offers, or that K-Pop boy bands offer, or that male pop stars have offered their female fans since pop was invented. Imagine if your boyfriend had the personality and empathy of your very best girlfriend. Who wouldn't want someone like that?

Izzard was a cultural phenomenon, her popularity soaring as she essentially became a national treasure. And all the while she was visibly, unapologetically trans even if she didn't personally use that term or female pronouns back then. I was a huge, huge fan and for some years she didn't disappoint: when I went to see her on the *Sexie* tour in 2003 she came on stage in a leather skirt, black tights, heels and a red corset padded out with fake boobs. I stared at her from my front row seat in absolute awe as she delivered a killer set in equally killer heels.

Izzard wasn't just cute and funny. She was a trailblazer for trans visibility, the "executive transvestite" that everybody loved. And she wasn't the only person blurring gender lines: my NMEs, Melody Makers, Select and Vox magazines devoted covers to the incredibly beautiful Brian Molko of Placebo, the sometimes-androgynous Shirley Manson of Garbage and the starkly confessional Manic Street Preachers. Even Kurt Cobain donned the odd summer dress, looking awesome in eyeliner.

I recently wrote about my decades-long crush on Shirley Manson, and the jaw-dropping effect of her appearance in the *Androgyny* music video, for a friend's fanzine: "when Manson rocked up in tuxedo, stockings and heels the inside of my head must have looked like the bridge of the USS Enterprise under alien attack: explosions everywhere, people being thrown around the place and everything getting thrillingly, life-threateningly hot." Manson's been a vocal trans ally as well as a brilliant rock star for as long as I can remember, and I'm absolutely in awe of her.

Androgyny and gender non-conformity seemed to be everywhere. I remember being particularly confused by an NME cover in 1991 showing Blur dressed as Blondie from the *Parallel Lines* cover, singer Damon Albarn as Debbie Harry in a short dress, ombre wig and high, high heels. I was confused because I couldn't stand Albarn and certainly didn't fancy him, but in that photo I kinda did. And I definitely wanted to wear that dress.

My music magazines, CDs and Eddie Izzard cassettes were like messages from another, better planet. I might not have lived there, but I wished I did.

Crash

When I was 26, I drove too fast, lost control on a wet corner and spun my car backwards and forwards across an A-road at rush hour. It wasn't the happiest moment of my life, but it may have been the luckiest: while every single panel was deformed and the axles broken, I was fine. Somehow the car had avoided going under the front of a 40-ton lorry and left me in a field with nothing more serious than a sore thumb and a profound sense of embarrassment.

The car was a write-off, and as I mouldered at home over the next few days I had plenty of time to think. In much the same way that a funeral makes you want to have sex, having a near-death experience makes you ask yourself some pretty big questions about your life. Such as, why are you wasting it?

I was miserable. I'd drive across the Erskine Bridge during my morning commute, wondering how best to position the car to drive off the side. I'd sit in the car park listening to BBC Scotland, envious of the people being paid to have a laugh with one another. I'd somehow get through the day at work and then either go to the pub or just drink too much at home. And then I'd go on the internet and argue with people or visit the crossdressers' forums and sites.

In addition to the friends I met up with, I also had a few disasters. I had to flee Nice N Sleazy in Glasgow after an hour that felt like a year with two young German guys who, I quickly realised, were only funny and interesting online; I pretended I needed the toilet and made a run for it. I met people who smelled overwhelmingly of soup. And I fell in love with a girl who hadn't quite realised she was a lesbian, an unrequited crush that culminated in the worst thing imaginable: seeing U2's Popmart tour not once, not twice, but three times. In one week.

Thinking about my disastrous meetings, I had an idea. I'd see if I could get someone to let me write about them.

I'd long wanted to be a writer, but my desire to escape school meant I didn't do the necessary courses at university. That was how you got into journalism: you studied, you got a wee job at the local paper, then eventually you headed off to Fleet Street or to a magazine.

But the internet changed that. I was a huge fan of a magazine called .net, an irreverent and very funny guide to the internet and new technology, and its masthead listed an email address for the editor, Richard Longhurst (a few years later, Rich founded LoveHoney, the Amazon of sex toys). So I emailed him my story idea about the horror of meeting internet pals in real life.

"That's one of the worst pitches I've ever had," he said. But he also said that my email made him laugh and he asked me to pitch more. So I sat up until 4am crafting ten killer pitches, which Richard hated even more than the first. But he told me that he liked the cut of my jib and asked me to write about journaling, the then-new phenomenon of people sharing their daily lives online. I wrote three thousand words of interviews and jokes, and then Richard and his fellow editors started offering me more commissions. I quit my job six months later and I've been a full-time writer ever since.

Being a writer has been my dream job since I realised that you can't be an astronaut if you're scared of heights.

The writing bug really bit me at school when I became obsessed with *Smash Hits*. It was a pop music magazine that I adored, especially when Neil Tennant – later of Pet Shop Boys – edited it in the early 1980s. It filled me with a love of language, and especially of language that could be used to make people laugh or that could prick the pompous. Or better still, both. It was joyful and hilarious, and I was lucky to be reading it in its imperial phase. Neil Tennant coined that term to describe the brief period when a band or artist is at the very height of their powers, and I think it applies to pop music magazines too.

That irreverence, that sheer joy of wielding words, was also apparent in the weekly music magazines whose ink I'd absorb every Wednesday in my teens. The writing was so fierce, so funny, so full of references to things I'd never read. *NME*, *Sounds* and *Melody Maker* assumed you were as smart, as well-read and as passionate as they were, and reading them felt like being in the best kind of club. I timed it right, too: my generation of *NME* and *Melody Maker* writers weren't the ones who now peddle reactionary horseshit for right-wing newspapers; they were the Simon Prices and the Sylvia Pattersons (who started at *Smash Hits*), writers of great talent and even greater enthusiasm.

David Hepworth, who created *Q Magazine* and *The Word*, two of my favourite (and now sadly defunct) music monthlies, once said that getting the latest issue of a good magazine was like receiving a letter from a friend. That's how I felt about the magazines I fell in love with, and it's how I've tried to write ever since.

I've been writing for a very long time and I still don't really understand how it works. Sure, I know the craft of it all, the tricks and the tropes and the rules to break with gay abandon. I love that side of it very much: I'm never happier than when I'm referencing *Green Eggs and Ham*, pulling off a perfect pun or getting annoyingly alliterative. But that's just the mechanics of it, what Truman Capote would dismiss as typing, not writing. I know how the typing works. It's the writing that remains mysterious to me. It feels like magic, or maybe alchemy: turning the base metal of a blank page or a neglected guitar into the gold of a piece, a post or a pop song. I've been doing it so long that I go into a flow state, completely oblivious to the world around me, without even trying.

When I write, I lose myself.

Same with gigs, with live comedy, with video games, with books, with all the busywork I fill my days with to try and escape from my own brain. When I'm in the moment, lost in the music or the laughter or the drama, the critical voice in my head that never shuts up is briefly drowned out. It's like floating on my back in warm Floridian sea water, my ears underwater and the sounds of the world suddenly reduced to a bass rumble. It feels like I've disappeared completely.

But disappearing requires a constant diet of distractions. Trying to escape from myself makes me feel like I'm a shark, constantly swimming so that I can breathe. I know that if I stop, I'll sink. And if I sink, I'll drown.

Writing isn't very lucrative and it's a very precarious way to make a living, but it does give you certain freedoms, such as choosing your own hours and what work you do. And you get invited onto fun things like radio programmes – the very ones I'd envied in my previous life – and to write books.

It's also really handy if you're trans.

I was still living with my parents, but during the day I was able to live more like the person I wanted to be – albeit subject to panic-inducing surprise visits from my dad, from couriers or from friends bunking off work. But most of the time I was able to crossdress without incident, something that made me feel really good. And I was able to muck about on the internet and call it work, and that made me feel really good too.

The shame always came back eventually. Many trans people will recognise what happened over the next couple of years: I got back into the cycle of guilt and purging. I'd promise myself I'd stop all the trans stuff and I'd get rid of all my female clothes, but then the trans stuff would come roaring back and I'd have to replace my clothes all over again. But when I was 29, I knew I was purging for the very last time.

I was in love.

Love changes everything

It's January 2001. I'm standing, quivering with nerves, outside the Starbucks at Hillhead Subway station in Glasgow. I'm waiting to meet the woman I love, and there's just one little problem. I don't really know what she looks like.

Her name is Liz, and we haven't actually met yet. Not in real life, anyway.

In 2001, meeting people online was for weirdos and losers. But in a coincidence you'd dismiss as too far-fetched if it were written into a romantic comedy, we both joined Match.com to take the piss out of the people who used it and ended up being one of their success stories instead. Not that we told the website that: we didn't want people to think we were weirdos or losers.

Today there's nothing unusual about meeting new people online: my friends meet almost all of their dates via apps. But back then online dating was new and strange. People had been using technology to meet, date or hook up for years – USENET had dating groups and CompuServe and AOL had dating and adult forums – but online dating was still seen as something normal people didn't do.

I was on the site because I was short of work and hit on the idea of online dating sites as an easy thing to write a feature about. Liz was on the site because she'd been thinking about writing a novel featuring online dating, or perhaps writing an exposé of the odd things men on online dating sites think will make them more attractive to women. But we ended up meeting each other instead.

Match.com enabled you to browse and receive messages for free, but if you wanted to send messages then you needed to take out a pricey subscription. That meant women didn't need to subscribe: it didn't take long before your inbox would be inundated with messages from men, most of whom hadn't read your profile and a few of whom would send you headless torso shots or endless pictures of their cars.

Liz wasn't looking for a date on Match.com, and neither was I. But I never wrote my article, because instead of writing about daft men, I saw Liz's profile and fell for her immediately. She was beautiful in her profile photo and her bio was the perfect mix of seriousness, self-deprecation and irreverence. My own profile gleefully nicked a Spike Milligan gag – it said I was looking for a rich widow with a heart condition for rollercoaster rides and extreme sports – and used my most smouldering guy-in-a-band photos, because there's nothing sexier than a broke, unsuccessful musician with unrealistic career expectations and an exaggerated sense of his own importance.

We hit it off immediately. From the get-go we sent each other huge messages, firstly on the site itself, then in endless emails, and then in MSN conversations that'd run into the wee small hours as we talked about our lives and our hopes and our dreams of the future.

We sat on MSN all day when we were supposed to be working – more dangerous for Liz than for me, because she had a real job – and then moved to night-time phone calls that lasted until our phone batteries beeped in protest. Our near-constant communication compressed time and removed all the obstacles to getting to know each other, and we talked more in those first few weeks than some couples manage in an entire marriage. I can't remember which of us said "I love you" first – I think it was probably me – but we both felt that we'd found something really wonderful. So what if we hadn't actually met yet?

But of course, I'd already learnt the hard way that how people appear online isn't necessarily what they're like in real life. We had no idea of knowing whether the photos we'd sent each other were representative or even recent, and we had no idea if in person we'd discover something that was an absolute deal-breaker. Would Liz turn out to be as unfunny as the German guys I'd sneaked out of Nice N Sleazy to avoid? Would she like the real me as much as she liked the online me? Would she even turn up?

I was starting to wonder. I'm hilariously, obsessively punctual: I hate being late for things because I feel that if I do I'm being disrespectful, so I always turn up hours early for everything. When I was younger I was so early for a job interview in Glasgow that I managed to befriend a busker, take over for him for three-quarters of an hour, go for a few pints with him because I'd made him a lot of money (I was skinny in a suit, looked cute and played songs people actually knew) and then discover the hard way that lunchtime drunk is no way to rock up to an important interview. I wasn't quite so bad this time – there was no busker and no Dutch courage – but I was still ridiculously early.

Liz wasn't. She's one of those people who really tries to be punctual but just isn't, and it wasn't until I'd finally decided that she'd stood me up that she fell out of the hastily-commandeered taxi she'd hailed from her flat just a few hundred yards away. She was late, and she was two inches shorter than she'd said in her profile. But she didn't smell of soup.

Liz was exactly how I'd imagined and hoped her to be. She was as pretty as her picture, whip-smart and funny with lots of stories to tell. There was an immediate chemistry between us that made my usual shyness evaporate, and our weeks of hours-long late-night calls meant that we already felt we'd known each other forever. A few weeks later we were taking a city break in Amsterdam; a few months after we first met online, we were engaged.

We got engaged a lot earlier than either of us had intended. I knew I wanted to marry Liz, and the combination of two bottles of red wine and the absolute certainty that Liz was my soulmate made me decide that there was no need to wait. We were in Oblomov, a now-defunct restaurant in Glasgow's Candleriggs with an Eastern European theme. Maybe it wasn't the wine. Maybe the overwhelming smell of cabbage is an aphrodisiac. Either way Liz said yes, and I repeated my proposal on bended knee once we left the restaurant. The following morning we called our respective families and they did their very best to pretend they didn't think we'd gone completely mad.

We didn't admit to meeting on Match.com until years later, because everybody knew that the only kind of guys you met on internet dating sites were probably crossdressers with massive debts who were wanted for murder.

Well. At least I wasn't wanted for murder.

I told Liz about my crossdressing very early in our relationship. If it was going to be the iceberg that sank our relationship, I wanted to hit it before a break-up would be too traumatic. But when I revealed the iceberg to Liz, it was clear that it wasn't even an ice cube. She was curious, asked a few questions and nodded when I said it was something I didn't do any more.

I was serious. When I was with Liz, all I was interested in was Liz. And when I wasn't with Liz, all I thought about was seeing Liz again. The trans stuff vanished. I was fascinated by clothes, but I wanted to see those clothes on Liz, not me. That's what I told myself, anyway.

I think many people have experienced the honeymoon period in a new relationship, the period when you're convinced that you have found your person and that person means you will now become the very best version of your best self. You try to become the person you want to be for them, to shed your vices and amplify your virtues, and it lasts until the first time you fart without leaving the room.

I really thought I could be that person forever, and I pushed the trans stuff down as hard as I could. I couldn't completely silence the car alarm, couldn't make the feelings go away. But what I could do was fight them. Love gave me the same kind of strength that enables smokers to pick a date to quit, for alcoholics to agree to start the 12 steps, for gamblers to vow to bypass the bookies.

I moved into Liz's flat after a few months and worked from the spare bedroom. Liz had a job with a technology company nearby and worked long hours, so it seemed obvious that as the person who was at home all day I should take charge of the cooking, the food shopping and the clothes washing – the same domestic arrangement we'd keep for over a decade. Liz used to joke that I'd make someone a good wife one day.

Life was great. I was in love, we were both making decent money and we could afford to have a fantastic social life. Liz was climbing the corporate ladder and my job was getting more fun by the day: I was contributing to lots of magazines, co-writing a whole bunch of books, and I'd started making more frequent appearances on BBC Radio Scotland.

Trans identity is rather like The Terminator: just when you think it's finally dead, an arm shoots out of the rubble.

I don't remember exactly when the car alarm in my head became too loud to ignore, but I do remember being under enormous pressure. Publishing was having one of its periodic crises as the internet started to damage the industry: magazines were closing, rates were dropping and late payment went from occasional irritation to constant source of financial panic. Spending even a short time as me helped me cope.

When the desire to dress came back, I didn't wear Liz's clothes, and not just because I'd have stretched them beyond recognition. The idea felt like a betrayal. So I returned to my old friend the Next Directory, which by now had embraced the internet. I'd get a few things delivered and spend most of my working day in a stretchy skirt, opaque tights and a plain top. I'd occasionally try breathtakingly daring acts of gender non-conformity, such as wearing a plain black women's t-shirt to Tesco or boyfriend-cut women's jeans to the BBC, but I was far too scared to try anything that people might actually notice.

When another magazine closed or another threatening financial letter came through the door, I'd crossdress and feel an enormous sense of calm. The rest of the time I was in a constant state of anxiety.

I kept the clothes hidden, but I knew I had to tell Liz. And it was probably a good idea to tell her about the financial hole we were falling into. She was fine about the former and frightened by the latter. But we worked it out. We sorted out the financial issues, and Liz was perfectly fine with me dressing when she wasn't home.

Everything was good. Work picked up again, Liz got a new and very well paid job, we bought a semi-detached house in the suburbs and we adopted Megan, the most laid-back black Labrador you could ever hope to meet. We knocked through walls, got the house just-so, entertained and socialised and barbecued and holidayed and talked about the future we'd build together forever.

PART TWO

BLACK HOLES AND REVELATIONS

Numb

I am holding Liz's hand and I can see her blood gushing onto the hospital floor. I am talking to her and trying to keep her awake and trying not to notice the calm but considerably more urgent movements of the nursing team and their demands for more blood. One of the nurses joins me in talking to Liz, who is fading, and I can see the worry the nurse is trying not to show. At some point somebody hands me our baby and I am absolutely terrified for baby and mum alike.

It's October 2007 and I've just become a dad.

The panic was an emergency C-section with a lot of blood loss: Liz had been misdiagnosed with Braxton-Hicks contractions and turned away from the maternity unit when it was actually the real thing. Her body spent three days trying to get an 11lb 3oz boy out of a 5 foot 3 inch woman, causing pain I can't imagine and resulting in massive contractions that wouldn't stop. I'd later discover that it's just one of the many potential horrors of childbirth that we try not to let newly pregnant people find out about, and that cisgender men don't discuss.

Becoming a dad made me think there was something very wrong with me. The magic of fatherhood, the world-altering, personality-changing joy of bringing new life into the world, simply wasn't there. I felt that I was failing Liz at the time she needed me most. I felt stupid and useless and guilty.

The National Childbirth Trust (NCT) says that rates of depression in new dads (the figures they quote are from studies of cisgender men) are double that of the general population. First-time dads are particularly vulnerable, and the symptoms peak between three and six months after the baby is born. I was one of those dads.

I now understand that while partners and spouses don't go through the huge hormonal changes that the birthing parent does, their hormones — testosterone, estrogen (which men have too), cortisol, vasopressin and prolactin, according to the NCT — do fluctuate. And while of course we don't experience the same physical demands and sleep deprivation, we do experience broken sleep and mental stress. I worried constantly about Liz, and about the health of our baby, and about money, and about whether I was really capable of being a dad, and about all the other stuff that becoming a parent makes you worry about. And that provided plenty of fuel for the depression I'd so far managed to keep at bay.

I loved our son with all my heart, but I found those first months really hard. I had expected my life to change, but I hadn't expected the changes to be negative: I was supposed to transform from a completely clueless chap into an all-seeing, all-knowing, DIY-doing dad who had the answers to life, the universe and everything. But I didn't. If there was a meeting where all those secrets were spilled, I didn't get the invitation.

My memories of those months are cloudy and mostly negative. I remember feeling hopelessly out of my depth, increasingly certain that there had been a terrible mistake and I'd been given a role — "dad" — that I was completely unable to do. I was convinced that our baby hated me, that I was utterly useless as a parent, that I was letting Liz down. I couldn't even fulfil my stereotypical role as the sole breadwinner: long-established magazines were shutting down, freelance rates were being slashed to well below minimum wage and I found myself threatened with a defamation suit for criticising a website's terrible graphic design.

Threats of defamation are often used to silence legitimate criticism: there's no legal aid for targeted individuals, and companies can face horrific legal costs even if the case is groundless. So my publisher did what I've since learnt that critics of transphobic authors do when they receive a vexatious nastygram: they backed down for fear of financial ruin. The publisher settled out of court, told me that they were absolutely on my side and then fired me shortly afterwards, slashing my income by more than a third.

Trying to work felt like typing through treacle. I'd stare at empty pages during the day, drink far too much at night and on the very few occasions I was home alone and awake enough, I'd try to make myself feel better by crossdressing for comfort.

While all that was going on, we were trying and failing to get pregnant again. I know that sounds strange given Liz's horrendous experience and my sadness, but we had always envisaged having a nuclear family and having one child made us want a second even more. We also believed, based on no evidence whatsoever, that having a new baby was bound to be easier second time around. We were also well aware of our – well, my – age: I was already 35, and we'd been told that the older the father, the higher the risk of health problems for the baby.

So of course Mother Nature took one look at our best laid plans and decided to mess with us. It took five frustrating and often very upsetting years to conceive our second son, and Mother Nature did her best to kill Liz again during childbirth. This time the weapon was bradycardia, which is when the heart slows and slows until it stops; once again Liz was saved by the surgical team and our little family of three became four in late 2013. I turned 41 a few weeks later.

I didn't know childbirth was so dangerous; as a man, nobody ever told me. But talking to other parents I learnt that our experience – Liz's experience – was not unusual, and that horror stories abound. Pregnant people and new parents still don't get enough support, but social media has helped a little bit by enabling them to talk about their experiences, to share information and support one another.

After our first child was born I encouraged Liz to check out two online spaces in particular that I thought would be helpful: Facebook (which at the time had fewer UK users than Friends Reunited, MySpace, Bebo or Windows Live Spaces) and the parenting forum Mumsnet.

If you travelled back in time to tell us how toxic those spaces would later become, we wouldn't have believed you.

When our second child was born, I was evicted. The spare bedroom where I worked needed to make room for a cot and all the baby paraphernalia, so my computers and guitars needed to find a new home. We tried to get our house extended, but a series of cock-ups meant we ran out of time: we didn't want months of building work when we had a newborn in the house. So I got a garden office instead, spending happy days painting and furnishing it to the constant soundtrack of Chvrches' first album.

I had a better handle on the parenting thing this time around, but there was one unintended consequence of moving to a garden office. I had nowhere to be myself.

There wasn't room to store clothes out there, and I couldn't dress in the house: we had a regular stream of visitors. Dressing and then going to the office wasn't an option either, because the neighbours would see me or I'd need to answer the door to one of my many courier deliveries (I was reviewing a lot of computer hardware at this time) when Liz wasn't home. The car alarm grew ever louder.

Playing video games

One of the ways I was able to experiment safely with my gender expression was by playing video games.

Video games have a special appeal for trans people: in addition to the usual escapism from the everyday, some of them enable you to play as the gender you feel you are, not the one you were given.

For many trans people, the first such games were MMORPGs, massively multiplayer online role-playing games. Many of those games enabled you to play as all kinds of characters from humans to hobbits and space aliens. As many trans people discovered, when you communicate with other players in an MMORPG they're quite happy to stay in character, so if your character is female you'll be addressed as such. That isn't always a good thing – there's plenty of misogyny, homophobia and transphobia online, and online games aren't immune to that – but if a game is well written and acted, I'm not playing it. I'm living it.

Many games offer little more than the opportunity to play Grunty McGruntface, a space marine who runs about space shooting space Nazis with his collection of overcompensatory space guns. But when a game is well written with relatable characters I will absolutely climb between the pixels and not just play the character but become her. During the pandemic I was Ellie in *The Last of Us Part II*, weeping throughout the closing hours as my quest for revenge made me lose my humanity.

Before I made sense of all the trans stuff, I was Commander Jane Shepard.

Commander Shepard is the hero / heroine of the first three *Mass Effect* games, a sci-fi series that enables you to explore far-flung galaxies and battle an incredible variety of enemies. While it's possible to play the game as a man, Jane, or Femshep (a portmanteau of Female Shepard) as she's known in the fandom, is the best version of the character. That's because she's voiced by the wonderful Jennifer Hale, who can make even the daftest dialogue sing. Jane is much better company than her male equivalent, and you can completely customise the way she looks – hair colour, facial structure, eye shape, jawline, hair, makeup… given enough time, you could create a Jane Shepard who was an idealised version of your feminine self. So I did, and she saved all of humanity. You're welcome.

I played the *Mass Effect* games again years later when they were remastered and reissued. As with the original titles, one of the things you can do in the game is pick Shepard's outfit for when she's not encased in ballistic armour. I think it's telling and funny that years ago, my Shepard's off-duty outfit was an impressive and impractical tight leather dress; today, it's combats and a hoodie. I've also realised that the dark red I've been dyeing my hair for years now is the exact same colour my Shepard had, which amuses me immensely: when I was creating my Femshep, I was clearly trying to make the me I so wanted to be.

Mass Effect also offered romantic options beyond the usual straight man/woman binary: depending on your choices in the game you could romance other characters of various species and genders. It caused a lot of controversy at the time, because while gamers seem to have no problem with inter-species alliances (the human-man-shags-sexy-space-chick trope that goes back to Star Trek), same-sex attraction was beyond some people's – boy people's – limited horizons.

It's a shame that the game wouldn't let my character have a relationship with the character she really fancied, the gorgeous and super-smart Miranda Lawson: the developers decided to code her as straight, so romance was only an option if you played as John rather than Jane. I clearly wasn't the only disappointed player: the internet was soon packed with fan fiction in which Jane and Miranda were an item.

I think there's more to Miranda's appeal than the perfection of her polygons. Miranda was a digital version of the Emmy-nominated actor Yvonne Strahovski, who lends the character her distinctive and expressive voice and makes the character really live. Miranda is much more nuanced and interesting than the copied-from-*Aliens* badass lady space soldier we tend to see in games: she has a complex history, family issues and a lot of guilt about the genetic engineering that gave her her powers. As she opens up to Shepard there's a warmth and vulnerability to her that you don't get with, say, the monosyllabic, metal-clad Marine you play as in *Doom*. She was interesting, and if there's one thing I'm attracted to more than anything else it's people who are interesting.

Mass Effect, MMORPGs and other games where you can be a girl, such as *Deathloop* and the *Dishonored* or *Destiny* franchises are very different games, but they all offer trans people something really important: the opportunity to inhabit your preferred gender, if only for a while.

Nowhere to run

We were both shattered by the demands of work and children. I was drinking too much again, and I'd put on a lot of weight from all the empty calories. I had developed a skin condition, a terrible scaly facial rash the doc thought might be an allergy and that no amount of borrowed concealer could hide, and I'd grown a big reddish beard to try and hide it. I felt fat, and useless, and ugly. On the very rare occasions where I felt safe to crossdress, nothing fit. I'd look at my flabby, bearded, crossdressed self in the mirror and feel nothing but shame and disgust.

But at least I was feeling *something*. Most of the time I didn't. Music, my drug of choice, didn't excite me. I'd meet friends with a raincloud over my head. I found it hard to do any work, and would blow my top at the slightest thing.

That really didn't feel like me. I'm not prone to anger: I like to think I'm patient and pretty easy-going, probably too much so. And one thing I really hate is conflict, so I do my very best to avoid it completely or de-escalate it when I encounter it. I'd rather write a passive-aggressive blog post about you than punch you or yell at you. So when I completely lost my shit at a guy who'd had the temerity to beep at my sleep-deprived and thoroughly crap bit of parking as I drove my baby to the chemist, I realised there was something very wrong. I'm the kind of person who'd rather die than complain or send my plate back in a restaurant, but here I was trying to pick a fight with a man who had muscles in places I don't even have places. I was lucky he didn't tear me limb from limb.

The GP diagnosed severe depression, prescribed sertraline and referred me to counselling for mental health and alcohol misuse. Both were pointless, because I've since realised that depression and drinking were symptoms, not causes.

It didn't help that my mental health counsellor was incompetent: she told me to think about the "starving brown babies" in Africa who had it much worse than me and that I should "find yourself a wee part time job". On one of my first appointments she asked the set questions, one of which is "have you made any serious plans to kill yourself in the last seven days?" When I told her that I had indeed made serious suicide plans three days previously, she said brightly, "Well at least you're not feeling like that today!", and ticked "no" on her iPad. And technically she was correct, because right then I wasn't thinking of suicide. I was contemplating murder.

The sertraline helped, and I think the act of naming my tormentor, of putting up my hand and admitting that I wasn't coping, was helpful too. I lost weight, cut down my drinking and started to feel better about myself. And after about a year, the depression came back and hit me like a freight train.

My suicidal thoughts were so frequent and so all-consuming they were really scaring me. It felt like I'd let a demon into my head to provide a constant commentary on how much of a fuck-up I was and how everybody would be better off without me. Minor parenting fail? Why don't you kill yourself? Minor slip-up on air? Why don't you kill yourself? Minor amendments from an editor? Why don't you kill yourself? And the demon was making plans it wanted me to implement.

I read everything, trying to understand how I could be doing everything right and still be depressed. The GP changed my dosage. I tried mindfulness and iron supplements. And then I had a blinding flash of inspiration from the most unexpected source: Derren Brown, the illusionist, artist and professional trickster.

I'd bought his book, *Happy*, which is his attempt to discover the secret to human happiness. I hoped it might help. And it did, by blowing the doors off the closet I was in.

"If you have something to come out about," Brown wrote, "you should come out." And he went on to explain why.

Fireworks went off in my head.

Things will never be the same again

A man goes to the doctor and says, "Doctor! Doctor! It hurts every time I do this!"

The doctor looks at him and sighs. "Well," he says, "stop doing it, then."

Derren Brown was my doctor.

According to Brown's book, keeping a secret is like carrying a heavy bag of rocks everywhere you go. I'd been carrying mine for decades, and I was so tired that the only solution I could come up with was suicide.

Brown's book paused and looked at me, at the saddlebags under my eyes and the flaking skin around my T-zone. It sighed.

Well, it said.

Put the bag of rocks down, then.

Put the bag of rocks down?

I hadn't thought of that.

I hadn't thought of it because I had told myself that coming out was a terrible thing that I couldn't possibly do. The effect it would have on Liz, on our children, on our families! Mired in misery, my mind was convinced that coming out was a much worse thing than me killing myself in my garden office and leaving the fresh corpse for the newly widowed Liz or one of the kids to discover. Brown's book helped me understand how ridiculous that was.

I realised that I'd reached a fork in the road and didn't have reverse gear. I could take this fork here and keep trying to protect my secret, keep trying to stop being trans, and ultimately the road would take me to my own death. Or I could take the other fork and accept that the trans stuff went much deeper than I wanted or had been willing to admit, a road that might lead to the end of my marriage.

I knew that by telling Liz I was risking absolutely everything we'd built together. Liz had married a man who occasionally crossdressed, not someone who presented as female in public. By coming out as non-binary, which is how I thought I understood myself at the time, I wasn't just asking her to accept my gender identity. I was asking her to hope that our children, our families, our friends, our neighbours and our colleagues would accept it too, and to deal with any consequences if they didn't. That's an awfully big ask.

I didn't want to wreck my marriage. But I didn't feel that I had a choice any more. I had never lied to Liz about my gender stuff and I wasn't going to start now.

So I came out.

The act we act

Of all the things I expected about coming out, I didn't anticipate it leading to me chasing Pokémon around dark streets with a small child while dressed as a witch. So here's my top tip: don't come out to your partner on Hallowe'en.

I'd agonised over how best to tell Liz what I was thinking. How do you tell someone who loves you that they don't really know who you are? Do you sugar-coat it, make a fuss of them before making an announcement, or do you blurt it out during an ad break? It's safe to say it's not something you should do over text – "OMFG I'm trans LOL KTHXBYE" – or even worse, emoji, or over the second bottle of Oyster Bay. But this was a really big deal, and just busking it seemed like it was almost certainly going to kick off, get sidetracked or be hopelessly misunderstood.

I decided this was too important to risk misunderstanding, so I decided to write Liz an email. I'm not a big fan of discussing really huge personal things in writing. There's too much scope for misinterpretation, for what's meant in one way to be taken in a very different way. But this was different, because there was so much I wanted and needed to say and I wanted Liz to be able to read it and think about it without feeling pressured to react straight away. I think that's better than blurting out a bunch of half-thought words and having the other person react in shock.

I wrote an email and rewrote it and rewrote it and rewrote it a few times more. I started with reassurance: I wasn't having an affair, questioning my sexuality, joining the Tories or taking up golf. But anti-depressants weren't shifting my near-permanent gloom and I'd come to realise that depression was a symptom, not the root cause. The root cause was that I was trans. Not trans as in transitioning to become a woman, I didn't think, but trans in the sense that I felt I was non-binary: I needed to be more feminine than men are traditionally supposed to be, not just behind closed doors but in my everyday life.

I finished with more reassurance and then explained what I meant about embracing being trans instead of trying to hide it.

I think if I can blur the lines a little bit, find ways to be comfortable in my own skin without frightening the horses, scaring the kids or petrifying the post lady, to accept my difference as a gift rather than a source of shame — double the fashion options! No need to go out with crap skin! — I'd be a lot happier for it and the future would look a whole lot brighter. And let's be honest, it's much more fun than golf.

My timing was awful. As a freelancer I don't really know what day it is, let alone what's happening tomorrow. And I had the added brain fog that comes from agonising over what to do and how to do it. So Liz received my email on the morning of Hallowe'en 2016, a day that was absolutely packed with things to do. In addition to work we had kids to dress up, a house to prepare for guisers and various everyday domestic dramas to deal with, so we had no time to talk.

"I got your email," Liz told me, sadness coming off her in waves. "We can't talk about it right now." She was right. This was not a conversation we could have during a hushed moment in the hallway, or between loudly spoken demands from the kids. I felt like I'd pulled the pin of a hand grenade and dropped it into our home; I knew it was going to go off but I didn't know when.

When Liz told me we'd talk later, my brain immediately began jumping to conclusions: she looked desperately unhappy, so as the day progressed with virtually no communication I felt my limbs grow heavier and heavier. All I wanted to do was climb under the duvet and stay there, possibly forever.

Unfortunately my kids and the other kids in the street had other ideas: we had guising to do and guisers to endure. So we dressed in the fancy dress outfits Liz had bought weeks before, plastered on fake smiles and tried our best to laugh at kids telling jokes that were old even when we were the ones telling them to our neighbours while dressed as Darth Vader.

And today we were dressed as witches.

Liz had bought us fallen angel costumes, basically the same as sexy witch costumes but with longer hems to stay on the right side of decent. We'd thought the costumes would be funny, but they didn't feel so funny now: I'm pretty sure that when other parents complimented me on my legs my haha-thanks were completely unconvincing.

If that wasn't mortifying enough, once we'd finished guising my eldest demanded that I take him out to catch Pokémon. We'd given him an old phone and installed *Pokémon Go* on it, and he was obsessed with it — so I spent the evening of my coming out pounding the streets in a highly flammable dress, laddered tights and the feeling that something very, very bad was going to happen after the kids went to bed.

I've only ever been in one serious relationship so I don't know if this is normal for everyone, but on the odd occasion when I upset Liz by doing something stupid such as drinking too much at a wedding we would dance around it with exaggerated politeness — so if it was something I'd done during the day or the night before we'd give the kids dinner, put them to bed and then go through the usual evening ritual where I'd cook and pour wine and we'd talk about nothing in particular. We wouldn't talk about The Thing until the food was on the table and we were well into the first bottle of two. It was a Stepford Wives version of us, the two of us playing the roles of devoted spouses rather than unexploded bombs whose timers were ticking. The exaggerated normality and perfect politeness of those occasions was our way of trying to take some of the heat out of the conversation we knew was coming.

I don't remember the words, although I know we talked about how deep I thought this stuff went (I didn't know), whether I was attracted to men (I'm not) and whether I wanted to have surgery (I didn't). But I remember feeling heartsick and insubstantial, weightless, like a gust of wind could lift me out of the chair and carry me across the room. I remember the skin on my arms and neck prickling, the familiar feeling of ice in my stomach, my ears starting to ring as my vision narrowed, the corners fading into black and the tiniest of tiny white dots dancing in my field of view. I've experienced identical physical sensations in only one other context, which is when I've been ill and about to faint.

I felt like we were like an old photo that had been left in the sun, its colours already losing their lustre, and I couldn't undo the damage: Liz was desperately upset and I couldn't change that because the mess wasn't because of something I'd *done*; it was because of something I *was*. And I couldn't ask Liz to return her new-found knowledge like it was an unwanted gift or a top in the wrong size. I'd pulled the pin, and all I could do was wait to discover just how much damage I'd done.

I felt like I did when I was five, looking at the wreckage of my beloved *Six Million Dollar Man* doll after I'd tried to work out how his telescopic eye worked and destroyed his head instead, or like I did on any of the very many occasions when as an adult I'd try to do something practical or positive and just ended up making everything so much worse. It's a feeling of utter hopelessness, a sinking feeling, the knowledge that something terrible has happened or is happening because you fucked up because fucking up is the only thing you appear to be here on Earth to do.

I remember we talked a lot and for a long time that night, and the next, and the next, over a constant thrum of existential dread. Liz was trying to map out what was to come in a kind of sonar, her searching questions helping her see the shape of our possible futures. I don't know if it was after three days or a week or longer or less, but as we talked and talked and things started to feel less massive, less urgent, we started to discuss how we would find a way to get through this with our marriage intact.

I've got the power

If you play video games you'll be familiar with the power-up, the reward you get for doing something good in the game. For example, in a space shooting game you might start off with a ship that's slow and whose guns aren't much better than pea-shooters. With each power-up, your guns get better, your shields stronger, your ship faster.

I think being out in even a small way is a power-up. Trans people are generally very vulnerable. We've had years of being told that we're broken, that we're mentally ill, that we're unattractive and unloveable. A 2020 Stonewall study found that 16% of people say they are prejudiced against trans people. One third of that group said they felt "disgust" towards us; one quarter said they felt "resentment".[1] So if and when we take our tentative first steps into the world, our trans powers are far from fabulous. We're expecting to be verbally abused at best, or maybe even attacked physically.

But each time you push yourself, you get a power-up. Your trans powers grow stronger and you unlock the next power. I moved from going about my everyday business in black jeans to black jeans and a nice top; to black jeans, a nice top and clear nail polish; to black jeans, a nice top and coloured nail polish; to black jeans, a blouse, coloured nail polish and some subtle eyeliner… each time I didn't have a horrible experience, I gained another power-up.

It's the same with revealing my trans identity to, or just being visibly trans with, other people. Every bit of acceptance, no matter how grudging or qualified, takes me one step further away from the terrified and ashamed person I used to be. It's like beating the end-of-level boss in a video game: frightening at first but just another obstacle to overcome.

But it works like video games in another way, too. When you're defeated in a level, you lose all your power-ups; if you die, or if you just stop playing, all your progress and power-ups are gone. Getting a negative reaction to how I present, whether it's a sour look or a stage whisper or a shout, has the same negative effect: my power-ups need to be earned all over again. And if I stop playing...

I'm writing this at the very end of 2021, and it's probably not a spoiler if I tell you that in 2020 Glasgow went into a COVID lockdown and stayed there for most of the following 12 months. During that time I lost all my power-ups. The first time I went to the pub again post-lockdown, I was just as scared as the first times I went out in public as me.

Those first times were fraught. Liz agreed that for the sake of my sanity I needed to find a way to be myself without getting murdered, but we weren't exactly sure how that worked. We decided that rather than coming out to anybody at all, the best approach would be to slowly and subtly make my presentation more feminine. So the black Wranglers were gradually replaced by black Per Una, Autograph or Next jeans. The band T-shirts were replaced by Breton tops and stripy jumpers from Gap. I now realise that getting rid of the band T-shirts was a mistake. If you happen to have a Bob Mould Beauty & Ruin tour shirt in XL...

The wider world might not have noticed, but I did. I turned up for my first ever outside broadcast, in Coatbridge shopping centre, wearing black M&S jeans, a cute red and black Gap shirt and a pair of low heeled Chelsea boots. And I felt fabulous and attractive all the way to the empty shop we were broadcasting from, where I discovered that we didn't have any heating. It didn't matter what I was wearing; it stayed warm inside my winter coat. The fact nobody could see my fabulous outfit didn't matter, because I wasn't doing it for anybody else. It's like the cliché of wearing lucky pants or your best bra for a date: the rest of the world might not know you're wearing them, but you do and it puts a spring in your step. It was another power-up: although I'd never been so brazen before, I didn't feel as scared as I thought I would. I felt taller, more confident. More me.

I decided I'd test the waters a little bit with my BBC colleagues in the days before Christmas, turning up in the studio with glittery nail polish and the cover story that my entire family had done it. That was nearly true: our three-year-old was currently fascinated by nail polish, and Liz and our eldest had been mucking about with various colours. But the fantastic festive fingernails, as I described them when the presenter commented on them on-air, weren't part of that. I wanted to see if anybody would notice, or care.

Few noticed, fewer cared.

I upped the stakes a bit for the radio team's Christmas night out, wearing my now-usual uniform of women's jeans and shoes and a unisex top but with fantastically festive dark red nails with silver and gold glitter throughout the polish.

I was busted, of course, possibly because I'd been so determined to get the polish right – a process that took an incredibly long time, because my hands are damaged from years of computers and guitars and shake very badly – that I'd done too good a job. It clearly wasn't a case of man grudgingly submitting to someone else's fun idea. One friend cornered me and asked nicely whether there was anything else I wanted to tell anybody about, and another friend noticed the polish and immediately mused on how it was one thing to meet trans people through featuring them on the programme, but quite different to suddenly have someone you've known for years come out as trans. Bear in mind that all I'd done was wear nail polish.

I think people pick up on all kinds of cues. One of the people that would come out publicly in response to my coming out on Facebook – more of that shortly – told me that they'd guessed I was trans years before. I can only assume there's a trans equivalent of gaydar that enables women and trans people to notice the tells that you're trying so hard to hide, so when you do finally decide to let some of you into the public eye nobody's really very surprised. And you often find that people are much more open-minded than you might imagine, and dealing with much more than you might have considered. One friend didn't ask whether I was trans or not, but the nail polish did lead to a conversation in which he spoke very honestly, movingly and frequently hilariously about his experience of having a teenage child in social transition.

When you've spent your entire life absolutely certain that there is nobody else like you, that there is something uniquely broken and shameful about you, that if people found out the truth about you they would shun you and you would lose everything in the world that you value… to be greeted with love and acceptance is incredibly powerful. It tells you that some, and maybe all, of the negative things that you believed for all these years aren't true.

What I took away from that night, other than a truly exceptional hangover, was a new motto, a very old slogan given fresh new life by my worst fears completely failing to materialise:

Those who mind don't matter, and those who matter don't mind.*

---

* I've seen the quote misattributed to Dr Seuss, but he never said it and despite what some magazines claim, it doesn't appear in *The Cat In The Hat*. The earliest known use of a very similar phrase was in *Punch* magazine in 1855. I'm fascinated by and can talk for hours about this stuff, and yet I'm still single.

★

On New Year's Day we made our annual pilgrimage to Luss, a small and very beautiful town on the banks of Loch Lomond. It's something we did every New Year from when our eldest child was very young, and we remembered its powerful magic because our first trip to Luss coincided with them finally sleeping properly.

This New Year, I did Luss in a kind of girl mode: a little bit of makeup, a nice top and jeans, low heeled boots and a women's parka. I got a few looks from some of the people in the coffee shop but others happily helped to take photos of my family without any apparent discomfort or horror. The only actual comment was from the woman at the checkout, a thirty-something woman with fantastically coloured red and orange hair who saw my nails, grinned like a Cheshire cat and demanded to know how I got them so fabulously shiny.

You become very good at reading faces when you're trans, I think. I'm just in from a supermarket shop where I told the woman at the checkout, "Wow! You have great nails!" – because she did, fantastic fuchsia talons interspersed with equally sharp silver shards; she'd got them done as a wee treat in advance of her pal's hen party – and I think the woman in the coffee shop had exactly the same expression as I had in the supermarket: that whole "I like what you're doing and I want to know more" face. We had a brief and fun chat about the pros and cons of doing nail polish properly versus doing it half-arsed and getting on with your day, and I left the coffee shop walking on air.

The people who matter don't mind.

The people who mind don't matter.

We are family

Many trans people won't have anything to do with the BBC, and I completely understand that. The BBC in England has been the subject of endless complaints and multiple protests by trans people and allies over what they believe is a deliberate, deceptive and dangerous anti-trans editorial policy that repeatedly platforms anti-trans bigots, amplifies their scaremongering and then circles the wagons when the pieces are proved to be groundless.

But there's another BBC, and that's the BBC I've worked with here in Scotland for around two decades.

I regret not going to university, but being a regular on BBC Radio Scotland feels very much like the next best thing: I've met so many extraordinary nice and funny runners, researchers, producers, presenters and guests. I've always loved radio and for many years was incredibly envious of the people who do it. To be invited to take part, even after nearly two decades of being a fairly regular contributor, feels like an enormous privilege to me.

It also felt enormously fragile. I'd spent years convinced that if my colleagues knew who and what I really was, that'd be the end of my exciting and glamorous radio career. But now I was coming out to the world, I knew that I'd have to come out to the BBC too. And in truth, I had no idea what the response would be.

So early in the New Year, I came out as trans to all of my colleagues at BBC Radio Scotland. The reaction was better than I could have possibly hoped, and for some time I couldn't talk to my BBC friends without feeling myself welling up.

Close friends knew. Some of my colleagues knew. But what about family?

My oldest child was nine, dealing with all the complex things that happen at that age such as peer pressure, shifting friendships and growing awareness of his body, and he had definitely noticed the changes in how I looked. He made me necklaces, complimented my stripy tops, told Liz he didn't like one particular boat neck striped top I'd worn because it was so different from what I normally wore. I worried that he was finding the changes worrying.

I've always tried to give my children a feminist perspective – to fight against the other kids' received wisdom telling them they can't be interested in X because that's for not for boys or not for girls, something both of my children have heard many times since they were very young – and I've made a conscious effort to reinforce their choices without negating the alternative, so for example when one child shares their hatred of Disney Princesses I'm supportive but also point out that wearing a cute dress and being able to kill a man with a single punch aren't mutually exclusive. If you wish, you can look really fierce while also destroying the patriarchy and curing cancer.

It's one thing to talk about that and another to actually flout gender norms, though. To have a dad go from depressed and fat to trans, fabulous and slightly less fat isn't exactly a subtle change. Liz and I talked about it a lot and while Liz felt we shouldn't label anything, I argued that we could avoid that while also making sure we gave our eldest the opportunity to share their feelings. For the first few months that seemed to work very well: Liz and I both spoke to him and carefully tried to gauge his feelings, emphasising the fact that he could talk to us about anything at any time, but there weren't any questions – or at least, there weren't yet. "To be honest," he says today, "I just wasn't that bothered. It really wasn't a big deal." I hope I won't find out in his memoirs that we messed it up.

Coming out isn't an event. It's a process. And the next step was to come out to my family, and to Liz's.

I still hadn't come out to my mum or my dad, bar an amused conversation when my mum spotted the string of pearls I was wearing one evening. She asked if I was getting in touch with my feminine side, I laughed and said yes, and that was it.

I had a complicated relationship with my dad, so I put off telling him. But I knew I had to. The thought of him finding out second-hand from someone else, stumbling across a picture of me presenting female or hearing me talk about being trans on the radio, which was something my colleagues were keen to have me do, was too awful to imagine. When a few years previously, I'd blogged about having depression, my dad appeared to be furious. So I decided to email him about this before word reached him from someone else. After several days without a response, he sent a cautiously positive reply.

I don't think you fully appreciate how much something is weighing on you until that weight is taken away. The days between my emailing my dad and him responding were filled with worry, and I became more and more pessimistic with each successive day. If he were going to disown me, and I had become utterly convinced that that was why he wasn't responding, I wished he'd hurry up and do it. So his reply came as a huge relief. I'd filled a whoopee cushion of worry while I waited in limbo and his reply meant I could sit down hard on it.

Looking back, though, something was off. If you were a proud parent and one of your adult children emailed you huge news, news so big you couldn't quite process it right now, you'd still reply straight away. Wouldn't you?

I know I would. I'd write something like "Wow, that's huge! I'm sure you've got lots to tell me, so let's get together soon. When are you free? Love you x". I'm a different generation from my dad, and I know I'm a lot more emotionally demonstrative since I came out, but even if you weren't me you'd still send *something* straight away, wouldn't you?

Wouldn't you?

My mum usually came for dinner once a week, and when she arrived that evening she complimented me on my shirt – pink and blue plaid, clearly from the women's aisle – and my jeans, a pair from Next, boot cut with loads of costume gemstones on the back pockets and hips. "They're amazing. I wish they made those for women," she said, as Liz choked back a laugh. I looked for the twinkle in her eyes that indicated my mum was messing with me, but she was deadly serious: she thought this was a new fashion.

Mum didn't know much about jeans, but of course she did know that I'd crossdressed when I was younger – so when we sat down and had the talk it wasn't a surprise that she wasn't surprised. We had a long chat, all the longer because every third word was punctuated by my three-year-old jumping on my stomach, and she listened intently and said how pleased she was that I was happy. And then things got really emotional. I asked her if she wanted to see a photo of me in girl mode, and she said yes. So I found the photo I was using online, a fairly poor headshot with a dodgy wig but some pretty good eye makeup, and passed her my phone.

"Who's that?" she asked.

"Eh? It's me!"

She looked again.

"Oh my god, you're pretty," she said.

She held the phone in both hands, zooming in for a better look. I didn't say anything. I was lost for words.

"The daughter I never had," she said.

Liz told her parents that evening too. They were a bit baffled but otherwise unfazed.

★

The following evening I continued my ongoing, frustrating and increasingly expensive quest to get the hang of putting on makeup. Part of the problem was purely practical: shaky hands are not great when you're trying to do eyeliner: it means every eye is a smoky eye whether you intended it to be or not. But a bigger part of the problem is that as with clothes, I'm coming to makeup with absolutely zero knowledge or experience. So to me, going into the No.7 aisle at Boots is rather like being thrown into a kitchen with every kind of food imaginable and being told to cook something amazing. Cook what? With what? How?

I went from a skincare and beauty regime of "wash face in shower every day" to the tyranny of choice. To take just one example, mascara, what's the difference between Colossal Mascara Lengthening And Volumising Mascara, Lash Lift Look Lengthening Volumising Mascara, Total Temptation Waterproof Mascara, Sky High Washable Mascara, Great Last Waterproof Lengthening Mascara, Great Lash Big Mascara, Colossal Big Shot Waterproof Mascara, Express Lift Up Mascara, Intense Black Multiplying Mascara, Total Temptation Mascara For A Conditioned Feel and Sensational Richest Black Mascara? And that's just Maybelline. The beauty displays in Boots were like the enormous, fully stocked gun racks in The Matrix, stretching to the far horizon not with M-16s but with makeup.

People who use makeup well have gone through many years of trial and error to find the good stuff. I didn't have that luxury, and I was too scared to actually test anything in store, let alone ask for advice. So I busked it. I went for L'Oréal foundation because I'd tried L'Oréal Men Expert make-up years before (it was ahead of its time: basically primer for men) and No.7 concealer because it was on special offer. My lipsticks were Rimmel, because that's the easiest section of Tesco's beauty aisle to escape from if spotted, and my eyeshadow was whatever was on 3-for-2 at Boots.

After the usual fiasco, I finally forced my face into something

I was reasonably pleased with, so I took some photos to get a better look at my own fabulousness. It turned out that somehow – the hoop earrings and heavy lids, I suspect – I'd made myself look like Bono, the singer from U2. And not in his younger, good-looking days. I looked like Bono does now, a little old Irish man with sprayed-on hair. I posted the picture to Facebook and didn't think anything more of it, until the following morning when someone responded to it with a picture of a bearded transvestite and a single word: "TWINS!" The photo was of somebody pretending to be Kenny Everett's ancient bearded lady, Cupid Stunt, who I remembered so vividly from the 1980s. And given my friendly, open, warm and welcoming approach to the world, I naturally assumed the fucker was doing it deliberately to mock me.

He probably wasn't; I've since become very adept at figuring out whether something is a mistake, tone-deaf or deliberate. I suspect that he thought "Ha! Eyeliner! That's like a tranny thing!" and hit Google for a funny tranny pic because, y'know trannies are funny. If it hadn't been the Kenny Everett character it'd no doubt have been David Walliams and Matt Lucas instead.

I was annoyed, but it was early and I didn't want to start a fight so instead of posting something angry I went for a shower. Thinking about it as I stood under the water I realised that the problem was pretty simple: I'd come out to the people who matter most, but I hadn't come out to everybody. So the only way to prevent any future ha-ha-you-look-like-a-tranny pics was to come out on Facebook. As the meme goes: joke's on you. I'm into that shit.

At the time I wasn't aware of others coming out on Facebook, but I've since seen lots of people do the big reveal on Twitter. At the time Facebook just seemed like the obvious place to post: it hadn't really started hiding all the good stuff in people's news feeds at that point, so I knew my post would be seen by all my friends and acquaintances. If there was a bad reaction I could just unfollow, or block, or quit Facebook altogether and leave the country.

"Hey everyone," I wrote. "If you haven't guessed from the profile pics, the posts, the makeup, the song lyrics or the risking a kicking by wandering around Glasgow in eyeliner, over the last couple of months I've come out as trans. It's great, and Liz is awesome about it. The label is non-binary — basically Eddie Izzard — and I'm quite happy to answer any questions because it's no big deal. If you're uncomfortable with that please unfriend or unfollow, though, because shit is gonna get fabulous :)"

Shit did indeed get fabulous. Over the next few hours I was inundated with more than a hundred likes, replies and private messages, many from people who already knew I was trans and just wanted to support me publicly, but the majority from people I wasn't sure would be entirely cool with the trans thing at all. One person even admitted their own trans-ness in the comment thread, another person came out to me privately, and I discovered the deepest, darkest secrets of many others who confided in me. My phone pinged with endless messages of support and congratulations, often from the most unlikely people.

Two things were clear: I know a lot of really great people, and many of those people were going to regret offering to help me with my makeup.

Later that day, the guy who posted the photo that had annoyed me so much sent me an embarrassed private message. He was horrified he'd caused offence, and thought my coming out was both cool and brave. He said if I ever needed support, he had my back.

People are often better than you think they are.

Cherry Lips

Red lipstick is powerful magic. Cleopatra knew it, crushing thousands of beetles to make the red stain that signalled status and power. The first Queen Elizabeth believed her deep red lips scared off evil spirits. And in a coffee shop in Scotland somewhere in the early 21st Century, the marks it left on a coffee cup made a trans woman cry because they said, you are here! You exist!

The trans woman wasn't me, but I told her story on BBC Radio Scotland. I'd been asked to take part in a documentary about the power of red lipstick, and in particular its use in the iconography of pop music. The producer thought of inviting me not just because I'm a pop music obsessive, but also because the previous fortnight I'd come out as trans on live radio with a little bit of help from Kaye Adams and a Debbie Harry tribute act.

At first I was adamant that I wouldn't talk about being trans on the radio. My BBC colleagues knew that that was temporary, because if there's one thing they knew about me it's that you just have to point a microphone at me and I'll start talking. So of course my dignified silence lasted about a fortnight. At the end of January, even more nervous than when I'd first come out, I drove to Pacific Quay in Glasgow to come out on live radio to several thousand people.

One of the reasons I decided to come out on air is because throughout my radio career I was terrified that someone else would do it for me. On a cold Monday in January, or a warm Monday in April, or a blisteringly hot Monday in July, or a bitter Monday in November, I'd sit in the studio trying to stay quiet while laughing at the face Fred MacAulay or Kaye Adams or Julia Sutherland or Sanjeev Kohli or Susan Calman had just made, or the joke Kevin Bridges or Frankie Boyle or Mel Giedroyc just dropped, or I'd wait for Travis or Glasvegas or Michelle McManus or Tommy Sheridan's interview to end so I could take my usual seat when they vacated it. And at some point in the next fifteen minutes my life would be over, because we would open the phone lines to the listeners and one of my teenage bullies would take the opportunity to tell Scotland that I was a tranny.

I felt like that every fourth Monday, when we took calls. The rest of the time I thought my bullies would text instead. Either way, everybody in the team from producer to presenter would soon know my terrible secret and that'd be the end of my radio career.

Coming out on air gave me the opportunity to turn the tables, to weaponise my most shameful secret. If I was going to be outed, I'd be out on my terms.

It's a weird experience hearing your name on the radio at the best of times, but when it's trailing a programme about your biggest, darkest secret it's particularly jarring. I'd popped a beta blocker to calm my nerves but I was still a wreck. I'd barely slept for worrying, my skin had flared up so badly no amount of makeup would hide it, and my newly pierced ears had picked up a mild infection that made them exceptionally sensitive and very uncomfortable inside headphones. I wasn't exactly looking or feeling fabulous. And to make things worse traffic was unusually chaotic, so despite leaving much earlier than usual I nearly didn't make it on time.

Of course, I needn't have worried. Kaye, an empathetic and accomplished interviewer who can usually make me crack up live on air, and fellow guest Dr Sarah Kennedy, a gender dysphoria expert who rather brilliantly is also Debbie Harry in a Blondie tribute band, made the time fly, and despite my potentially risky decision to allow listener questions nobody demanded I be burnt at the stake. Quite the reverse: my Facebook feed, Twitter, email and the programme's own social media filled with mainly congratulatory, positive comments, and the majority of questions might have been phrased awkwardly but were warm-hearted and interested: listeners wanted to know if I was going to change my name, why I'd got married if I knew I was trans, what advice I'd give my teenage, closeted self. I was quite surprised to see some people talking about how the programme had made them cry.

I also did a short video for the social media people, sharing addresses of websites for LGBT+ people and their families in the comments section. In its first day online it was viewed 38,700 times, and it went on to be viewed 65,000 times. I can't watch it without cringing with embarrassment at how earnest I was and horror at how crap I looked, but at the time I was surprised by how few negative comments there were: one "I identify as a fire hydrant. I wasn't born as one, I don't look like one, I don't have the same parts as one, but if you don't refer to me as a fire hydrant you are ignorant", one "they're everywhere" and one comment that I needed to up my game in terms of presentation (I wasn't presenting female when I did the video). And I did get one actual Nazi urging me to follow the advice of the theme song from MASH ("Suicide is Painless") to "do us all a favour". But that was it. I'd expected all kinds, but the majority of comments were positive.

I wasn't bothered by the comments. I've been a writer with an online presence since the late '90s, so I'm used to being called the odd name; such comments are rather like midges in that they're both insignificant and annoying. But commenters and social media posters have become an awful lot nastier to trans and non-binary people since then, both in terms of viciousness and volume. When the same bit of the BBC, The Social, made a video in early 2020 about non-binary poet Gray Crosbie trying to get a haircut, Piers Morgan posted the video to Twitter, which led to thousands of screaming transphobes descending on Crosbie's personal Twitter account. As the BBC reported, the video "attracted hate from around the world."[1]

There was no hate waiting for me when I got home. My eldest had left some little parcels for me. Using loom bands, those little elastic bands you can link to make things, he had very patiently made me a necklace, a bangle, a ring and some earrings.

In the coming days I was contacted by several journalists, radio producers and TV researchers who wanted to talk to me, and for me to talk on air. In the end I refused all but one, the lipstick documentary.

Scotland's trans panic hadn't really kicked off yet and the majority of people who approached me seemed to be nice enough and well meaning. But it was obvious that at least one TV researcher I spoke to was fitting me up for a look-at-the-weirdo piece; and as a journalist I'm well aware of how easy it is to paint a picture with the bits you choose to use and the ones you choose not to, either deliberately or accidentally. I didn't want to risk an ill-thought-out comment making me look foolish in print, or being misrepresented online or by another news outlet.

One of the programmes I was offered sounded interesting, as it would be a simple interview in a studio. But that interview was conditional on being able to first send a crew to my home to film my wardrobe, to film me getting dressed and to film me putting on my make-up in order to introduce me. That isn't just invasive; it's actually damaging. I understand the fascination with the coming-out narrative and before and after revelations, but that perpetuates the idea that being trans is some kind of performance, that a trans person's identity is merely a costume that can be put on or discarded at will.

I politely declined the offers of Sunday newspaper spreads and of evening news magazine items. I'm glad I did. As *The Guardian* reported,[2] when football photographer Sophie Cook appeared on BBC Newsnight to talk about trans identities she received over 1,000 abusive messages including death threats. In an hour. When my friend Cara from the charity Gendered Intelligence spoke about trans issues on Radio 4, I saw the first abusive posts start appearing on her Twitter feed within ten seconds.

Thinking about it now, it was a mistake to go on air at all. The bit of trans people's stories that the media wants to focus on, the big ta-da! of coming out, is the time when you're at your most clueless and vulnerable. We don't invite toddlers on air to opine about the human condition, because they haven't lived. And now I think we shouldn't invite newly out trans people to opine about being trans because they haven't lived either.

When I went on air to talk about being trans, I had no more experience of living as an openly trans woman or of being a member of the LGBT+ community as I have of being a frogman in the Belgian navy. I don't even know if Belgium *has* a navy. I didn't know any of the things I know now. I hadn't read any of the trans history and LGBT+ history and feminist history I've inhaled since. I didn't know the thoughts I was having were neither new nor insightful.

I was a newly hatched egg who thought I was an adult human chicken.

I really regret going on camera, on air and on mic during this period. I was naive, foolish and ill-informed, so I was taking up oxygen that should have been given to people who actually knew what they were talking about. And I hadn't thought of the possible consequences of coming out so publicly to so many people.

One of the things that I hadn't considered about doing radio was that other people would hear it. That sounds silly, I know, but in my head the group of people I knew were radio listeners did not include any people who knew me or my family. But of course, it did. Many people Liz and I knew heard it, often by accident: they were listening to the radio while doing something or driving somewhere and suddenly there I was.

I hadn't considered that me blabbing on about My Truth and My Journey on national radio meant there was a very good chance that some of the school run mums would hear it, and that they might talk to our kids' school friends about it – not necessarily in an approving or positive way. The thought of our children hearing other people talking about me was unbearable, so after getting the okay from Liz I decided to have a chat with our eldest to explain what was going on.

Children are very matter of fact, but they're also very vulnerable, so I think it's important to reassure your children that no matter what else might be going on, you'll always be there to love them and protect them and be there for them. And that's what I said. I explained that the clothes and makeup might change, but I wouldn't. They were like wrapping paper. Underneath I was still his dad, and I still loved him from the bottom of my heart. That would never change, and neither would I. But from time to time I'd wear what I felt like wearing, even if it wasn't what other dads tended to wear.

He got it straight away, and we had a long and often hilarious conversation about sexism, gender stereotypes and silly rules. By coincidence Donald Trump had said that day that he expected his female staff to "dress like a woman",[3] and the inevitable online backlash used the hashtag #dresslikeawoman[4] for mass sharing of photos showing women pilots, bishops, surgeons, coroners, builders, doctors, musicians, soldiers, police officers, engineers, suffragettes, political protesters and astronauts. It was glorious, inspiring stuff and we scrolled through endless images, my son wide-eyed throughout.

A few days later I turned up at the BBC to do my regular slot. On the way out the team ambushed me with beautiful

flowers, thoughtful gifts – Prosecco and make-up – and a card signed by everybody. On the front it said:
Let the adventures begin.

PART THREE

WE SINK

Fa Fa Fa Fa Fashion

Clothes are hard, especially if you're coming from a position of complete ignorance: what looks brilliant on eBay can make you look like Mr Blobby in the mirror. But getting it right can feel electric. There's something about even a perfectly ordinary, everyday interaction with others that feels super-powered when you're rocking a look you really like, and since coming out and losing my self-consciousness about being trans I've had very many joyous moments with friends, family and colleagues where nothing remarkable happened but I felt happy and confident and fabulous. When you've spent decades being awkward and shy that's absolutely exhilarating.

But getting it right is also really difficult to do, because you know absolutely nothing.

Imagine if you just popped into existence as the you you are right now, with none of the experiences you've had or knowledge you've gained. Your body, your brain, your entire existence is a blank slate – but to the people around you you're just another adult and there is stuff that they expect you to do.

But you don't want to do what they want you to do, because your egg has just cracked and your world is new. Everything that other people take for granted and have long since stopped noticing is overwhelming you, and you feel like the first creature who has ever seen these colours and smelled these scents and had these insights and by god you want to tell everybody about how *amazing* everything is and have you seen the sun and the sky and the colours and the grass and the flowers and the…

It's very annoying, I know. But it's so exciting to experience it, to finally get to be a full person rather than the half-person you policed yourself to be. Unfortunately that exhilaration can be really damaging. It distracts you as you drift into the pink fog.

The pink fog is something I first read about on trans-related message boards. It's when you get so caught up in yourself and your gender stuff that you drift away from reality.

In my desire to do everything, to wear everything, to explore all the possibilities I'd been denied and to be the super sexy person I'd had to hide from the world for so long, common sense and a sense of proportion often got lost in the fog.

I became an eBay addict, accumulating lots of really stupid purchases that I was too old or too tall or too broad shouldered to wear, or which no self-respecting woman would wear to anything other than a fancy dress party. I bought dresses for the parties nobody was inviting me to, activewear for the exercising I had no intention of doing, bikinis for the beaches I wouldn't be sunbathing on.

Imagine doing a trolley dash in Primark, but you're blindfolded and you've been drinking Prosecco for three days straight and instead of a trolley you're sat on a Vietnamese pot-bellied pig and it's not Primark it's a bin and the bin is on fire.

My eBaying was very much like that.

It was as if I was drawn to the things that would make me look my worst: bodycon dresses that made me resemble some kind of bondage potato; tops that strongly suggested I was pregnant with a fully grown Danny DeVito; skirts so short that there was a distinct risk of my testicles popping out like a photobomb by Right Said Fred. I didn't wear any of these things outside, of course, but that didn't stop the second-hand shopping spree. Things got so bad that the eBay app refused to let me add any more items to my watch list until I agreed that I didn't need as many handbags as Imelda Marcos had shoes.

The pink fog is about more than buying stupid things you don't need, don't suit and can't afford, although that's part of it. It's also about wanting to make up for lost time, to come out of a decades-long winter and feel the sun on your face for the very first time. That all feels perfectly natural, and positive, because your whole life has led up to this. But the people around you haven't had that adjustment period, and for some of us the pink fog can make us push beyond what other people find comfortable or make us appear to change very significantly in a very short period of time. That can make life difficult for the people you live with or the people you work with.

I didn't think my own pink fog was very dramatic and I did try to notice its wispy tendrils before they got hold of me. I tried not to change too much too quickly: I didn't wear a skirt around the house, let alone outside, until more than three months after my initial revelation to Liz, and I made a deliberate effort to dial down the fabulousness – so when I went out I dressed like any other faintly harassed shopper, and when I went to work things I'd keep my outfits simple and the makeup subtle, or what I thought was subtle. I now realise that I looked like an enormous five-year-old who'd been playing with her mum's makeup. But despite my many mistakes, I constantly tried to analyse what people around me were wearing, hoping to discover how I could blend in as much as possible.

There were practical reasons for my lack of flamboyance too. I hadn't much experience of things women my age learned long ago: how to navigate stairs in heels, how to get out of low chairs without flashing your pants, how to get in and out of cars or sit when you're wearing a skirt, how to walk in really high wedges, how to pick things up from the floor when you're wearing a pencil skirt and so on. I already knew that going out in a skirt would attract much more attention than a more androgynous look. I didn't want to add to that attention by staggering around and falling on my arse or going face-first into the oven chips in ASDA.

I think I practiced some psychic self-defence too. I'd turned down TV, radio and newspaper appearances because I wasn't quite ready to do them, let alone deal with the fallout if I were presented as someone to mistrust or mock. And while my trans superpowers were building up nicely, I wasn't quite ready to face the world as a man in a skirt just yet. I needed to get used to the idea in my own mind, to reach the point where a skirt was just another thing I wore, part of my armour against double-takes, stares or comments. So initially at least I kept the skirts and heels for wearing around the house and made most of my mistakes in private.

When it came to friends, family and colleagues I kept in mind an old comedy sketch from The Fast Show, in which an earnest young couple would respond to any piece of dinner party conversation by saying, "And when you think about it, that's really quite like the story of Jesus, isn't it?" I was very mindful of Derren Brown's argument that being different was just one piece of information about you; people didn't need to hear that information from me again and again and again. My trans identity was a big deal to me, but it wasn't and shouldn't be a big deal to anybody else.

Coming out is exciting and all-consuming and euphoric. But eventually the momentum slows and the euphoria fades, and you're left with a simple realisation: everything has changed, and nothing will be the same again. Sometimes that's a good feeling. Being true to yourself is powerful; Whitney Houston was right when she sang that learning to love yourself is the greatest love of all. But being yourself is pretty damn tiring too.

If you don't fully transition, or if you do transition but don't pass as your gender, there will never be a day when you can wear whatever you want without anybody noticing. You'll never walk into a busy room without turning heads, or walk through a busy street without being hyper-aware and a little bit anxious and afraid.

The first time out in a skirt or makeup or both is exciting and frightening. The second time less so. A few more times and it strikes you that you're dressing for Groundhog Day: any time you go out in feminine attire, you'll be aware of being around people who haven't seen you before and who will notice you.

It's the same when you travel anywhere, or meet anybody new, or even answer the door. The freedom to dress as you wish quickly becomes tempered by the desire for an easy life with no alarms and no surprises. "What shall I wear today?" is soon replaced with "How strong do I feel today?" The desire to wear something nice battles with whether you can be bothered with the cartoon-style double-take from the twentysomething woman in the comedy club, the smirks of the young man on the top deck of the bus, the stage whispers of the teenage girls in Tesco, the death stare from the middle-aged woman with keys to a Range Rover in her hand and the *Daily Mail* in her shopping trolley.

The initial stages of coming out feel rather like being strapped to a space rocket, the roar and speed and sensation of it all overpowering everything else. For weeks I was so excited I barely slept, my brain racing through everything that had happened that day and what might happen the next. But sooner or later the rocket runs out of fuel and you find yourself far from home with no idea what to do now. Things the euphoria overpowered start coming back again, whether they're the everyday stresses and strains of life or trans-specific issues such as the sadness you feel when you look in the mirror and still see yourself. And of course if your coming out has had a negative response from your partner, friends or family then there's the fallout from all of that to deal with too. Even online abuse directed at other people can ruin your day.

One minute I'd be elated and full of joy, the next so sad I could barely speak. The sad feelings weren't as deep or as long-lasting as when my depression had nearly wiped me out, but they were pretty unpleasant nevertheless. I spent a few afternoons under the duvet, my internal monologue refusing to let me sleep but not letting me concentrate enough to get any work done either. Whenever I thought about the future I could only imagine negatives, such as Liz leaving me for somebody more masculine.

This is in no way unusual, because while coming out addresses one really big issue it isn't a magic cure for everything in your own head, and it doesn't magically make the world a nicer place either. I followed all kinds of trans and non-binary people on various social networks and platforms, seeing them dealing with their own Groundhog Days: coping with anxiety, dealing with personal issues, drowning in debts. And if that wasn't enough many of them were also dealing with being misgendered by strangers, shunned at work, shoved in the street, harassed on the internet, mocked in the newspapers and ridiculed on TV.

I watched endless video diaries of people trying to come to terms with what their identities mean, and often noticed the smiles that didn't quite reach the eyes when they tried to put a brave face on the negative things they had experienced or were experiencing. That's not to say they didn't have rich, fulfilling and authentic lives. Of course they did. But they reminded me of the women's march protester with the sign, "I can't believe I still have to protest this shit."

Underneath it all is the knowledge that all the cards are stacked against you. The body you're in doesn't fit the gender you need to express yourself as, so if you're not young and slim and pretty your best efforts will always fall short. In my head I'm as gorgeous as Emma Stone. Unfortunately my mirror begs to differ. No matter how excellent the eyeliner, how luscious the lipstick or flawless the foundation, whenever I looked in the mirror I didn't see a pretty woman, or a pretty anything. Just a fortysomething bloke in makeup. Less Emma Stone, more Fred Flintstone.

Even on good days you'll see your reflection and wonder what the hell you're doing. You'll ask yourself again and again if coming out as trans was a terrible mistake. And there's no shortage of people happy to tell you that it was.

Shout, shout, let it all out

I didn't marry to deceive. I married because I was in love. I thought that love had cured me of my sadness and my weirdness. I genuinely believed that I could be Mr Right, and for a while I think I was, or at least as close as I could get.

When married people come out as LGBT+, there's often a negative reaction from the wider world and if they're well known, the press too. The person (it's usually a man, or someone who'd tried to be) is cast as duplicitous, a deceiver, someone who used his partner as a human shield to hide his dirty little secret and robbed her of the best years of her life. I saw lots of that when TV presenter Philip Schofield came out as gay in 2020. I don't think he was trying to deceive anybody either, except maybe himself.

What Schofield and I both did to ourselves was effectively conversion therapy: we fought to try and make ourselves "normal", to deny what our own brains and bodies were trying to tell us, to refuse to see the signs that we were who we were trying so hard not to be. And the more people depend on you, the harder you try to fight it – and the more awful the consequences if you can't fight any more.

I didn't realise it at the time, but my coming out put Liz and I into two separate and very different time zones. Having spent all my life fighting my gender stuff, now that I was out time felt painfully slow: there were so many things I needed to do and say and change and experience. Everything had been broken for so long and I was racing against time to make it all better.

But for Liz, time wasn't moving slowly. It was moving ridiculously, frighteningly quickly. "It was like an out of control train," she told me recently. "It was terrifying."

When Liz said she wanted to find a way to make things work, I didn't interpret that as "okay, let's take it easy and see where it takes us." I interpreted it as permission to kick the closet door clean off its hinges.

I often use the analogy of throwing a hand grenade into a relationship because I think it's a good way to describe the sheer speed and force of what coming out can do. One minute your husband is an ordinary guy who occasionally likes to explore his feminine side. Then, when you least expect it…

Boom.

Liz knew I crossdressed from very early in our relationship, but she thought it was an occasional thing, not my entire identity. And that's what I thought too for a very long time. I wasn't keeping it a secret from her; I didn't tell her because I didn't know either.

Liz had already had to deal with much more than she signed up for. She had seen the funny, excitable, enthusiastic man she'd met and married turn into someone much sadder; my mental health issues turned me from a little ray of sunshine, albeit sarcastic sunshine, into someone permanently under a cloud. Our marriage was already under enormous strain because of that and because of my precarious career, and my coming out made that strain so much worse.

I can't speak for Liz; her story isn't mine to tell. And I can't speak for other trans people or their partners. But I think I understand now what I didn't consider at the time, which is that coming out can be a very frightening, confusing and disorienting experience for your loved ones.

When a partner comes out, it raises very big questions about them, about the world you live in, and about you. I try to imagine what would have gone through my head if I'd been the cisgender partner and Liz had come out to me. I think my worries would be pretty universal: How deep does this rabbit hole go? What will the neighbours say? What effect will this have on our kids? Will I still be attracted to her, or her to me?

Not all relationships flounder when one partner comes out. But sooner or later they all need to deal with the same question: what happens if the person you married can't be the person you married?

I was oblivious to all of this. I didn't so much come out of the closet as roar out of it on a glitter-powered rocket cycle, waving the Trans Pride flag and putting all of eBay on credit cards I already couldn't keep up with. I binned my boring boy clothes, wore skirts to the shops, talked about being trans on national radio to thousands of people and spent months getting dirty looks from old women in ASDA. And in the meantime Liz got texts from school run mums offering support or digging for gossip. It turns out that wasn't the best way to do it.

I feared Liz would reject me when I came out to her, but she was fiercely protective and utterly supportive. Bar the odd bit of fashion advice (and occasionally, wardrobe theft) she never asked me to tone down my presentation. As long as it was safe, age- and place-appropriate and wouldn't get me killed, she was absolutely fine with it.

I thought that meant Liz was absolutely fine with all the trans stuff.

Liz was not absolutely fine with all the trans stuff.

In April, six months after I'd come out to her and four months after I'd started coming out to the wider world, we both accepted what had been increasingly obvious for some time: our marriage was in trouble. We made an effort to try and get back to normal, to make Friday night date night and go back to how things used to be, and I put most of my feminine side away because I really didn't want to lose Liz. But I could feel our shared future slipping in and out of focus. Our date nights felt forced, awkward silences where we'd never had awkward silences before, the pull of smartphone screens so much stronger than the strings holding our relationship together.

And then one morning I opened the iPad we shared and saw that Liz hadn't closed the tabs.

The tabs that were open were property websites and advice columns about the effect of divorce on children. I don't think she'd left the tabs open deliberately; when Liz gets tired it hits her like a tidal wave and she'll stop doing whatever she's doing immediately and head for bed. But clearly, we needed to talk.

So that night we talked, and Liz said:

I love you, but I don't think I'm in love with you any more.

I knew this feeling. I'd felt it nearly twenty years previously when my tyre blew out and my car slewed across a rush hour road. Then, like now, my brain slowed time until it almost stopped. Sounds slowed too, shedding semitones until they were no more than faraway rumbles. There was ice in my abdomen and I felt sick. I felt an incredible dread, unable to affect the outcome and forced to see it approaching in cruel slow motion.

I love you, but I don't think I'm in love with you any more.

Everything had changed. I looked different, smelled different, walked different. When I asked to explain the last one she talked about our most recent date night, when we'd walked to a restaurant at the bottom of the hill from us. I'd been wearing simple low-heeled boots, but Liz's mimicry of my walk suggested some kind of pathetic horse.

At the time, I didn't understand. For months, I'd constantly checked with her that everything was okay, that she wasn't uncomfortable with anything, that she wasn't embarrassed or worried or anything else. And the response was always positive. She'd raved about how much better I smelled, and how she loved the way the house smelled when she came home now.

She'd told me I looked great, that she still fancied me, that she was looking forward to summer nights on the decking drinking rosé in matching floaty dresses.

Liz told me that she'd been saying all that not because she believed it, but because she was trying to be supportive.

She told me that I wasn't the man she married. She felt different about me, couldn't articulate why or how, but something big had changed. When we'd gone out to a concert the night before – me taking it easy in jeans, a simple top, trainers and minimal make-up – it had really struck her. I was no longer her husband.

I asked questions, but the answers weren't in the words. They were in the spaces between the words, the too-long gaps between question and answer. We cried, and we hugged, and we tried to pretend that everything was going to be okay when it very clearly wasn't going to be okay. The eyes that I'd spent so many hours gazing into could barely meet mine now; the voice that used to make laughing threats to hunt me down if I ever dared leave no longer put a price on my head. Like time travellers who'd accidentally stood on a butterfly, the futures we'd planned together were already starting to flicker and fade.

PART FOUR

RIP IT UP AND START AGAIN

Wrecking ball

In April 2017, around a hundred days after my radio interview, six months after I came out privately to Liz, thirteen years and eight months after we got married and sixteen years and four months after we first told each other we loved each other, Liz and I became legally separated.

Love and Pride

It's a rainy Saturday in July and so far I've been yelled at by a drunk, accused of abominations by a street preacher, smiled at by a bearded nun, rendered numb below the knee by horizontal rain and fallen on my arse in a packed Subway carriage. It's not even teatime yet.

Moving to Glasgow suited me. I found a pub where the staff were lovely and made me feel welcome, and I started to feminise my clothes again. I became much more practical in terms of what I wore, dressing more appropriately for my age and my surroundings instead of just buying whatever was cheap on eBay. There were still fashion disasters, but not quite so many.

I'd already transitioned my wardrobe from fully male to fully female before I'd separated from Liz, and in Glasgow I settled into a routine where previously forbidden female things were just normal. I shopped carefully, looking for things that would actually fit rather than grabbing whatever looked okay. I epilated my legs – I now know what lawns feel like when they're being mowed – and spent many hours trying to copy everyday makeup tips from YouTube. I dressed in obviously female clothes while I worked, only changing into something less so if I was going out somewhere I wasn't sure of. I wore wedge shoes and sandals around the flat to try and get used to walking in heels. I still do that latter one from time to time until I remember that I'm 6'1" and don't need the extra height or risk of sprained ankles.

Something shifted during this period. I no longer considered my female clothes to be crossdressing: they were my clothes. The only time I felt that I was pretending to be somebody else was when I presented more male, for example to do the school run: that was when I was crossdressing, trying to fool people into seeing me as somebody I wasn't, reducing my Technicolour world to shades of grey. The rest of the time I was just being me.

In July, that me went to Glasgow Pride.

That probably doesn't sound like a big deal, but when you've spent decades being ashamed of who you are there is something profoundly liberating and energising about standing among thousands of people just like you for the very first time.

Pride is often portrayed as a party, but it began as a protest – and as a trans person, there was plenty to protest about. The same week that I attended Glasgow Pride, heavily armed neo-Nazis and gammon-faced grandfathers in MAGA hats were screaming "fuck you, faggots" at US Pride marchers. The UK anti-trans panic was building up steam, with articles published in national newspapers claiming that people like me were predators, child abusers, a threat to free speech and enemies of feminism. Other Pride marches had been interrupted by anti-trans protesters, and bad actors were doing their best to get the L, G and B to throw the T under the bus.

I was apprehensive about the prospect of having to run a gauntlet of anti-LGBT+ people on the streets, or worse, anti-trans activists trying to disrupt Pride itself. But the main reason I kept equivocating over whether or not I'd actually go was because the simple act of going to Pride felt like an enormous step and I was genuinely scared of taking it.

Pride is for the LGBT+ community, but like any community there are schisms within it. Some cisgender gay men don't want to be associated with camp gay men or trans people; some transsexuals consider anybody who hasn't had surgery a tourist undeserving of the term trans; and so on. And the marketing of Pride, particularly the post-march events, looked pretty stereotypical to me: endless photos of cute, young, toned cisgender men and the odd outrageous drag queen. I really didn't know if Pride really was for people like me, or if the T in LGBT+ was only added out of custom – so I feared being looked at as not trans enough, not LGBT+ enough. It was the same impostor syndrome I'd always felt, but this time I feared being seen as an impostor at a party supposedly for me. I wasn't sure I was ready to push myself this far out of my comfort zone.

When I was feeling a bit braver, I made the mistake of posting to Facebook to say that I was kinda sorta maybe thinking about going. My BBC colleagues spotted the post and asked me if I'd be up for recording an item for radio about what it's like to go to your very first Pride. The offer of money to talk about myself was impossible to resist.

Saturday dawned, and I decided to mix Pride with practicality. I wore a tartan kilt skirt – it was Pride *Glasgow*, after all – and black tights, but I put Doc Martens on my feet in case I needed to make a sharp exit or kick someone. I did a reasonable job of my makeup, walked out of the front door and got my first weird look within five seconds when a young couple from a nearby flat damn near broke their necks doing a double-take. That didn't bode well for my travel plans, which involved taking the Subway into town then walking across Glasgow's busy shopping streets to get to Glasgow Green. It didn't help my nerves when I saw the Subway information screens warning about the system being busy due to a big football match. I loathe travelling in Glasgow when the football's on: I'm an easy target for boozed-up blokes' jokes.

But my fears were wrong this time. I got a few warm smiles from young women I didn't know, and as I walked through Glasgow I gained extra confidence from seeing the rainbow flag bearers, queer couples and bearded nuns – the charity, protest and performance group The Sisters of Perpetual Indulgence – walking the same road. I was only yelled at once, by a poor soul clearly the worse for drink long before lunchtime. And I was amused rather than appalled by the bible guy preaching eternal damnation through a megaphone as I clumped past him, his face as clenched as the fist holding his microphone. 5,000 marchers, 50,000 supporters, Irish popsters B★Witched and Scotland's First Minister Nicola Sturgeon were getting ready to show that he was on the wrong side of history.

It's a shame nobody told the cops. As I arrived at the event, I saw a small group of young trans protesters and allies being manhandled and thrown to the ground by the police. They were protesting the bone-headed decision to let Police Scotland lead a march whose origins were a protest against police brutality and corruption, and as far as I could see the protestors were completely non-violent; five people were arrested and later released without charge. I later learnt that another LGBT+ person, LGBT Unity convenor Embrima Kalleh, had been stopped and searched for "wearing a cagoule on their head"[1] under anti-terrorism powers that don't appear to have been used against any of the white people wearing similar cagoules. This happened within view of the Pride party buses, their corporate-logoed rainbow flags fluttering as their sound systems drowned out the protest.

Despite that jarring introduction, I still found Pride to be positive: it made a big difference to my confidence and my feelings about being out. To stand in a park with thousands of people who think your darkest secret is something to celebrate, not hide, is incredible. It was so powerful that I stayed while Glasgow did its summer thing and delivered freezing cold rain that came in sideways, soaking me all the way through to my bones.

Eventually the weather won and I walked back through Glasgow to no reaction whatsoever. I got on the Subway, the subject of idle curiosity for a few young women, then successfully blended in by standing up, misjudging where the bar was and falling on my arse in the busy carriage. Nobody laughed apart from me.

I'd originally planned to change into jeans and a t-shirt before going to the pub for dinner, but I decided that if I could walk through Glasgow in a skirt I could damn well wear a skirt to the pub. I swapped the kilt for a knee length black denim skirt and my rain-soaked tights for a fresh pair and went to my new local.

I thought it would be quiet. It wasn't. There weren't any free tables, so I had to stand at the packed bar for a couple of drinks. The bar staff were their usual friendly selves and greeted me with smiles, but I was utterly terrified. It didn't help when I noticed a couple of young women who spotted me and giggled. When my table was ready I was called a little early, so I had to stand there, quite clearly a very nervous bloke in a skirt, until the table was fully cleared. My post-Pride confidence faded fast.

When I'd finished my food I got up to leave, and a mixed table of people I assume were students called me over. "Excuse me!" one of the young women said. "Excuse me!"

I moved over, mentally bracing myself for whatever humiliation she had in mind.

"I just wanted to tell you that you look amazing," the woman said, her friends nodding. "You look amazing and I hope you have a really great night."

I mumbled my thanks but my heart was soaring. I didn't look amazing, but her words certainly made me feel that way.

When I got home I had a serious go at my make-up, tried a bunch of wigs and took many selfies. In male mode I find it hard to smile to order, but in female mode the smiles were genuine and reached my eyes. I spent a lot of time just looking at those photos, thinking.

Going out in obviously female clothes had been terrifying, but it had felt strangely calm too. Everything had felt right, like all the pieces of something were in their right place. During and after Pride I was treated as, and felt that I was, a normal person doing normal things in a normal day. And that feeling of rightness only disappeared when I was pulled out of it by the sight of my reflection, by the double take of a stranger, or by having to make myself look less feminine for fear of how others might react. Then I had the sinking feeling of not being who I am in my own head, of being seen not as a person, but as a freak.

I realised I wasn't non-binary. I was very, very, very binary after all.

Just not the male one.

That night, I posted on a trans forum where I'd made some friends. "OMG," the title said. "I'm trans. Like, trans trans."

Shit.

Sexy! No no no

I love autumn, and I particularly love it in Glasgow: the dear green place becomes even more beautiful when the seasons change, its parks and avenues aflame with blazing reds and brilliant shades of warm citrus and burnt ochre. On a nice day it's absolutely breathtaking: it makes you feel incredibly alive. And if you're single, incredibly lonely. These are days you want to share with someone, someone you can kick through leaves with and make friends with other people's dogs with, to talk animatedly over dinner with and walk hand in hand down chilly streets with.

I'd always considered myself to be a loner, but that's not true. It's just something I told myself to draw the sting of being lonely. Liz was right when she said I'd make someone a good wife: without somebody to laugh with, cook for, make big plans with and generally make a fuss of, I'm half a person.

So I did something I hadn't done for fifteen years. I signed up for a few dating apps, vividly aware that the last time I'd used any I was much younger, much thinner and a completely different gender. And I soon discovered that I wasn't remotely ready for any of them, not least because they're very different from the ones I'd previously used: the emphasis on photos is great if you're young, pert and beautiful but not so good if like me you look more like a neglected sofa and your self-esteem is virtually zero. And so many of the photos are weird: I was baffled by the profiles that used so many image filters you couldn't tell if the poster was actually human, or the ones that had so many people in shot it wasn't clear if you would be dating a woman or an entire ward of Mormons. I also began to wonder if there was some secret lesbian rule I didn't know about that meant you had to take all your dating app photos on a racing bike halfway up a mountain.

I didn't dare swipe right because the women who looked cute and interesting were clearly way out of my league, but I did attract some attention on some of the apps I tried. Unfortunately that attention generally came from two kinds of people: men who don't read dating app profiles, and women who don't read dating app profiles. The former were men who fetishised trans women and automatically assumed that I'd be gagging for a shagging even though my profile made it clear I was only interested in women and feminine people; thanks to their unsolicited image sharing I've now seen more weird-looking penises than the average urologist. And the latter swiped right despite their profiles' adamant assertions that they wouldn't date someone who already had kids, someone who didn't want to give them children or someone who was transgender.

That last one is very common. I'd hardly be a catch if I weren't trans – I'm overweight, middle-aged, asexual-ish, separated with two kids and a pretty precarious career – but of course I am trans, and that reduces the number of people who might be interested in dating me to approximately zero.

I'm not really exaggerating. A 2018 study[1] reported that just 1.8% of straight women would consider dating a trans person. The numbers were slightly more encouraging among lesbian women, 29% of whom would be fine with a trans partner. But even among trans and non-binary people there was only a narrow majority who would be OK dating a trans person: 52%.

I know you only need one person to like you. But after decades of being told that trans women were freaks, undateable and unlovable I wasn't entirely sure that if the roles were reversed

I'd date me either: why date a middle-aged trans woman when you could have someone younger, prettier and cisgender?

The big problem I had, and have, with dating apps is simple. The very thought of dating terrifies me because with the exception of Liz, I've never dated anybody as an adult – so I'm absolutely certain that meeting any woman from a dating app will result in a humiliating rejection. Maybe she just won't turn up. Or maybe she will turn up and her face will fall when she sees my height, or my body shape, or my hands, or my Adam's apple. Maybe she'll keep a poker face until she hears my voice or notices that other people are pretending not to look at us. Maybe we'll get past all of that and she'll decide I'm really boring. Maybe she'll fake a phone emergency or her own death, or somehow we'll get through the date and step outside and she'll say "Look! A squirrel!" and run away.

This is internalised transphobia, I know. But it's incredibly hard to overcome it, to see myself as someone that other people might find valuable, let alone attractive or loveable. So I did what I'd done since my teens and decided that you can't lose a game if you don't play. I rationalised: my life was in too much flux. There were too many unanswered questions about my future, about my transition. How could I expect someone to love me for who I was if I didn't know who I was?

I purged the apps like I used to purge my clothes, knowing that sooner or later I'd be back to repeat the cycle all over again.

I may not have known who I was, but I knew I was starting to feel a lot happier. Others noticed too. "We're fine with the trans stuff," my brother told me. "It's the happiness that freaks us out." I hurled my car around Scotland's twisty bits before the world woke up, grinning my face off and howling along to Faith No More. I cried with joy against a festival crash barrier when Peter Hook of Joy Division played Love Will Tear Us Apart, a song I love and thought I'd never hear live. I felt my heart soar when friends got in touch for no good reason and made me feel loved.

I delighted myself by slipping terrible jokes into serious articles I wrote. I grinned at unruly kids and big-eyed babies.

I used to be the kind of person who hates bus stop conversations with strangers. Now I'm the kind of person who starts them.

But was that person non-binary? I'd thought so when I first came out: I knew I wasn't comfortable being a man, but of course I didn't have a female body. So when a friend referred to me as a "trans woman" in a Facebook post it took me a moment to realise who she was talking about, because I knew the label of trans woman didn't apply to me. Nearly a year after coming out, though, I wasn't so sure any more. The more female I presented, the more comfortable and happy I felt. And the more comfortable and happy I felt, the more I wondered if I needed to do more than just change my presentation.

In previous chapters I've said that I didn't have severe dysphoria about my body; just an overwhelming sense of *meh*. But that was starting to change. The more I moved through the world as me, the more disappointed in my body I became.

I'd spent endless hours looking at trans women's HRT transition timelines, the photographic evidence of the cumulative effects of hormone treatment and improving make-up skills. I actively searched for timelines of middle-aged MTF trans women, trying to see what was the result of HRT and what was just better lighting, good makeup and a cute smile.

Looking at such images wasn't new, nor was the strong yearning I felt to be one of the people in the pictures. I've had those things since I've had internet access. But something was different now. I no longer saw the photos as pictures of transformations that, for me, would be impossible and unattainable.

I started to see them as maps of the possible.

What struck me wasn't the physical transformation; it was the difference in the way they looked at the camera, the smiles reaching their eyes. Even relatively minor physical transformations looked spectacular because of the difference in the way people held themselves and looked at the camera.

Each timeline was the same story: unhappy people finally becoming happy in their own skin. I wanted to feel that too.

Have you seen *The Matrix*? In 2020, director Lilly Wachowski confirmed what every trans person already knew: the 1999 film she made with her sister Lana – who, like Lilly, hadn't yet come out – was a trans allegory. It told the story of Thomas A Anderson, an ordinary Joe who takes a red pill that enables him to finally see reality and discover his true identity. In the US at the time, oestrogen pills were red. Anderson realises he is not the man everybody thought he was: he's really Neo, he's the messiah and he knows kung fu.

I didn't know kung fu and I'm definitely not the messiah but I felt pretty much like Neo did. Everything had changed. I wasn't non-binary. I was a trans... something.

I wasn't sure what I was. But I knew that when I went through the world presenting fully female, everything suddenly made sense. And while that was very positive, I was also feeling the strongest negative emotions: loss, and anger. For me self-discovery wasn't a cosmic microwave ping that announced the dawn of the new me and the dawning of a golden age. I was frightened and sad and angry. Because if I was a trans woman, then like Thomas Anderson I'd spent my whole life trying to be somebody I wasn't instead of living the life I should have lived.

I felt myself grieving the loss of that life, angry at the sheer unfairness of it all to me and to the people around me, of having everything turned upside down when I was already more than halfway through my allotted three score years and ten. Like a teenager, I felt that everything was so unfair.

I felt like I'd become the punchline to a joke everybody was in on except me. I was so certain of who I was, and it turned out I was completely wrong. Sometimes I wish that I'd taken the blue pill and made it all go away.

Shame shame shame

I didn't want to be trans.

No matter how validated you feel in an event such as Pride or in any trans-friendly environment, to be trans is to live in a world that has spent a very long time telling you that trans people are deviant and disgusting. Inevitably, that sticks. There's still a big part of me that's ashamed to be trans and expects the world to treat me badly because of it.

That shame is why I used to purge the clothes I spent so much money on, and why I'm so certain that nobody would want to date me. I see it in other trans people too, in the attempts to carve out a hierarchy of transness that just so happens to put people like them at the top and people like me far beneath them. And I see it in my own reaction to other trans people.

I've already mentioned comedian Eddie Izzard – who now describes herself as transgender – joking about the difference between "weirdo transvestites" and "executive transvestites". Few people would nominate themselves for the former category: of course we're going to think that we're Audrey Hepburns to others' Fat Slags. But when you've been exposed to decades of anti-trans sentiment, you do absorb the prejudices. You don't want to be seen as one of, or lumped in with, the weirdo transvestites.

It took me a very long time to attend any LGBT+ anything. That's partly because many LGBT+ groups have an arts and crafts element, and as a newly out middle-aged trans person

I didn't want to waste any valuable time making pots when I could be getting the hang of smoky eyes instead. But it's also because I've absorbed all the homophobia and transphobia that's in the wider culture, and which was particularly toxic when I was growing up.

I hated the person I used to be. I compensated for my own self-loathing by trying desperately to make people like me, and if that meant not challenging their casually expressed misogyny, their racist jokes or their homophobic slurs then that was a price I was willing to pay. Not least because I agreed with some of it. I hadn't had my own red pill moment yet, so I had no reason to believe that the newspapers my parents bought every day and weekend were lying about lesbians, about immigration, about trans people, about feminism.

Remembering it makes me want to climb under a rock, but in my late twenties I definitely espoused the view that if you didn't realise you were transsexual until middle age then you were probably having some kind of mid-life crisis. And what's the point of coming out when you're that old, anyway? And imagine if it was your dad! Now he's your mum!

What's worse than the folly of youth? The middle-aged ability to remember every stupid squawk of it.

And it wasn't just talk. When someone who worked for the same company as me transitioned from male to female when I worked there in my mid-twenties, I didn't want to be anywhere near them. Maybe I feared that if I stood too close, I'd catch transsexualism too.

I understand now that I was profoundly ignorant and fearful, my very straight and white worldview largely shaped by the printed prejudice and misinformation that thumped onto our doormat every morning.

I'm writing this over four years after I first came out, and in the time since I've come to realise that pretty much everything I thought I knew about trans people was wrong. I hadn't been hearing the voices of trans people; I'd been hearing the voices of the people who wrote about trans people in newspapers and magazines or talked about them on radio and TV. As I've since discovered, many of those people are biased and in some cases extremely bigoted against trans people; others just don't do their homework and regurgitate long-discredited arguments.

And of course, when I finally got over myself and started going to LGBT+ things, everybody was lovely, I had a great laugh and nobody made me do any pottery.

But some of the absorbed prejudice is still there. I gawk when I see someone I think might be trans. I stare if a TV programme about trans issues includes very big, overweight trans people in too-short, too-tight skirts even though I've been the very big, overweight trans person in a too-short, too-tight skirt. The very same judging people do to me, I do to other trans people.

It's taken me a while to realise that I'm projecting. A few years before I came out, I was at a concert by an old favourite band and looked around at the sea of greying and balding pates, of expanding waistlines in old tour t-shirts, and I thought, "Shit! This place is full of old guys!" Of course, I was one of them. But deep inside us everybody still thinks they're sixteen, so there's a disconnect between what you see and your own self-image.

It's the same with trans people. I judge other trans people because inside my head I'm sixteen, slim and cute – so when I look at fortysomething trans people doing their best with what God gave them, often in clothes a decade or two too young for them, I'm judging because deep down I know I'm looking at a mirror. I'm Groucho Marx, not wanting to join a club that would have me as a member.

I think to be able to do this trans thing successfully, to go through life attracting the wrong kind of attention when you don't want any attention at all, means suspending disbelief a little bit. That's why something as simple as being misgendered hurts, and why a sour look or comment can ruin your entire week. I don't need anybody else to point out my flaws. I'm a harsher judge than any stranger could ever be.

Wildest dreams

I've loved Taylor Swift's *Wildest Dreams* since the very first time I heard it in 2014, the line about being remembered as someone in a nice dress at sunset knocking me sideways. That was exactly how I imagined myself, how I wanted to be seen: smiling in a summer dress beneath a fiery sky.

That wasn't a new feeling. I'd felt that yearning since the 1990s when I'd played The B-52's *Dry County* on heavy rotation, imagining swinging on a porch in lazy, hazy summer days. I knew I'd never be seen as pretty or even cute, but I'd be happy with carefree.

Unfortunately carefree was the opposite of my reality. For me to don a summer dress was more of an engineering project because my body was the wrong shape. It was flat where it should be full, full where it should be flat. Uncomfortable underwear and silicone boobs could only do so much, and no matter how careful the makeup or well positioned the wig I didn't dare venture outside because I knew I didn't look remotely feminine. The best I could manage was looking almost right in a single selfie photograph, the other unsuccessful shots quickly deleted, or to catch a fleeting glimpse of myself in the mirror.

Standing in a nice dress staring at the sunset? I was a gorilla in a cheap dress struggling to take a selfie.

The problem, of course, is that women's clothes are designed to be worn by people who have female-born bodies, and female bodies differ from male bodies in some very obvious ways. There are all kinds of variations in our individual shapes, but the typical differences are that female bodies store fat in different places and have different proportions to male ones.

A typical cisgender woman's widest part is her hip line, which is wider than her natural waist; my widest point is my shoulder line, which is much the same width as my waist. A cis woman's waist is on the same level as her belly button, which in turn is in line with her elbow joint, but my waistline is below my belly button and elbow joint. Women's bodies are more curved, men's more angular and more muscular.

There's only so much I can do with control top pants and fake boobs when I have a male body. But what if I could take my male body and make it more female? Could HRT do that for me?

HRT (hormone replacement therapy) uses some of the same HRT medications that many post-menopausal women take. The specific medicines and dosages may vary, but the intention is the same: to adjust the levels of hormones in the body to achieve a desired outcome. Results vary from person to person according to their genetics and the age at which they begin treatment, but HRT's effects on a male body can be significant.

If you're a cisgender woman and think you might need HRT, you go to your GP and they give you a prescription. If you're a trans woman, you can't. The NHS routes all trans healthcare through the gender identity clinics (GICs), a desperately outdated, underfunded and overstretched part of the desperately outdated, underfunded and overstretched NHS mental health services. The GICs are a throwback to the days when being trans was considered a mental illness and have a terrible reputation for gatekeeping and for ever more horrific waiting list times. So many trans people self-medicate: they buy their HRT over the internet.

I'd originally ruled out HRT altogether, because I didn't think I wanted to take it. And when I started to think that I did want to take it, I ruled out self-medication because I believed it was dangerous. And it is, in the same way that buying any medicine over the internet is dangerous: I've written my fair share of pieces about lethal diet pills and about pills made from whatever was lying around the factory floor to know that. But the longer I'd been waiting to see the Gender Identity Clinic the more frustrated I felt. I'd been on the waiting list for the Sandyford Clinic, the GIC for Glasgow and the West of Scotland, for eleven months already, I was middle-aged and the clock was ticking.

I decided to go to a private counsellor and found the half-dozen sessions helpful. My counsellor pointed out the inconsistencies in my beliefs during the very first session: on the one hand I was saying that I was proud of being trans, that I was happier than I'd been before, that I'd experienced nothing but love since coming out. And on the other, I clearly still believed that being trans was something deeply shameful that the world wanted to punish me for.

Despite counselling, I was riding a wave of sadness over my identity: I desperately wanted to be able to present as female without attracting negative attention, and my inability to do so was making me miserable. What had previously been mild gender dysphoria had become painfully strong.

If there were a magic pill I could take to give me a female body, I'd take it in a heartbeat. There's no magic pill, but there is HRT. So on an overcast September morning I drove through another of my red lines. I started HRT.

Remember how awful puberty was? Some of us pay to go through it twice. Going on HRT makes significant changes to your body over a period of several years, and while I knew it wouldn't undo the changes made by my first, male puberty – I'd still have facial hair, an Adam's apple and a very deep, resonant voice – it would change my skin, my fat distribution, my musculature and my metabolism. It also made me cry a lot.

There's a lot of misconceptions about what HRT can and can't do for trans people and a lot of misconceptions about trans people's biology too. I recently saw an anti-trans activist on Twitter claim that trans women don't have pelvises. Another claimed that trans women on HRT aren't allowed to use elevators. Some people refuse to believe that trans women can grow natural breasts, but any body will if it has sufficient oestrogen levels. For those of us who transition long after male puberty the results are often modest and our breasts will look smaller and will be more widely spaced because many trans women's ribcages are larger than cisgender women's ribcages. But they're still perfectly natural.

Just like normal puberty, an HRT-induced second puberty takes a long time. I didn't go to bed a 40AA and wake up a 40DD; reaching an A cup, like I eventually managed after a few years, is considered pretty good going.

Trans women who self-medicate don't do it blindly. I know in my own case I did so much studying I could probably do a pretty good job as an endocrinologist. When I get my blood test results back I'm the one reading the levels and asking the GP to adjust the prescription. So I knew what I was letting myself in for.

I knew that after a few months on HRT my body would begin to change where it stores new fat, although sadly it doesn't move the existing stuff around. My skin would start to soften and my body hair would reduce, redistribute or just disappear. My hair loss would slow or perhaps stop, my face would get rounder and my nails would break more easily.

I also knew what HRT would do to my genitals. As someone who's on the asexual spectrum and wasn't in a relationship I wasn't alarmed by the prospect of them shrinking – which they did – but the prospect of painful erections did worry me, because if you're a prostate owner you need to clear out the pipes from time to time as a maintenance measure. As I would later discover, they really were painful – but it wasn't long before they stopped altogether.

HRT would lower my libido and make me need to use the toilet more often, which was cruelly ironic given the growing controversy over trans people's bathroom use. It would almost certainly make me infertile, which wasn't a concern for me but might have been if I were doing this in my twenties.

I was more interested in the emotional effects than the physical ones. I had read countless descriptions by trans women of feeling more emotional, feeling things more acutely, of feeling less sad and less uncomfortable in your own skin. That was what closed the deal for me.

For trans people moving from male to female there are two main kinds of medication to take: one increases the amount of oestrogen in the body and the other suppresses testosterone. After a lot of research and a lot of abandoned shopping baskets, I found a reputable online source for both kinds of medication and ordered a three-month supply. It took around two weeks to arrive.

I felt like I did before I came out, knowing I needed to make changes so I could feel better and frustrated because I was still waiting for a first assessment at the gender clinic. Any NHS prescription was definitely months and maybe even years away.

I don't believe in magic pills, but the tiny blue estradiol tablet and the white, Aspirin-sized spironolactone one would have massive consequences if I took them. If I did, I'd be setting in motion a chain of events that would force me to change the way I saw myself, and which would change the way other people – family, friends, healthcare providers and complete strangers – would see me too. I would no longer be a feminine man, or non-binary, someone happy in his identity but blurring gender roles. I would be in some form of medical transition, which would mean I was what I'd told myself I didn't want to be for so long.

A transsexual.

Was I sure that was what I wanted? Did I really want to live as, and be perceived as, a trans woman, with all the risks and negatives and difficulties that entailed? I didn't know. But I knew I wasn't comfortable in my own skin, and I needed to be. So I swallowed the pills without a second's hesitation.

Now I know kung fu.

What's the story?

Everybody has a story, and the Sandyford Gender Identity Service wanted to know mine.

I thought I had a pretty good idea of what my story was by now. I was a trans person – not a trans woman, not yet; I wasn't even sure if I'd use the women's toilets even if I somehow became 100% female-looking. I wanted to present female all of the time, and to do so with as little artifice as possible.

The letter from the Sandyford clinic arrived halfway through my third week of self-medicated HRT: after nearly a year I had reached the top of the waiting list and should call for an appointment. I did, and was given a date four weeks hence.

In the oversubscribed and under-resourced world of NHS gender clinics, four weeks was a heartbeat away. Today the waiting lists are much longer; the same clinic that I had to wait 11 months to see now takes four years between initial referral and first assessment, and it's falling further and further behind. For one English clinic the predicted wait is currently seven years; in another, current clearance rates mean new referrals can expect to wait twenty six years. Some trans people will die before their first assessment date. And those are the waiting times for first assessments, not treatment.

I'd been advised by many people that the Sandyford would want to know who I was, how I felt, what I wanted. I was pretty sure I didn't want any kind of surgical intervention, but I did want to stop self-medication and continue hormone treatment under medical supervision. And if there were other changes that could help me feel more comfortable – electrolysis to remove hair, for example, or voice therapy to find a more feminine way of speaking that didn't sound daft – I'd want to try them too.

I also decided to push my boundaries a bit more. I'd presented as male with eyeliner and androgynous clothes a lot, but I'd always left the wigs at home. So on quiet November Wednesday evening, two days after my "tranniversary" of first coming out, I went to the pub in a jumper dress, leggings, boots and a long red wig.

The first thing anybody said to me was "wow, you look great" – an untrue but kind compliment from one of the bartenders, who was working the bar that night and who has since become a good friend – and I ended up having conversations with him and his colleague about the whole trans thing. I knew them both already and we'd spoken about trans stuff before, but to do so while presenting female, sitting at the bar while customers came and went without saying anything (other than "hiya" from a couple of pub pals), felt quite amazing. Another power-up.

One of the reasons for pushing that particular boundary was because of the trans whispers about gender identity clinics: if you don't present fully female at your appointments, the whispers say, they don't take you seriously and you may be denied treatment. While that certainly used to be the case – the BBC documentary *A Change of Sex*, first broadcast in 1979 and now available on iPlayer, will have you shouting at the screen when you see how the gender clinics used to treat trans women – I wasn't sure that was the case any more, although I've since been told some real horror stories about some gender clinics, so perhaps I was wrong. But after a year mouldering on a waiting list I certainly didn't want to take any risks. If I were going to present female then I didn't want my first time doing so to be in the clinic waiting room. I'd be nervous enough. So the pub was a trial run for that (although it turned out to be premature:

on the day of my appointment the clinic called to cancel and reschedule for the following week).

I also discovered something: getting ready, walking there with the wind in my hair – a really weird feeling when your head's sported a number two crop for a decade-plus – and sitting at the bar in fully female presentation felt natural, or at least it did when the initial terror wore off and the heart rate monitor in my smartwatch stopped panicking. The guys at the bar checked to see if I was feeling a bit calmer once I'd had a couple of drinks – I'd admitted I was terrified when I first walked in, although I'm pretty sure they'd already worked that out from just looking at the state of me. I got scared again when the bar started to get busy and boisterous groups of young men and women arrived, but while I got a few strange looks that's probably to be expected when you go to the gents toilet wearing a wig, skirt and tights.

I still felt extremely vulnerable. But I also felt a sense that everything was in its right place. I wasn't hiding anything: I'd come out as myself and that felt pretty damn good. I was starting to realise that I'd rather be the ugliest girl at the party than one of the boys.

I couldn't help compare last year's me to this year's model. Last year's me was lost and full of fear, scared to even tell the Sandyford's answering machine that I was trans. This year's me was doing something I could have barely imagined back then: going through the world as me, at least some of the time. Many of the things I'd feared had come true, but I wasn't just older and wiser. I was stronger too, and despite everything, happier.

The counselling sessions I'd just completed had been really helpful, and I was starting to feel mentally different as hormones changed my body chemistry. The first few weeks of HRT had been hard – I felt a severe sadness and could barely get out of bed. I worked mornings and then spent much of the afternoons under a duvet; I had vivid nightmares every night for the first few weeks and started the days more tired than when I'd gone to bed – but things improved quickly and I started to feel much better. I also noticed more evidence of HRT working its slow magic: My skin became very dry, especially on my head, and I developed what looked awfully like teenage acne – albeit much worse than anything I'd had in my first puberty. My hair felt shaggy, the bald spot on my crown appeared to get a little bit smaller and I smelled a lot better.

The only other obvious effect was embarrassing: my boobs began to grow, and they became painfully sensitive. Cis men like to joke that if they somehow acquired breasts, they'd spend all day every day playing with them – just happily massaging their own boobs all day long without a care in the world. They don't imagine spending all day feeling like somebody's going at their tits with a cheese grater or accidentally banging a boob and feeling like somebody just slammed a car door on it.

I've never found my boobs erotic. In my early days of HRT I found them intensely itchy and sometimes painfully so. I started wearing bras not because they're cute but because if I didn't my clothes would chafe in places I really didn't want chafed. I turned to padded bras not because I was trying to look more busty, but because I needed all the protection I could get. Even something as simple as pulling on a tight top felt like being attacked with sandpaper, and my youngest's endless enthusiastic ninja leaps onto my chest from on high damn near killed me. The combination of his love of jumping on me and their body apparently consisting entirely of elbows and knees brought me very close to using words they wouldn't want him to repeat at nursery.

When it comes to physical appearance, HRT weaves its magic slowly and imperceptibly. It's rather like drawing a single dot on your skin with a blue biro every day: if you check your progress daily or weekly you'll hardly notice the change. Look in the mirror after two years, however, and you'll be the same colour as a Smurf. When I looked at a photo of me I'd taken a few days before I came out and a photo of me I took 13 months later, I could barely believe I was looking at the same person.

This puberty was a welcome one. People commented on how contented I seemed, and I did feel a lot more positive than I'd been feeling for quite some time.

But when you're trans there's always someone happy to pour a bucket of shit over your head. The person holding this particular bucket had discovered that I was going to the Sandyford Gender Clinic and sent me the worst email I've ever received, an email that told me at great length that I was not and never would be feminine. It's something I still hear in my head whenever I look in the mirror and don't like what I see. Over many, many words the email informed me that I was making a fool of myself and that I was dementedly and selfishly destroying the lives of my children.

I responded in anger. A few days later, when I was out for dinner, a notification on my phone told me that there was a sequel to the first message. If the first message was the worst email I've ever received, the second one made that one look like a good-luck card. It was a work of deliberate, calculated viciousness and it had me crying in the restaurant toilets for some time.

That's not my name

One of my favourite musical stories is the tale of pop singer Arnold Dorsey, whose career was flatlining in the mid-1960s. His manager decided that what he really needed was a more memorable name, so he borrowed one from a 19th Century composer and Engelbert Humperdink was born. If it weren't for that canny decision, the world would never have got to hear "Please Release Me", let alone the inimitable "Lesbian Seagull" on the Beavis and Butt-Head *Do America* soundtrack.

You don't have to stick with the name your parents picked for you. People change theirs all the time: because another actor has the same name, because they want to disguise how posh they are, or simply because they don't like it. Bono from U2 took his name from a hearing aid shop. bell hooks is a much more intriguing name than Gloria Watkins and was a tribute to hooks' maternal great-grandmother. Lady Gaga trips off the tongue in a way Stefani Joanne Germanotta doesn't. There's no way John Wayne would have become an icon of American masculinity if he'd stuck to his real name, Marion Morrison. And of course, trans people change their names to reflect the person they actually are, not the person whose name they were originally given.

Changing your name isn't hard to do. But choosing a name is incredibly difficult. I've been involved in the naming of two humans, three dogs, a guinea pig, a goldfish and God knows how many bands, and the hardest name of all to choose was the one I have now.

Many closeted trans people have a name they'd rather use than their given name, but I didn't. Before I'd come out as trans I'd used various aliases online to hide my identity, but I didn't identify with any of them; now I was openly trans I just used the name I'd been born with even though it often jarred with my presentation. On the internet in the past I might have been a Jenny or a Mhairi, but in the real world I used the name I was given.

By the time I completed my counselling sessions I still wasn't sure whether I'd ever consider myself a trans woman, but I was starting to feel very much at home in my trans identity. Things that previously seemed loaded with significance had become completely normal, from makeup and hair removal (originally an exciting transgression; now, a right royal pain in the arse and various other places) to wearing obviously female clothes. I pruned my wardrobe, getting rid of clothes that were too tight or too young or too short and shoes with heels that were too high. As an openly trans person there was no illicit thrill to dressing in female clothes, applying makeup or wearing a wig; they were just things I had to do in order to see myself in the mirror, things I needed to get the hang of if I were to be gendered correctly in public, things I'd often wish I didn't have to do.

Although I wasn't entirely happy with the way I looked, I was a lot more comfortable in my new-found trans identity. I found that if I came across as cheerful and confident, other people responded to me in kind. From beauty consultants on make-up counters to dentists, waiting staff in restaurants, sales assistants in supermarkets and strangers in pubs, people treated me as the person I was: someone who was cheerful and confident and jaw-droppingly gorgeous. Okay, maybe not that last one.

Should that person still have a boy's name? I wasn't so sure any more. He was starting to feel like somebody I used to know, somebody I used to be, someone I'd been close to but from whom I'd drifted apart. When I got my makeup right and the hair just-so and looked in the mirror, the person I saw didn't look like him.

I found myself doodling names on scrap paper, trying them on to see if any fit, like a primary school kid imagining who they might marry.

My given name, Gary – inevitably, hilariously and constantly defaced on my secondary school jotters to say "gay" – had been an accident. I was supposed to be Stephen, but my dad swapped it at the registrar and what was supposed to be my middle name became my first name. It was a name that became associated with deeply uncool people, perma-tanned Essex wide boys in Ford Escort XR3i cars with dizzy girlfriends in white stilettos, and I never liked it or its even less desirable diminutive, Gaz.

I am not and have never been a Gaz. Gaz is one of the lads, has top bantz, loves his bird almost as much as his wheels, is a right laugh. Gaz is a commercial radio DJ, a zany TV presenter, runs a mobile disco. In the film of his life, he'd be played by James Corden.

As any parent can testify, choosing a name isn't easy. It's harder still when you're trans, because you've already got a name that everybody knows you by and that you're used to saying and hearing. I found that some names I really liked just didn't work, the syllables and plosives getting caught in my throat. Others – such as the Gaelic names I love so much and find so beautiful, such as Mhairi and Niamh, Aoife and Siobhan – would mean a lifetime of spelling them out. And others were too old or too young, names that were popular before I was born or long after I became an adult.

If I were going to have a female name, and I still wasn't sure if I wanted to, I'd need to find a name that was age-appropriate, easy to remember and to adjust to, and reasonably gender neutral when spoken aloud – something I felt was important for my children, because while an androgynous dad with an androgynous name isn't unusual an androgynous dad called Debbie is.

I searched for a name that felt like it fit who I was now, not who I used to be. And I found it in Carrie.

Carrie was age-appropriate, gender-neutral when spoken (thanks, Cary Grant), almost identical to my given name and associated with some really kick-ass women such as the actor and author Carrie Fisher, the guitarist, writer and composer Carrie Brownstein, the actor Carrie-Anne Moss (Trinity in the Matrix films) and the singer, vocal coach and presenter Carrie Grant. And of course, Carrie was also the eponymous hero of Stephen King's novel and the 1976 film of the same name starring Sissy Spacek, in which a shy teenage girl unleashes her extraordinary powers after being humiliated by her classmates. That seemed fitting too.

Carrie.
Carrie M.
Carrie Marshall.

I wrote it again and again on envelopes, practiced introducing myself in the mirror – "Hiya, I'm Carrie" – and took it for a test drive: I changed my name on Amazon and eBay and other places that didn't matter, the initial weirdness of seeing a female name on my deliveries and the odd looks from couriers soon becoming just as normal as all the other changes I'd been making. I started to look into the practicalities of changing my name: how to do it (it's different in Scotland than in England and Wales), who to notify, what potential problems might occur, whether I should consider voice training so my speech matched my moniker. I talked to myself in mirrors, smiling.

Hi. I'm Carrie. That's right. C-A-R-R-I-E.

I changed my name on a few discussion forums and changed my profile photo too, a favourite and unusually flattering shot of me in makeup and a long red wig that looked spookily like one of my female cousins. I wasn't going out like that just yet, but I felt it looked like the me I felt I was, not the me that kept turning up in photos. I used the same photo as my profile picture on Facebook and Twitter, but decided to keep my given name there for the time being. Almost everybody I know is connected to me on those two services, and I wasn't ready to make any announcements just yet.

Say my name

I was still very uneasy with the idea of describing myself as a woman: it was something I constantly agonised over, because while I was certain that I wasn't a man I still wasn't entirely comfortable with the opposite label. Hormones hadn't dramatically changed my appearance or my shape and of course I hadn't had surgery, so I felt more comfortable saying that I lived in the middle: not necessarily a man or a woman, but a trans person. I think a lot of that was to do with the increasingly loud anti-trans sentiment I was seeing in *The Guardian*, the *Sunday Times* and online: writers and interviewees expressed their horror at the thought of anyone assigned male at birth claiming the label of woman, and my fear of conflict and of making other people uncomfortable made me wary of claiming a label some people didn't think I had any right to use.

But the world doesn't like ambiguity. It wants you to tick a boy box or a girl one so that its callers can sir you or madam you, so that a faraway stranger can be certain about what shape your genitals are when you're renewing your home insurance.

Most public and private sector organisations' computer systems and paperwork are binary. It soon became apparent that the system as it stands can't cope with female names and pronouns if the gender isn't also female: good luck getting ID in the name of Ms Ladyname if the gender marker remains M.

So the evening before my first Gender Identity Service appointment, I posted completed paperwork to the National

Records of Scotland to legally change my name to Carrie. After a few weeks my amended birth certificate would come back in my new name (but with the gender marker still saying male), enabling me to start the long process of changing my identity in the wider world. It feels like endless form-filling and postal order-enclosing: you need to tell a surprisingly long list of people, many of whom charge a fee for letting you keep their data up to date and putting your new name on a bit of printed plastic.

My list included the DVLA, HMRC, DWP, EHIC, TV licensing, the electoral registration office, my mobile phone provider, the Scottish Qualifications Authority, ALCS, PRS, my library, my old occupational pension provider, the NHS, my bank, my credit card company, my landlord, Safe Deposits Scotland, my work clients, The Passport Agency, Companies House, my Tesco, Nectar, Boots and Sparks cards, my dentist, my breakdown cover, my energy provider, my insurance companies, my magazine subscriptions, my social media (I had to say goodbye to my Twitter verified blue tick, which you can't keep if you change your name; it still hasn't been granted to me again), my broadband provider, my Subway and Scotrail smartcards, my accounts with Amazon, Apple, eBay and Google and every other online service... I'd usually miss a few, and many of the forms I sent were rejected because I didn't fill out section 32 subsection 3(b)21 in the right colour of ink. I became horribly familiar with the sound of official government forms coming back through the letterbox for clarification.

I also got used to having this conversation with bemused baristas every time I went to a coffee shop. I hope there's a special circle of Hell exclusively reserved for whoever decided it was a good idea to write customers' names on coffee cups:

Them: What's the name?
Me: Carrie.
Them: Gary?

Me: No, Carrie.
Them: Sorry, Karen.
Me: No, sorry, it's Carrie.
Them: Kerry?
ME: No. Carrie. With a C.
Them: Ciara?
Me: No. Carrie. C-A-R-R-I-E.
Them: Carrie?
Me: Yes, Carrie. Like Carrie Fisher. Yes.
Them: OK. (Writes "Harry" on cup)

It's not just coffee shops. Have fun persuading your Uber driver that the 6'1" you is the same Carrie who booked the ride, or being looked at by entire waiting rooms when you give your name to the receptionist, or being questioned on entry to a gig because the name on your ticket is a woman's name. One reason so many trans people apparently embrace gender binaries instead of blurring gender lines is because to be in the middle is an enormous pain in the arse.

Such irritations aside, I was already certain that changing my name had been the right thing to do. But I hadn't changed my gender: in the eyes of the law I was still a man. That's because changing your name doesn't change your legal gender. For that you need to apply for a Gender Recognition Certificate, a document created by the 2004 Gender Recognition Act. I wasn't sure I wanted one, as the process is famously invasive, time-consuming and prohibitively expensive.

But changing my name still felt big in a way going on HRT hadn't. Even when I first started noticing external physical effects, they didn't feel as big a deal as saying "Hi, I'm Carrie." Maybe that's because HRT didn't feel like such a visible step, or maybe it's because I knew that if the HRT didn't work out I could just stop and my body would largely return to its previous state: reversing a formal and public name change seems much more awkward and difficult. Maybe it's because HRT doesn't require any changes to documents or any public announcements or emails to employers.

Maybe it's simply because you can hide the changes made by early stage hormone treatment under a thick jumper. You can't do that with your legal identity.

Changing your name isn't just a bit of administration. It's a planted flag, a line in the sand, a declaration of intent: this is who I am. It's a weary commitment to spending the rest of your life telling people that no, it's not a mistake; that's your name. It's the knowledge that people will hear your name and then your voice and feel the two don't align. It's the beginning of years of double-takes, bureaucratic bullshit, ID cards issued in your old name (sometimes accompanied by looks of abject horror from people who knew the old you), the odd client putting you on their system as Carrie Fisher and other misunderstandings.

It's the fear you're disappointing your parents by discarding your given names, the worry that your children will be judged for something they have no control over, the knowledge that the rabbit hole you're exploring goes much deeper than you ever imagined, the fear that you've committed to something that'll see you spend the rest of your life alone.

Flip your wig

The gender clinic made me cry. I didn't even realise until the doctor asked if I needed a moment.

My initial assessment was six days before my forty-fifth birthday, a year and two weeks after I'd started to come out as trans. I cried a lot during the hour-plus conversation; the psychiatrist seemed nice enough but her questions took me to some pretty dark places. I think sometimes we bury our feelings quite deeply in an act of mental self-defence, and digging them back up again brought all the emotions flooding back.

I was told to expect a second assessment with the gender clinic the following January before being assigned a doctor to oversee my treatment, a process that would take a few more months. While I waited for the next step I did what I'd promised the doctor I'd do and investigated how to stop self-medicating and continue with HRT under proper medical supervision.

My NHS GP was perfectly happy to treat me but wasn't keen on prescribing anything without first getting the Gender Identity Service's say-so, so an NHS prescription – known as a bridging prescription – was not on the table. It's worth pointing out that my GP is perfectly happy to prescribe HRT to cisgender women: it's the same medicine, the same monitoring, but my GP does not feel adequately trained or informed to prescribe it for me. So I contracted with a private GP to prescribe and monitor HRT until I could move onto the NHS treatment pathway.

My private GP was GenderGP, a trans-friendly practice that has been demonised in the press and hounded on social media (but vindicated by a tribunal[1]) for allegedly handing out HRT like candy. That wasn't my experience: HRT wasn't even up for discussion until I'd satisfactorily completed specialist counselling, had a full blood workup and discussed the situation with my NHS GP. Although I was already on hormones it took four months to persuade GenderGP to actually prescribe anything. And even then the prescription was still a cautious one.

Getting into the NHS system would save me a great deal of money in the long run, because in Scotland NHS prescriptions are free for everybody. Private GPs charge for everything from setting you up on their system to writing the prescriptions, as well as charging quite a lot for the medicines themselves. It was definitely worth the money, but it was already quite a lot of money.

Before anybody would prescribe me anything I had to get my blood work done, testing not just for blood cell count and other common factors but also for any signs of liver or kidney problems, diabetes and other health issues that might make HRT or my specific medications dangerous. If I'd messed up my body by self-medicating hormones, the blood work would quantify the damage. The results were exactly what you'd expect from a red meat-eating, sedentary journalist whose idea of exercise is padding to the fridge.

GenderGP changed my prescription from oestrogen pills to patches, which are safer for older folks like me but which felt as big as dinner plates and left incredibly adhesive gunk when I took them off three days later. I hated them and asked GenderGP to put me back on the pills.

Now that I was really feeling the effects of HRT both physically and mentally I was certain that I was on the right road, and that meant I needed to start thinking about presenting full time as female: the Gender Identity Service would expect it and

I wanted to do it anyway, or at least for as much time as possible when I wasn't with my children.

I started dressing in more obviously feminine clothes and shoes all the time, wore light makeup during the day, kept my nails permanently polished, wore skirts and shoes and wigs on nights out. I started walking with more confidence. When I went out I wasn't apologetic any more, hoping nobody would notice me: I made a point of being in the centre of things, not the periphery, of taking my rightful place at the bar, in the audience, on the train. I wasn't ashamed any more. I was proud of who I was.

Although I soon realised that I really needed to get a better wig.

All this self-actualisation is fun, but it's also expensive: if you want a wig that doesn't look cheap, you can't wear a cheap wig. Hair is more complicated than it looks, and that means the fibres of your wig can't just be dyed a solid uniform colour if you want it to look realistic. That's obviously not an issue if you're dressing up as Xena: Warrior Princess for a fancy dress party, but it's a problem if you want hair that looks normal. And I wanted to have hair that looked normal.

Buying a wig is a very strange experience. I made an appointment online and went to a boutique in Glasgow's Pink Triangle, the windows either side of it full of sequins and improbably large jockstraps that reassured me that this was not a place unfamiliar with the Ls, the Gs, the Bs and the Ts. It's not a bit of Glasgow I'd spent much time in; even now I've yet to visit any LGBT+ venues, imposter syndrome telling me, as it did before Pride, that I'm not queer enough to be welcome.

The boutique itself looked and felt like a film set for something baroque that would feature a lot of face powder, tea in china cups and heaving décolletages in corsets. The main room evoked the lobby of an expensive and long-established hotel, something built in the days of empire. The shop floor was largely empty of anything but furniture, the only indication that it was a wig shop were a few model heads in the corners. I was welcomed warmly and ushered into a side room of exposed brick and highly polished wooden flooring, on which sat a white dressing table and a high-backed chair. I took the chair and looked through thick tomes of trichology to try and find the wig with my name on it. The books were huge and heavy, like those big Bibles you see on altars but with a lot more pictures.

I already had a vague idea of what I wanted so we soon narrowed it down to just three possibles. One was too short, one just didn't look right and one was a beautiful design in the worst possible colour, a very pale blonde that emphasised the redness of my face. I was reassured that we could find the perfect colour, because of course it's impossible and financially suicidal to stock every variant of every wig. We tried a few different ones and settled on a reddish light blonde similar to my own natural colour.

I came close to crying when I tried the wig on. It wasn't the right colour, but it was the first time I'd worn a wig that looked like it belonged on my head – and because it was long, it made my face look thinner as well as more feminine. I didn't see a man with a wig in the mirror. I saw a woman who'd made a bad dye decision.

As a man, hair didn't matter to me: I wanted long hair when I was younger but family disapproved and friends mocked, so I got it cut short again and adopted a Walter White crop when male pattern baldness became obvious. But as a woman hair matters to me a lot, because so much of our culture's ideas of femininity are wrapped up in it.

This is something that is definitely different for girls. Male pattern baldness isn't exactly welcomed by men, but the culture says that if you experience it, you just shave your head – and in our culture shaved men's heads are considered to be sexy, strong and virile. Scroll through the action movies category on Amazon Prime or Netflix and it's a symphony of slapheads leavened by the odd appearance by Keanu Reeves. Now scroll through the rom-coms and period dramas and see how many of the female protagonists have hair loss. It won't take long.

When Natalie Portman shaved her locks for a role, she suggested that internet commenters would think she had cancer, was gay or was a Nazi. And some people surely did: while she was of course slagging off clichés about short-haired women, many people are very invested in those clichés and like to perpetuate them.

So much of my self-esteem comes from other people responding to me as a woman. And lots of people make their decision on whether to do that based on my hairline.

I have long and very red hair now and I get my brows and lashes coloured regularly, but whenever I went into a shop COVID-masked so that only my eyes and the top of my head were visible my visibly receding hairline meant that I was still gendered male before I made a single sound. I'm very used to it, so it doesn't sting like it did at first, but it's still one of those things that makes you mouth "oh, for fuck's sake" behind your mask.

I like having long hair – it's yet another of those little things that just feels right – but if I want people to respond to me as me I need to tie it up and slap a wig on top. And as much as I like the way I look when I do that, I don't like what feels like the artifice of it, the fact that if I were to go back to someone's flat, as unlikely as that is, they'd see me without it in the morning. Also, I'm scared it'll fall off when I headbang on stage.

I'd eventually find a solution to the headbanging problem in early 2022 thanks to something called a hair mesh integration system, which I currently have on order. Hair mesh integration is similar to hair extensions, but the synthetic or human hair is woven onto a mesh that's then attached to your head semi-permanently. I assume that's with glue, but who knows? Maybe it's with special hair nails. It lasts for a year-plus with adjustments every nine weeks or so, and it's very expensive – although not quite as expensive as I feared. I was expecting it to cost thousands, but it turns out that I still have quite a lot of hair that my hairdresser can work with so the cost will be around £400 up-front and then about £120 every three months. It's still a lot of money, I know. But it's a lot less cash than a hair transplant, which I know I can't afford even on credit. And I think it'll be worth it. It'll be worth it to get up in the morning and see me. It'll be worth it to feel that I can just walk out of the flat with no preparation, no effort, and be gendered correctly. It'll be worth it to finally be able to go swimming again.

With the exception of one foreign holiday, I haven't swam since I came out. I'm too scared of abuse, of being yelled at because my swimsuit and boobs say woman but my hairline says man. Whenever someone on Twitter asks trans people what they'd love to do if they could be 100% guaranteed that nobody else would object, the answer is overwhelming: we'd go swimming.

I ordered the wig and paid £310. That's cheap for a non-cheap wig: human hair ones cost considerably more but this one, by the Jon Renau brand, used very convincing synthetics that could even be styled and straightened. Don't try that with an ordinary wig unless your chosen style is On Fire. And £310 is nothing compared to the cost of hair transplants or even just women's hairdressing: according to one of those spurious surveys companies do to try and get in the papers, Scots women spend £751 a year on cuts, colour, conditioning and curls. You can buy two really good wigs for that, or many more if like me you're good at eBay and bad at impulse control.

On my 45th birthday I spent another £100, this time on a different cliché: a tattoo, something I'd always believed I'd never get. I went for a stylised phoenix on my right bicep. A month later I'd get another tattoo, this time of a water symbol. I've since added more: a mermaid, a red heart and a butterfly. If you're ever watching a documentary featuring lots of trans women you can play a drinking game: one drink for every butterfly tattoo you see. I think when you're trans, getting tattooed can be even more significant than it is for other people: to be able to exercise autonomy over your body, even in such a relatively small way, feels empowering when autonomy is something you're largely denied. When I get inked, I don't need to languish on a waiting list or persuade any strangers that I'm sane.

Shake it off

Some things are very hard to get out of. The Labyrinth at Knossos was pretty tough, for example, although it's nothing compared to a Sky TV contract. For me, one of the worst traps to get caught in is the dress I know I'm probably too big for but decide to try on anyway. I should know better by now, but it always ends with me stumbling around my bedroom, dress pulled over my head like a parka in a playground fight, bumping into the furniture like a foul-mouthed sporting mascot having a particularly bad day.

Without hair removal, HRT and surgery, dressing when you're trans is a serious challenge. The old me had it easy. He'd shower, pull on whatever wasn't yet capable of going for a walk by itself and leave the house. As Carrie there's a lot more planning, a lot more effort and a lot more to deal with: as the automated checkout in my local supermarket might put it, there are some surprising items in the bagging area.

When I was going out anywhere I'd plan in advance what I was going to wear – androgynous? More feminine? – based not just on what I felt like wearing but where I was going and what sort of crowd I expected to be there. It's okay for the gender identity clinics to demand you live full-time in your desired gender before getting any treatment to help you blend in, but they aren't the ones walking down busy streets at closing time in a wig. There are still some places, times and crowds where looking like a man in a skirt is asking for trouble. That's probably not the best phrase, as it has echoes of victim blaming; of course assault is never the fault of the victim. But you wouldn't wear a Celtic football strip to a famously rough Rangers pub.

Once I'd decided on a theme I'd then try to plan my outfit from my head to my toes: not just the main bits of the outfit but the underwear (important if you're wearing something where you don't want a bulge), the shoes (flats? Biker boots? Something with heels? Something I can kick people with, or run in?) and jewellery.

With my outfit – or more likely, multiple outfits – set out on the bed it was time to deal with the practicalities. First of all I'd shower, keeping my face under the hot water to try and open up the pores before shaving as carefully as possible. I've never shaved anybody else – this would be a very different book if I had – so I don't know if this applies to other people, but my stubble grows in umpteen different directions so I can't just shave downwards, the direction least likely to make my face and neck look like I've been smacked repeatedly with a garden rake; I have to also shave up, and sideways, and at various angles to try and get completely smooth. That's a real challenge around the lips: if I don't do it well enough I'm really conscious of feeling the bits I've missed, but if I do it too much I'll slash my own face and spend the next half-hour trying to stem the bleeding with a styptic pencil (stingy, and no match for your face when it's doing an impression of a scarlet Niagara Falls) and little blobs of Andrex (mostly ineffectual, and likely to re-open the cut when I peeled them off). Having angered my face, the next step was to towel dry and apply so much moisturiser to try and cool it down that if you tried to grab me I'd shoot out of your grasp like a greased eel.

After that it was time to deal with the boys. I became adept at "tucking", which is a technique for minimising the bulge of male genitals that involves pushing the testicles upwards into your body and then pushing the penis backwards and securing it somehow. Some drag queens use Duct Tape. I'm more of a coward so I just wore tighter pants to keep things in place and cursed the fact that I had to do it at all.

With the unwanted passengers safely stowed, the next step was to do my makeup. If I applied it too early the makeup wouldn't fully cover the redness without me having to trowel it on; if I left it too late I'd have to rush it and end up with a look that wasn't so much day to night as day to nightmare.

Finally, I'd get dressed, look in the mirror, hate what I saw and sometimes, burst into tears. I'd try every outfit I'd already identified and then some more for good measure; each time, what I'd see in the mirror fell far short of what I'd hoped to see and what I'd imagined in my own head. By the time I was actually reasonably happy with what I was wearing – a process that could easily take an hour – my bedroom would look like someone had dropped a charity shop on it from a very great height.

Even when I started to get the hang of my presentation I still stood out. It wasn't just my height or my voice; there are tall, deep-voiced cisgender women too. It was also because of how I walked and how I sat and how I moved and in a million other things, the myriad mannerisms that mark someone out as feminine rather than masculine. I wasn't socialised as female so there's a whole world of stuff I've had to learn and even more things I've had to unlearn. For example, I find it almost impossible to navigate the hug/handshake/kiss on the cheek world of hellos and goodbyes, especially when the other person is male; it makes my brain go into panic mode. I think if I spot someone I haven't seen for a while in the supermarket I'll just hurl myself into the frozen peas until they pass. While I've become a lot more tactile and more expressive, I'm very aware that there's still something of the Eliza Doolittle to me – and sadly there's no Henrietta Higgins to help me navigate this unfamiliar world, even for a bet.

★

You know that dream where you're doing something in front of an audience – in the school assembly hall, maybe, or at a big work conference – and for no good reason you have to do it in your underwear? That's how I feel when I go out as me. In my old life I was completely anonymous, too old for women to notice me or for men to see me as a target or a threat. But riding the Subway into town is a vivid illustration of how that isn't the case any more. Everybody looks. *Everybody*. Some do it subtly. Most don't. And they look in different ways. Younger women generally clock me and go back to their phones. Older ones often double-take and then either look away and avoid further eye contact or give me a really hard stare. Only the oldest women don't seem to care at all; they've seen it all before.

And men? Men stare. Sometimes they stare with open disgust; sometimes they stare, sneer and turn to their friends to make some hilarious joke. Some stare purely to intimidate, their expression saying: what the fuck are you going to do about it?

The worst are the ones who've been drinking, because they don't just look: they talk too. I don't get the last Subway out of town for that very reason, and I also try to avoid the football crowds. But sometimes I can't, because the Subway breaks down and instead of taking the Outer Circle that goes nowhere near the football stadiums I'm herded onto the already-packed Inner Circle, which takes me past Ibrox just as the more refreshed fans are heading home. It's not all fans, I know. But the more vocal flag-wavers aren't exactly famed for their progressive politics, and it's absolutely terrifying when they clamber en masse into an already packed carriage. That's when I get singled out, usually by middle-aged men who, with exaggerated politeness, will urge me to sit next to them and make a big fuss when I decline, thereby ensuring that all eyes in the carriage are on me.

In my early days online, U2 fans used to curate lists of some of the dafter things Bono said. And one of the daftest, according to online lore at least,[1] was his 1992 interview with an unspecified US magazine in which he told the interviewer "Being a rock & roll star is like having a sex change! People treat you like a girl!... I know what it feels like to be a babe." He doesn't. But being obviously trans in public gives you a pretty good idea of what it might be like to be Bono.

Lose yourself

When I was a child, I tried to hide my femininity from my parents. And as a parent, I tried to hide it from my children.

It's not that Liz and I didn't want the kids to know that I wasn't like other dads. It's that Liz didn't want my youngest to know the word "trans" right now for fear he'd start talking about it in school. Four-year-olds have no filter, and she feared his being bullied or his friends' parents suddenly deciding their kids shouldn't play with him. I went along with it because I thought Liz was probably right: when my oldest was four, he took a daft joke seriously and informed his entire nursery class that I was actually The Incredible Spider-Man.

Like any self-respecting superhero, I needed to create an everyday identity. Wonder Woman became Diana Prince, an unassuming nurse; Superman became Clark Kent, a mild-mannered reporter; and I went backwards in time to inhabit the old me.

I approached school run clothes as camouflage, avoiding anything clingy, using too-tight sports bras to minimise my developing chest and wearing cardigans to hide the bumps. That presented some challenges when the school run happened on mornings where I then had to be somewhere else, because when I wasn't with my children I didn't present as male any more. I found doing so really awkward and uncomfortable, so I became an expert at the car park quick change: I'd wear simple, fairly androgynous clothes, keep accessories to a minimum and wear just enough makeup to hide the worst of my skin without being too obvious. Once the kids had been dropped off at school and/or nursery I'd pull a short wig from my bag and quickly brush it into shape while looking in the rear view mirror. I called it my daytime hair: a shortish blonde bob that was much less impressive but an awful lot less effort than my "proper" long wig.

But you can only hide so much, and one evening my youngest pointed at my chest and exclaimed delightedly, "Ha! Daddy! It looks like you've got boobs!" It did, because by now I was the faintly bemused owner of a pair of "Snoopy boobs", so called because of their resemblance to the face of the cartoon dog: they were small but they were definitely breasts, not man-boobs. I mumbled something about needing to do more exercise, but in addition to having no filter, four-year-olds have no respect for their parents' privacy either. A week later he barged into my room when I was getting dressed and asked why I had boobs.

I said the first thing that came to mind, which was that if you stop exercising your muscles get flabby. "So you have muscly boobs?" he asked. "Yes," I replied, oblivious to the mistake I was making. It turns out that when you're four and a half, there is nothing funnier in the world than the phrase "muscly boobs". He used it mercilessly for months.

Children ask a lot of questions, and my two were no exception: at six my youngest wanted to know why I changed my name, why I didn't live with mummy any more, why I didn't invite their friends over for playdates. Now a tweenager, my eldest wanted to know if I'd always felt the way I did, when I'd realised that I wanted to be more like myself, and whether being me made me happy. I always answered honestly and openly, but I tried not to take questions as an opportunity to stand on a soapbox or share too much information. I was torn between desperately wanting to tell them everything and knowing that too much information would be, well, too much information.

Rather that fact-bomb my kids and overload them with information, Liz and I hoped that we could instead try a positive version of boiling a frog. That's the idea that if you chuck a frog into hot water it'll jump out straight away, but if you start with lukewarm water and slowly raise the temperature in small increments the frog doesn't notice the changes. It's an urban myth that survives because it sounds so plausible, and while we weren't trying to fool our kids like the unnamed bullfrog-boiler we were hoping to make tiny changes rather than big ones. My gender presentation would inevitably change as my body changed and my hair grew, but by not making a fuss about it or doing or saying anything dramatic I hoped that having a trans dad would be something that my kids didn't really give much thought to: it was just a piece of information about me, no more interesting than the colour of my hair.

This would be our first Christmas as a separated family, and while I don't want to minimise the pain and sadness of a marriage break-up I think things were starting to get better. We'd started to find the right rhythm for the kids' time with me, our pickups and drop-offs weren't so emotionally charged or draining, and Liz and I were tentatively rediscovering the friendship we had before this all happened. We started to do and plan family things, not as partners or grudging exes but as friends again. We still planned to divorce, but we'd do so amicably.

One of those family things, a trip to see the Chinese Lanterns at Edinburgh Zoo, was soundtracked by Lorde's *Melodrama* on the car stereo – not deliberately, but just because that's what the stereo had cued up. The album had been a near-constant companion for me through it all – it's a superb breakup album by an impossibly talented artist – and as 2017 drew to an end I'd started to feel the way she does in the song "Hard Feelings", trying to care for herself the way she used to care for her partner. It hit hard, and I had to hide some tears on the drive home: I was still working through a lot of sadness and anger over being rejected, and as much as I could understand the reasons for it, it still hurt. That hurt was why our post-breakup conversations had tended to be terse text messages and drive-by exchanges across the driveway as I picked up or dropped off the kids. But rational me knew what emotional me was still working towards: Liz was the same person I'd fallen in love with, married and spent many years with, and we still cared about each other.

A few weeks later, my oldest and I watched *Star Wars: The Force Awakens*. He loved it, as I knew he would, but it turned out to be an unexpectedly emotional experience. He wanted to know the actors' names as well as the characters, and when we got to Leia – the imitable Carrie Fisher – it piqued their interest.

"That's the same name you have!" he said, delightedly. "Was that deliberate?" I said that it was, and we had a brief and age-appropriate chat about the general amazingness of Carrie Fisher.

Later, I had to explain the relationship between Fisher's Leia and Harrison Ford's Han Solo.

"So they were in love before, but they can't be together now?" he asked.

I said yes, that's right.

"But they're still friends?"

Yes.

"Like you and mum!"

I managed to croak a yes before making a hyperspace jump to the bathroom so I could cry without them seeing.

These are what they call hard feelings.

Merry Christmas everyone

My first Christmas as Carrie was tough. The pub that normally feels like a safe space felt distinctly unsafe during December as it was overrun by people in sober suits and sparkly dresses who didn't normally drink there or drink very much. As usual, freelance me had completely lost track of the days so I was quite surprised to find the pub full of office parties in the first week of December; after spending the evening being variously glared at and leered at by pissed-up, shaven-headed, banter-spouting thumbs in identical black single-breasted suits with identically loosened ties I vowed not to come to the pub as Carrie again until Hogmanay. That was a regulars-only, ticketed event where "civilians", as my friend Laura called them, wouldn't be admitted.

I had a few drinks on Christmas Eve but went home early because I was missing the children terribly: although my eldest didn't believe in Santa any more my youngest did, and I knew they'd be out in the front garden throwing reindeer dust (a mix of oatmeal and glitter) before setting out the mince pie, brandy and carrot that I wouldn't be there to eat, drink and leave ostentatious teeth marks in.

I woke early to the deafening silence of an empty flat, trying not to think about the excited unwrapping that'd be happening in the house. This was my first Christmas alone, my first Christmas as a separated parent, the first Christmas where I wouldn't be doing the rounds of relatives and in-laws. With Liz

I'd become used to extravagant unwrapping sessions at home before huge, hectic Christmas Day dinners at her parents' house where mountains of food were devoured by family and friends; this year I shared an M&S turkey crown in my flat with my kids, my mum and my brother and sister-in-law. As much as I love my family and as much as I tried to stay cheerful I couldn't help feeling an enormous sense of loss. The music didn't help, because of course all the best Christmas songs are about loss and loneliness. "Baby Please Come Home", my favourite Christmas song, is heartbreaking at the best of times, and I had to excuse myself for a few sobs between setting out the courses.

I've always used busywork to try and keep sadness at bay, but that Christmas I didn't have much real work to do and couldn't really motivate myself to do anything speculative. On the days I didn't have the kids I had a lot of time to think. Moving from self-medicating HRT to GenderGP-supervised HRT, which I did the day before Hogmanay, felt like another big step towards legitimacy: my hormone treatment was no longer a secret, my medication coming not from Hong Kong or Turkey or Tuvalu with the risk of hefty import fees but from a proper pharmacy via a proper prescription.

I realised that I resented the partygoers in the pub for making me feel that I couldn't be myself, for making me feel ashamed of myself, and I resolved not to give people that power in future. From now on I vowed that I'd try my very best to walk unafraid, to face the world on my own terms rather than accepting other people's boundaries.

At the beginning of January, everybody went back to work and I went back to being Carrie.

Permanently.

PART FIVE

WHAT IT FEELS LIKE FOR A GIRL

Call me

Muhammad Ali, Snoop Dogg, Eminem, Brad Pitt, Jude Law, Calvin Harris, Miley Cyrus, Whoopi Goldberg, Bono, Boris Johnson and my dad all have two things in common. One, they don't go by their birth names. And two, nobody's spending all day on the internet screaming their birth names at them.

Trans people call our old names "deadnames", because they are no longer being used. I killed Gary when I legally became Carrie: the person I used to be literally and legally does not exist any more. But unlike Brad, Bono and Boris I still have people using my deadname. And I'm not alone. For example, people who wouldn't dream of deadnaming Woody Allen – Allen Stewart Konigsberg – take great pleasure in deadnaming The Matrix directors Lilly and Lana Wachowski.

The Wachowskis, of course, are trans – and that means they're legitimate targets for the kind of self-proclaimed feminist who's a staunch defender of Woody Allen and other problematic men such as Johnny Depp.

Deadnaming happens from time to time by accident: someone who's known you as X for a decade will occasionally forget to call you Y. But most of the deadnaming of trans people and non-binary people I see online is deliberate and malicious. People do it to make it clear that they don't believe we are who we say we are: we are butterflies and they are chanting

"Caterpillar! Caterpillar! Caterpillar!"

People demonstrate their dickishness in another way: deliberately using the wrong pronouns to show that to them, we don't deserve the respect they give to dogs.

I'm a dog owner myself so I know how pet pronouns work: if you accidentally call someone's good girl a good boy or vice versa, the owner will correct you, you'll say sorry and you'll use the right pronouns. If you don't, the owner may set the dog on you.

We all use pronouns: that "we" was one of them. We talk about her car, his phone, say that he danced or she wrote. Those gendered pronouns are a relatively new development: in old and middle English, the most common pronouns for people – "he" and "heo" – were pronounced so similarly that they were effectively indistinguishable. Gendered pronouns didn't come along until the 12th Century when some bright spark came up with "she".

Before I became Carrie, my approach to pronouns was simple: I described myself as non-binary, so you could call me he or him and I really didn't mind. But when I actually became Carrie, that started to feel odd. I was doing a big work project that involved a lot of videoconferencing and went full-time as Carrie halfway through the project. I started to feel myself flinch when I was referred to as "he" during those meetings as I sat there in my wig, makeup and smart casual business attire.

It wasn't being done out of badness; I've experienced that many times and this was different. The person doing it knew me from before but had been perfectly respectful about my change of name and presentation, so I knew it wasn't a dig or anything like that. But every "he" felt like a paper cut, something that took full advantage of my basic fear that I was making a complete fool of myself by becoming Carrie.

It doesn't stop. Many months and a lot of hormones later, I'll be sitting with long hair, makeup and what are quite clearly tits under my t-shirt and the person I'm talking to will refer to me as "he" or "him" to the person they're with. The formula for correct gendering seems to be "get your tits (and your legs) out": if I'm in jeans, I'm referred to as him; in a nice dress, her. It also depends whether you see me first or hear me: the voice is a one-way ticket to Him Central.

There had clearly been another shift in how I saw myself. I still shied away from describing myself as a trans woman, but now the he/him stuff felt weird: Carrie might not have been born in a female body, but she had a female name and presented as a woman – so "she" or "they" was clearly more appropriate than "he". When I wrote about myself, for example if I was doing an author bio or commentary on some of my music on YouTube, the pronouns I used were always she/her.

This, apparently, is a bad thing. For example, in early 2018 the *Sunday Times* ran a why-oh-why piece titled "Revealed: The Transgender Email".[1] It contained the shocking news that Oxford University was asking students to include their preferred pronouns in their email signature. A predictable outcry ensued, and there was a similar one in 2020, also created by the *Sunday Times*, when the BBC suggested that staff might like to put their pronouns in their email signatures but it was okay if they didn't want to.

Like many things in the press, it was a manufactured outrage about people being asked to be nice to other people. A simple courtesy has become weaponised in the UK's increasingly unhinged War On Woke, with people going out of their way to be nasty to people in the name of triggering the libs. According to some of the high-profile anti-trans activists who regularly appear in the papers,[2] "pronouns are rohypnol"[3]. Rohypnol is the sedative rapists use to render their victims unconscious, so clearly that's a reasonable and sensible comparison to make.

If you really aren't sure what pronouns to use and can't ask, there's a perfectly acceptable and grammatically correct option that goes back to the days of Chaucer: the singular "they". The singular they has been in use for over 600 years and its validity was confirmed by grammarians in 1795, 1879, 1922, 1931, 1957 and the 1970s. But you know how crazy the word of grammarians can get, so you won't be surprised by the vicious wars against "they" waged by rival camps in 1795, 1825, 1863, 1898, 1926 and 1982.

The same arguments have raged in other languages, so for example in 1966 Sweden proposed the use of "hen" as a gender-neutral alternative to "hon" (she) and "han" (him). Take-up has been slow, though: "hen" didn't begin to enter common usage until 2010, and since then it has prompted a lot of debate and angry newspaper articles from people who have bad opinions for money.

If you can use the right pronouns for ships and Shih Tzus, if you call cisgender drag queens "she" but refuse to do the same for trans women, then I hope you step on an upturned three-pin plug in the middle of the night every night for the rest of your life.

Pronouns aren't the only issue you need to consider when you're presenting as the opposite gender from the one you were assigned at birth.

Where do you go to wee?

It's just history repeating

In the film *A Quiet Place*, Emily Blunt learns what it's like to be a trans woman going for a wee: in the post-apocalyptic world of the film, she has to navigate the world without making a sound for fear of alerting terrifying monsters with super-sharp hearing. For me, that's a Monday evening.

Like other women, I use the toilet to do my business, haul up my tights, fix my makeup and take mirror selfies if I'm feeling particularly cute and there's nobody else around. But unlike other women I try to time it so that the other cubicles are empty, even if I'm uncomfortably desperate to go, and if someone comes in just as I've finished I'll wait quietly until I hear them wash their hands and exit the room – something that would be more difficult with men because the stereotype of men not washing their big man hands post-pee is true of many.

Sitting in silence is harder than you think, especially if you have a stupid sense of humour and a sense of your own ridiculousness and the person in the next cubicle appears to have imbibed twenty gallons of Prosecco. Knowing you can't laugh even though the inhabitant of the adjacent cubicle appears to have smuggled an industrial pressure washer under their skirt makes the sound eleven times funnier, and I've sometimes had to reassure my friends on my return that no, I wasn't crying in the toilet – or at least, I wasn't crying tears of sadness.

I stay silent and seated because I don't want to make other women uncomfortable by my presence, and because I'm scared someone might make a scene. While trans people are overwhelmingly the victims of verbal, physical and sexual abuse in toilets, the press and social media says otherwise – so I'm scared of being singled out by someone loudly objecting to my presence or even attacking me. I'm much more scared of you than you should be of me.

But there's a long history of scaremongering about "others" in public toilets. In the US, segregated bathrooms were deemed necessary because a vocal minority of white women came up with various bullshit excuses for being terrible racists, so for example some claimed that using the same facilities as Black women would expose them to venereal diseases. Such claims were made until well after the Second World War, and in the 1970s and 1980s the same fear was directed against "predacious" gay men and lesbian women who couldn't reproduce and therefore had to recruit people, especially children, in public toilets and changing rooms for reasons never quite adequately explained. A vocal minority of straight women warned other women about the dangers of lesbians following their daughters into public toilets.[1] Bull dykes and lipstick lesbians were both vilified, the former for their supposed masculine hypersexuality and the latter for being "inclined to lure innocent girls… into a lesbian fantasy world, only to later betray them."[2]

Now it's trans people's turn the same rhetoric is rolled out: people who are overwhelmingly victims of violence and abuse are presented as a threat to you and to your children. "They are coming for your children" was said about Jews, and Black people, and immigrants, and lesbians, and gay men, and now it's being said about us.

By pushing the false narrative of trans women being dangerous predators, activists – whether faux-feminist or religious right – encourage the policing of women's appearance based on very stereotypical ideas of what is and isn't feminine enough. As we've seen again and again, that policing affects Black women, big women, tall women, women with short hair, lesbian women, gender non-conforming women and any other women whose femininity is considered lacking by strangers who have decided to judge them based solely on their appearance. There have been multiple reports of lesbian women bullied in bathrooms for the supposed crime of looking as if they might possibly be trans.

I'm scared of the self-appointed toilet cops, and if you're a woman who doesn't look like a 1950s white American housewife you should be too: I've seen anti-trans activists posting online about loitering outside public toilets waiting to inflict humiliation and violence on anyone who looks like they might be trans, I've seen anti-trans women boast about carrying weapons into toilets in their purses and I've seen cis women's very loud and very public outrage at sharing hospital wards with women who turned out not to be trans at all. Internet sleuths who claim "we can always tell" if somebody's trans have thus far identified Michelle Obama, Taylor Swift, Meghan Markle, Holly Willoughby, Jodie Whittaker, David and Victoria Beckham, Keira Knightley, and all of Prince Harry's ex-girlfriends as secretly transgender.

These people really scare me, because as far as they're concerned violence against me is entirely justified for no other reason than the fact I'm trans. They're happily making the world a more dangerous place for all kinds of women purely because they hate people like me so much.

The law is very clear on toilets: there's no law about who's allowed in which toilet (which is worth remembering if you're a woman in an endless queue for the ladies at a gig and there's an empty gents nearby). And common sense is pretty clear too: if you're in a skirt, tights and heels, let alone control underwear, a urinal is not the receptacle for you.

This is a storm over nothing that's got an awful lot of people, including me, terrified of going for a wee in case they get yelled at, beaten up or worse.

True Colours

Keanu Reeves's dog looking sad in John Wick. The war memorial in Glasgow's Riverside museum. Dropping the kids off at what used to be my house. All pop music. All of these things have made me sob my eyes out, often embarrassingly and publicly.

The crying was cathartic, a kind of mental housekeeping: my emotions needed a tidy up so I'd sort them out with a quick blub and then get on with my day or night. But the scale of it kept surprising me. One afternoon my youngest had urged me to sell my flat and move into a house to stay forever and ever because he really missed me; in addition to crying at the time I found myself bursting into tears again that night whenever I remembered it, which was a bit of a problem as I was sitting by myself in the pub at the time. I stopped counting after the seventh crying jag. Even at my lowest points pre-HRT, I had never cried like that.

Having lived the majority of my life as a man, the emotional changes from HRT were a surprise: I'd just assumed that boys don't cry because we're socialised that way. That socialisation is real, but I'd also found that a relatively small change in my body chemistry made me experience emotions very differently. I wasn't crying more because I was suddenly *allowed* to. I was doing it because I suddenly *needed* to.

After four months of taking HRT I felt like a completely different and considerably more emotional person. Where previously I tended to exist on a plane that started at "indifferent", went through "irritated" and ended at "quite pissed off, actually", my emotions were much more starkly defined and much wider ranging.

I didn't realise it at first, but one of the reasons I felt different was because feelings I'd had all my life were starting to fade. What had been normal for most of my life wasn't normal at all, and the HRT was making that increasingly clear.

If life is a video game, I hadn't been the principal character: I was an NPC, a non-player character who looks like the main player but who speaks words that aren't theirs, follows paths other people have programmed, and responds to others according to someone else's script. There are plenty of parts of my pre-Carrie life that I just can't remember, and the combination of that disconnection – a therapist would call it depersonalisation – and gender dysphoria made me dislike myself to the point where I'd let friendships wither and die. Because I didn't like myself I assumed that nobody else liked me either so I didn't do any of the maintenance that all friendships need from time to time. That I could lose friends by just not staying in touch proved to me that I'd been right: the friendships were shams all along.

I think a big part of it was that I didn't really have the kinds of friendships I have now. I had a similar attitude to friends as I did to dates: sooner or later people would find out my secret and reject me, so it was wise to keep people at arm's length. Friendships were based on shared circumstances, and when those circumstances changed the friendships fell away. So when I moved out of Ayrshire I lost touch with a lot of my Ayrshire friends; when I stopped playing in bands I lost touch with a lot of the people I'd met through music; and when Liz and I separated I lost almost all the mutual friends I'd got to know through Liz.

Social media played a part, too. With real-life friends, you only see a little bit of their lives, such as how they are when you're all having a laugh in the pub. But on social media you see much more; as the joke goes, it's a great way of finding out which of your former school friends have gone full racist. I've been genuinely saddened to quietly end online friendships with people who in real life I'd probably just agree to disagree with, but whose online presence primarily consists of posting links to right-wing publications and provocateurs. It's not censorship; I'm not asking them to stop posting. I'm just leaving the room, closing the door behind me and bricking it up so I can't hear them talk about Jordan Peterson any more.

HRT made me feel part of the world again, and my happier emotions were just as strong as my new-found ability to turn on the waterworks at the slightest provocation. Things that made me laugh made me laugh a lot more: a Jack Handey one-liner or a Frankie Boyle podcast or a Sara Pascoe book would leave me howling with laughter, drenched in warm tears, honking and insensible on a packed passenger train and unable to snap out of it despite the death stares of my fellow passengers. Something as simple as a fun pair of earrings would make my day, and a makeup or hair disaster would have me hooting.

Things that touched me touched me a lot more deeply, such as the kindness and thoughtfulness of the friends I'd made since moving back to Glasgow. I remember being rendered speechless while hosting a summer barbecue when my friend Aimee handed me a beautiful bouquet of flowers without fanfare or fuss; nobody had ever done that for me before, because flowers aren't things usually given to or appreciated by men. So Aimee's generous gift wasn't just pretty. It was meaningful too, a sign of how Aimee and my other friends saw me: as Carrie. I pretended my watering eyes were due to the smoke from the barbecue but I don't think anyone was fooled.

I was starting to feel much more positive. I smiled at strangers, struck up conversations in Post Office queues, chatted happily to wait staff and shop assistants and beauty technicians.

When you've been grumpy and shy for most of your life, that's very, very weird. Good, obviously. But weird.

Trans men report similar feelings of happiness, although of course the specific changes from taking testosterone are different to those from oestrogen. What we have in common, though, is that the right hormones enable us to feel more at home in our own skins. The constant alarm in our heads is finally silenced.

HRT changed the way I experienced emotions, amplified and magnified them. Whether that's better, worse or just different, I don't know. But the HRT version was certainly more vivid. As Liz put it, "It's like you've moved into Technicolor".

Everybody hurts

When I got the bus to my second gender clinic assessment, an older, clearly trans woman got on after me. When I got off, she got off too. We were both going to the same clinic and, to my great shame, I walked quickly to outpace her. There was a group of young men just in front of us and I thought that if they clocked the two of us (as the bus driver clearly had; he couldn't stop the sour look from spreading across his face when he heard my voice), they'd be twice as likely to shout at us.

They didn't even notice us.

I'm deeply ashamed about my behaviour that afternoon. Instead of acknowledging somebody whose experiences may well have been much tougher than mine and offering a hello or even just a smile in solidarity, I was embarrassed and chose selfish self-preservation instead. That's a really shitty thing to do.

It's something I then spoke to the doctor about during my appointment, the struggle I have with my own transphobia. I grew up being told that trans people were messed up, and part of me still feels that: one of the reasons I was having so much trouble with my gender identity – the pains I took to say I felt like a trans person, not a trans woman; my discomfort at describing myself as a lesbian even though my sexual orientation is to be attracted to women; my reluctance to use the ladies' toilets even when my presentation was 100% female – was because deep down, I still thought being trans was somehow wrong, a terrible fault rather than just part of the infinite and amazing variety of human beings.

I think part of it was that the woman unwittingly embodied something I'm really scared of. She slumped in the bus seat, staring fixedly at the floor, never raising her eyes. She carried herself in the manner of somebody who's learnt that attracting attention means attracting trouble; if I were to describe her in a word, it'd be downtrodden. And God forgive me, I distanced myself from her because I'm scared that I'll be downtrodden too.

I have two pictures of me in my head. In one, I'm liked and loved, the life and soul of the party, my personality all the positives I attribute to Carrie. I'm looking good, my life is a whirl of love and laughter, and I experience the world as a dynamic, attractive and vivacious woman who has a great relationship with her children, a flat that smells of really great cooking, and a really hot girlfriend.

And in the other I'm old and overweight, shapeless in frumpy florals, shuffling around a supermarket before returning to an empty flat and wishing my children would phone me.

For me, other trans people can be the Ghosts of Christmas Yet To Come, the most fearsome of all spirits. It's monstrously unfair to think of strangers in that way, I know, but it strikes at something deep inside me. I don't think I'm the only trans person to fear that the road I'm taking isn't necessarily the road to eternal happiness.

It's something I discussed with the psychiatrist during my appointment: not just my Christmas Carol ghosts, but whether I had doubts about any part of my transition from male to female. And I did, and I do. I am absolutely certain that I haven't made the wrong decisions, because I think I came to the point where there was a stark choice: be me, or be dead. But being trans can be incredibly hard sometimes. There isn't a week that goes by when the hugeness of all of this doesn't hit me, when it doesn't all feel utterly futile, when I don't ask myself what the hell I've done. We all have the little voice of doubt in our heads. My little voice often turns up with a full band and a wall of Marshall amplifiers.

The doctor wasn't there to provide answers, just to listen; to identify whether I had gender dysphoria and if so, whether treating it would help me live a happier life. The answers were clearly "yes" and "yes", so the appointment ended with a trio of referrals: to the medical team so they could take over my HRT regime; to a hair removal expert so I could do something about my facial hair; and to counselling services experienced in helping people tell the little voice in their head to give it a god-damn rest. I had my initial assessment two months later; the first actual counselling session was nine months after that. If you're keeping score, that's 28 months from my initial self-referral: it took from October 2016 to February 2019 to actually get any counselling. I wasn't in any kind of crisis, but the system is clearly failing trans people who are.

Walking out of the clinic felt really strange. It was all a bit of an anti-climax. When I'd first called in October 2016 to get an appointment, I was terrified. I was shaking so much I could barely hold the phone and my voice came out as a squeak. Seventeen months later I was standing outside the gender clinic presenting fully female, with a female name, on medically supervised HRT, with an official diagnosis of gender dysphoria.

It should have been a big deal, but it didn't feel like one. I knew I had gender dysphoria. It just took a while for the paperwork to catch up.

High voltage

For trans feminine people, facial hair is the stroke of midnight of the Cinderella story with you in the role of the pumpkin: the rasp of sharp stubble when you rest your chin on your hand breaks the spell in which you're totally getting away with being a girl. I'm relatively fortunate in that I have light colouring, so I don't get the blue chin that people with darker hair have to deal with. Makeup for people with darker facial hair is a real challenge: it can be hard to effectively cover shadow without looking like the slap has been trowelled on. Some women use a layer of blusher or even lipstick underneath foundation and powder.

I know rationally that nobody else can see my stubble, because while they feel like enormous steel cables to me the hairs aren't visible through my foundation. But just knowing it's there is enough to puncture the little happy balloon I'd spent my day in.

Shaving is a pain, both literally and figuratively. I've always hated shaving because my skin hates it; to have to shave twice daily as I had to do at the beginning of my transition is uncomfortable, and I can't imagine I was doing my skin much good by taking the top layer off so frequently. But even then, the stubble would be back long before midnight: if my second shave was in the early afternoon, my skin would feel like sandpaper by the time the sun was starting to set. That raised practical issues, such as: if I'm going to be travelling all day, what am I going to do to ensure I haven't gone full werewolf when the moon comes up? I started carrying an electric shaver in my bag. It's embarrassing to have to sneak away to de-fuzz, but not as embarrassing as being a woman with a five o'clock shadow.

It's something I simply hadn't thought about when I still presented as male, and in the early days post-coming out I was pretty sure I didn't need facial hair removal or anything like that. But it turns out I did: I just didn't realise it at the time because I wasn't being me yet.

Deciding to go for facial hair removal was another red line I'd vowed never to cross. It's very painful, can be very expensive – if you need electrolysis, which I did, the NHS only pays for a fraction of the treatments – and it's permanent. But like HRT, it didn't feel like a big deal any more. I didn't want to have stubble, so I needed to get rid of it.

I had my first hair removal assessment in late June 2018. It didn't last long.

"Hmmm," the nurse said. "That's a lot of red."

Red isn't good when you're being assessed for laser hair removal, which is the fastest and most effective way of getting rid of lots of unwanted hair. The laser needs pigment or it just passes through, and red, blonde or grey stubble doesn't have enough pigment for the machine used by the NHS clinic I was referred to. My facial hair is a mix of red, blonde and grey.

I shouldn't have been there, I was told, but that wasn't unusual: the gender clinics tend to send everybody even when they're clearly unsuitable for laser. So the next step would be for the nurse to email the gender clinic and for the gender clinic to approach the NHS for funding for electrolysis.

Electrolysis is a process where a highly skilled technician uses a tiny probe to remove all the money from your bank account.

I'm not kidding. At the time of writing I've spent over £15,000 on it, with several thousands still to go.

I was approved for 15 hours of NHS-funded treatment, the

maximum then available. But there are around 30,000 follicles in my face, each of which has to be individually stabbed and electrocuted several times before there's no more hair. 15 hours? Even 150 is a low estimate, and you can add even more if you're ginger. So once the NHS funding is gone you have to pay the rest yourself. To date that's been two hours a week for nearly four years at £64.80 an hour. I think I've got another year of treatment still to go.

It'll be worth it in the long run, because I'll have the smoothest face in the nursing home.

I'll be glad when it's done. My friend Aimee did several of my tattoos and reckons I don't feel pain. I do, but the pain of getting inked is nothing compared to the pain of electrolysis. Lying on a table for two hours as individual follicles are electrocuted and heated before the hair is yanked out with tweezers isn't a great deal of fun. My torturer tells me that it's worse for those of us with red hair: red hair is tougher, more resistant and requires more power.

It's particularly awful on bits where there isn't much fat, such as close to the jawline, and when it's done anywhere that bit of my face doesn't calm down for about four days afterwards. For the first 24 hours I look like I've shoved my face into a bucket full of wasps.

The literature tells you that most patients find electrolysis mildly uncomfortable rather than sore, but the patients they're talking about are cisgender women and their facial hair is usually many times thinner, much less dense and much easier to remove. When you see electrolysis illustrated it's always a shot of a serene-looking young woman with porcelain skin, not a middle-aged me shouting JESUS FUCKING CHRIST I FELT THAT IN MY TEETH and bursting into tears.

The main reason it's awful, though, isn't the pain. It's that in order to remove stubble there needs to be some stubble to remove. Although I don't have the kind of Desperate Dan chin that gives a five o'clock shadow fifteen minutes after shaving, it means I can't shave for the days running up to each electrolysis appointment – or immediately after the appointment, when the skin is angry.

What that means is that to keep a weekly schedule, I had to spend some of my week with facial hair: if I'm getting stubble yanked out of my face on Thursday, I can't shave after Monday morning. Living as me while also having stubble felt like a big step backwards and made me sad.

One day like this

It's a Friday in April and I'm wearing my new wig, the one I ordered months previously. It's a lot longer than the ones I'm used to, and I'm meeting Lo, a friend from London, at the BBC so I have to brave the River Clyde on a windy day. It's hilarious, especially if you're not used to having long hair, and I take some giggling selfies as the wind does its best to blow the wig off.

I'm in a fantastic mood. I've had the kids for the last few days and we had a really good laugh in the morning before it was time to go back to their mum. I've got a new song I've written playing on repeat in my headphones, a rock thing I'm absolutely delighted with. I'm smiling at strangers, letting the odd looks bounce off.

It's the second time I've met Lo face to face. I'm delighted to see them again and as we catch up in the BBC reception area, which has a café area that's open to the public, I hear a familiar voice: another friend, a young trans filmmaker. We hug, compliment one another and do the ten-second catch-up thing as she's off to a leaving do.

Lo and I finish our coffee and chat some more, then go exploring the riverside. I get to play the enthusiastic tour guide, pointing out some of the less salubrious bits and how the waterline is changing with lots of new development. We walk past tons of people including gangs of teenagers without comment despite my big voice and mad hair.

Lo is a musician like me, so we do the tour of the live music pubs and park ourselves in one of them. We only planned to pop in for a pint but the chat's so good and the beer so cold that we accidentally stay there for hours. We move on and have the best Indian meal I've ever had in my life, sharing some wine, ordering more beer and setting the world to rights until it's time for me to get the late bus home. We hug goodbye and promise to do it all again soon, and we both mean it.

The bus gets me home without incident and I make it back in time to sneak into the pub for last orders. There, a woman I have a massive, massive unrequited crush on gives me a megawatt smile and tells me I look pretty.

One day like that a year would see me right.

The queerest of the queer

I had already embraced the label "queer" to make sense of my gender and sexuality, my attraction to women and my desire to live as a woman, but I hadn't made the jump from identifying as a trans person to being comfortable describing myself as a trans woman.

And then I did.

Queer.

Trans.

Woman.

Like my official diagnosis of gender dysphoria, it looks like a big deal written down but it didn't feel that way. It was more of a "well, duh" feeling: once again I was just admitting what was bloody obvious to everybody else. I'd been on the brink of it for some time now; all I needed was a few hours with an affirming friend to take that final step.

It still felt incredibly liberating, though. Using the words made me feel like I was embracing my identity, not apologising for it; standing up instead of worrying about standing out; doing in real life what I was already doing online and in my music: being unafraid, unashamed of who I am.

I decided to face another fear and wear a dress to a gig: the band, Liverpudlian trash-rockers Queen Zee, were very queer and very trans-inclusive, and I thought – rightly – that if there was one gig where I needn't worry about being yelled at in the ladies it would be that one.

I picked out a particularly flattering, slightly fitted skater dress, teamed it with black tights and ballet flats, and looked at myself in the mirror.

I looked amazing.

Maybe not pretty, and definitely not sylph-like. But the stars had aligned, my makeup was perfect, my new wig was pretty spectacular and the tights emphasised the sheer length of my legs, far and away my best feature. I even had real if modest cleavage.

I was absolutely delighted: I looked and felt more like me than I'd ever looked or felt before. If twenty-year-old me had realised what forty-five-year-old me could look like with a bit of slap and some fake hair, she'd have been down the gender clinic in a flash.

I still wasn't as confident as I could have been, though. Wearing a dress to a gig for the first time was a daunting prospect, especially as I was meeting an old friend who hadn't yet seen me as Carrie: he was cool with the trans stuff, but I was a bit worried about how he might react to the sight of his old friend in a frock when the most extreme example of feminine presentation he'd seen me try was a bit of eyeliner that made me look like a New Romantic bassist from the 1980s. I decided to pop into my local pub to see some friendly faces and maybe have some Dutch courage before heading into town.

I'm glad I did, because when I walked in my friend Laura was there. "You look really pretty!" she said, grinning delightedly before adding "Is it okay for me to say that?" When I reassured her that not only was it okay, but it'd be even more okay if she could just say it a few hundred more times and maybe put it in writing too, she laughed and told me that "seriously, you look really hot".

One of my favourite things about being a trans woman is that I get included in the confidence-boosting compliments that men don't tend to exchange. There isn't the sexualised or lecherous subtext of some male/female interaction: I can say "oh my god, you look AMAZING in that dress" or "you should definitely buy that one, you'd look stunning in it" to someone I know without worrying about coming across as a creep, because I absolutely mean it and that's how it's interpreted. I know how a simple compliment from a friend can make your day eleventy billion times happier.

Before I came out, I never dreamed I would ever be told I was pretty, let alone hot, unless someone was doing it to mock me. One of the great sadnesses of not coming out until later in life is that you're stuck with a body that's developed in all the wrong ways, and without some pretty major interventions, the best you can do is try to camouflage the most obvious flaws. So I never imagined anybody would say anything positive about my appearance, or that if they did I'd believe them. But they do, and I do. I'll never be mistaken for a pretty young anything, but that doesn't mean I can't be proudly, unapologetically me. Whoever you are and however you identify, being happy in your own skin is pretty damn hot.

The Queen Zee show gave me the confidence to go to bigger and bigger gigs presenting fully feminine, and within a few months I was bawling along to The Manic Street Preachers' Motorcycle Emptiness at the 12,000 capacity Hydro. To say it was emotional would be an understatement: although I expected the Manics crowd to be welcoming, I still spent most of the day being really terrified of going to the show as myself. But my fears turned out to be groundless.

Thinking about it on the bus home, though, something struck me. Whether it was getting used to being me in ever bigger, busier places, walking through the centre of Glasgow in a dress, being visibly trans on public transport, using the ladies, travelling to with my new ID or any of the other heart-in-mouth moments that weren't so much beyond my comfort zone as on an entirely different planet from my comfort zone, I'd had to do them entirely on my own.

A young trans woman I follow on Twitter described the dynamic post-coming out as "silent abandonment" by friends, and sometimes by colleagues and/or family too. It's not unique to trans people – another friend who suffered a series of very serious health problems experienced the same thing when it became clear she wasn't just going to be in and out of hospital and cured in a week– but it seems to be a common experience: just when you need friends the most, your friends scatter.

My friend describes it as a "friend exchange": it shines a harsh light that exposes fair-weather friendships, but it also brings in new people or brings you closer to people you weren't close to before. That's been my experience too.

Everybody makes the right noises when you first come out. They tell you how brave and lovely and awesome you are and promise support. And then they disappear. It's not that they aren't supportive. It's that, you know, they'd love to meet up but work's really busy right now, or money's tight, or it's all a bit mad with the new flat and all that but let's totally catch up soon, they can't wait to see you and hear how you're doing. And the weeks become months and you're still going through every door with nobody at your back. It's a gift for the little voice of negativity, which immediately interprets it as "they're ashamed of being associated with you" and plays that again and again on a loop inside your head.

Even the ones who aren't ashamed to be seen with you can be wary. One of my male friends admitted that when he's out with me, his wife wants him to check in by text message every hour or so to reassure her that he hasn't been beaten up because he's with me. And of course, that makes you wonder how many other invitations have been declined by friends because they or their partners worry being with me will get them hurt. It's really upsetting to think about.

Being trans is a hard road to walk. It's harder still when you're walking it solo.

I don't walk it solo any more. I can thank my found family for that.

Many LGBT+ people have two families: their blood or adoptive families, and their found families. Found families are the friend groups we create based on shared interests and values, not necessarily shared genes or surnames. So far in this book I've talked about my family family, but not my found family.

Without my found family, I wouldn't be here.

It's different for girls

Since I moved to Glasgow and began living in the world as me, I've discovered a kind of friendship I'd never experienced when I was still pretending to be a man. My friend group is much more diverse, both in terms of what my friends do and who my friends are. The group is overwhelmingly female or non-binary. And it's introduced me to a kind of friendship that's much deeper, much more profound and much more life-affirming than any friendships I've ever experienced before. I have friends I would do absolutely anything for, and I know they would do absolutely anything for me.

Growing up male, I missed out on those kinds of friendships. I had friends, but not the kind you'd confide in, skip down a rainy street with or laugh with on a dance floor. I don't think I've ever written a song about one of my male friends, but I've written dozens about my female friends.

I sometimes feel sad that as a late transitioning trans woman, I didn't get to have those kinds of friendships when I was younger. But I'm also very glad that I didn't experience some of the other things my cisgender women friends did, such as:

- I wasn't paid significantly less than my colleagues for the same job, or sexually harassed at work, or discouraged from certain jobs or careers for no good reason.
- I hadn't been groped at gigs, leered at by relatives or been hit on by other people's husbands.

- I'd never had to worry about unwanted pregnancy or abortion, or fight for my right to abortion or contraception or other essential healthcare.
- I'd never had to consider whether my choice of outfit would attract unwelcome attention, or if my reputation would be used as justification for someone attacking me;
- I wasn't catcalled from building sites while still a child, didn't experience random abuse from men in vans, and wasn't followed home by strangers.
- I haven't been forced by a sexual partner to do something I don't want to do, and I'd never had to worry about somebody spiking my drink.
- I hadn't had death or rape threats on Twitter.
- I hadn't grown up with a constant barrage of attention telling me I'm ugly, or overweight, or unintelligent.
- I hadn't been the victim of coercive control or domestic violence.
- I hadn't spent every second of my life subject to a male gaze that objectifies me on the basis of whether men would "hit" or "smash" me or not.

As I began writing this chapter, a friend emailed with an example: that morning her friend, a forty-something woman, went to the post office. And in the street outside, which was full of people, an older man she'd never seen before exposed his penis to her and called her a "fucking whore" before disappearing into the crowd. What's awful isn't that it happened in the middle of the day, in a modern city in one of the most advanced nations in the world. It's that so many women have not just one, but many stories just like it.

And of course there are physical things too. I don't menstruate and I can't get pregnant, so I'll never have to endure the terrifying things Liz endured during her pregnancies and labour. I don't and can't suffer from painful periods or the often debilitating conditions some of my friends have had to deal with, conditions that their male doctors dismissed as "women's troubles".

There are many horrible things about being a woman. I consider myself very lucky not to have experienced many of them, and I don't feel the sense of loss about being unable to bear children that I know some other trans women do. But that doesn't mean that because I'm a trans woman my life has been constantly skipping through sunlit meadows either. Spending decades pretending to be somebody you're not and being so scared of the consequences of being found out that you stay in the closet until the choice is between coming out or killing yourself isn't exactly a walk in the park. And when you do come out you encounter not just homophobia and transphobia, but sexism and misogyny too.

I think it's important to talk about and recognise privilege, the advantages and disadvantages that some of us have because of our race, our class, our gender and all the other factors that affect the paths of our lives. But as with anything else trans-related, when it comes to trans people and privilege the debate is often very toxic and used to try and justify discrimination against or just abuse of trans women.

Anti-trans people claim that trans women are socialised as boys, which is generally true, and that they benefit from male privilege, which is also true. But they take those facts and use them to claim that as a result trans women, and in particular late-transitioning trans women like me, spend their entire lives oppressing women all day long and then decide on a whim to pretend to become women so they can oppress them a little more. To these anti-trans activists trans women are not women, are not oppressed and cannot *be* oppressed: they are the oppressor, incredibly privileged people having a little jolly by pretending to be members of an oppressed class. To some of the bigots, trans women are indulging in "womanface", our gender presentation a sickening parody, and we should be "morally mandated out of existence". I've seen anti-trans activists pile on a trans rape survivor to tell her that she was appropriating victimhood: they told her that she's not a "real" woman but a man indulging a "sick" fantasy of being female, that she'd clearly been "asking for it" and that she probably got a kick out of it.

Let's back away from the bigots and talk honestly about this.

I have *absolutely* benefited from male privilege. I've detailed some of it above. But male privilege isn't the only kind of privilege; there is cisgender privilege and heterosexual privilege too (and all the other kinds of privilege: class, race, education and so on). There is a huge difference between how the world works for straight cisgender men and how it works for people who are not cisgender or who are not straight, both before they come out and afterwards.

I haven't had the same experiences that you've had. But you haven't had the same experiences as many other people of your gender have had. If you're a white woman, you don't experience the racism Black women do. If you're a straight woman, you don't experience the homophobia lesbian women experience. If you're a rich woman, your life is very different from poor women's lives. If you're an abled woman, your life is very different from disabled women's lives. And so on.

The idea that trans women like me haven't experienced and cannot experience anything horrible because of our supposed male privilege is nonsense. Pre-transition and post-transition, our lives are very different from those of straight cisgender men. Straight cis men don't experience howling gender dysphoria or spend half their lives in the closet, for starters. And it's particularly galling to be lectured on privilege by people whose educational, financial and class privilege far exceeds mine, let alone most trans people's, and whose lowest low was when daddy wouldn't buy them a pony.

I'm much more privileged than many trans people. But I still lived in denial about who I am, trying to fit in a role I found increasingly difficult and terrified of the consequences of being found out. I was bullied in school and in my adult life too, and like other trans people I've struggled with mental health and suicidal ideation. In the US, 46% of trans men and 42% of trans women have attempted suicide, a rate almost ten times higher than the wider population.[1] Some privilege.

Privilege isn't permanent. Whatever male privilege I had vanished the moment I started to transition. When I first started presenting fully female I found myself being talked over in video meetings where previously I'd been considered an expert, my suggestions blanked until one of the men repeated them; when readers of my journalism disagree with me now the tone is no longer respectful but patronising and sometimes abusive; I've even had readers who think it's perfectly okay to track down my private contact details – details I don't share publicly anywhere – and send me text messages on a Saturday night.

We face the same gender pay gap as cisgender women, and sometimes worse: a late-2021 study by the Human Rights Campaign found that where cisgender women were paid 81% of the average wage, for trans women the figure was 60%. We are talked over, marginalised, and experience all the other delightful things men do to women in the workplace. And we also encounter additional issues that straight cis women don't: homophobia, biphobia and transphobia.

I've seen many trans women's accounts of constructive dismissal in the workplace as their performance and abilities were suddenly found lacking, their work suddenly and repeatedly subjected to much more intense scrutiny than before. Those of us who are freelance often find that formerly enthusiastic clients suddenly stop answering our emails when we come out. It may be illegal to discriminate against trans people, but that doesn't mean it doesn't happen.

The process can work in reverse too. Some trans men report feeling more valued at work[2] because men are more valued in many workplaces – although that doesn't apply to all trans men. The same HRC study that found trans women were paid 60% of their cisgender male counterparts found that trans men and non-binary people were paid 69%.

I'm not trying to win an event in the Oppression Olympics here. My life is much easier than the life of, say, a single mum struggling to survive on Universal Credit. But again and again we see affluent, middle-class, straight white women in the media claim victim status while denying it to people who have suffered much more than them – women of colour, working class women, disabled women, gay women, incarcerated women, unemployed women and many other kinds of women, whether cis or trans.

Women are an oppressed class. Of course they are. But some women are quite happy to perpetuate or even participate in that oppression in order to gain or secure status for themselves. Punching down is paying a lot of writers' and pundits' mortgages right now.

My experiences of being trans are exceptionally positive compared to many of the trans people I know and many more I don't, people who don't have my colour or class or good fortune. Their supposed privilege didn't stop them from being disowned by family, discriminated against in the workplace, sexually assaulted in private and physically assaulted in public.

I know most of my life experiences are different to those of cisgender women. But to be seen as female – whether you grew up female, transitioned to female or just blur gender lines – means being treated very differently from the way men are treated. If you walk in women's shoes the world instantly becomes a much harder place. My women friends know that very well, and as a result their attitude to my womanhood often reminds me of Bill Hicks' routine about gays in the military: if you're dumb enough to want to experience the world like we do, welcome.

Suspicious minds

I've been having a bit of a day. My car exploded on the way to a hospital visit necessitating a call to the hospital, a call to the AA and a call to the garage. I've spoken to nine people on the phone so far and every single one of them thought I was a man. It happens so often I barely notice it any more.

Sometimes, though, the difference between who I am and what I sound like means people don't believe I'm me. So when I call to do things like amend my car insurance, I enter some kind of conversational loop.

"Okay, and your name is…?"
Carrie.
"No, sorry. I need your name now."
It's Carrie.
"No, I mean your name. Who you are."
I'm Carrie. The policyholder. Carrie Marshall.
"But… but it says here, Ms."
I know. I'm transgender.
"But…"

Eventually the agent accepted that my name was indeed Carrie, but he clearly wasn't happy about it. I lost count of the number of times in our short conversation he asked "Are you *sure* there isn't anything else you need to inform us about?"

The agent clearly thought I was part of some dastardly plot

to defraud Direct Line, when all I wanted to do was insure my car. And it was such a contrast to the process of actually buying the car, where I got a genuinely good deal partly because it was the end of the month and the salesman had a commission target to hit and partly because I was trans. The salesman was a former nightclub owner who regaled me with tales of his more outré trans customers' shenanigans, and bent a few rules to get me a better deal than I'd hoped for, let alone expected. I'd bought it on the Sunday when the dealership was dead; picking the car up on the Monday from a packed showroom and dealing with multiple members of staff passed entirely without comment or incident. Everybody was nice to me, because most people are nice.

When I think back to how scared I used to be of so many things, I'm partly sad that I didn't face my fears sooner and mainly delighted by how my life is now. I barely recognise the scared, shy, unself-confident person I was when I first came out. I'm more assured, much happier and considerably better dressed.

When the obligatory idiot in a white Transit van yells at me in the street, I don't even pause. And when giggling drunks stage-whisper "That's a MAN!" in the pub I don't react, or let it bother me particularly. I'd rather they didn't do it, of course, but it just isn't important. I'm in a really nice dress, I feel really good about myself and my quiz team's going to win a £50 bar tab while they distract themselves by speculating about what's in my pants.

There will always be poorly trained insurance agents, groups of "lads" who cackle after I walk past and people in suits who disapprove of my very existence and will go out of their way to tell me so, but they're nothing compared to the very many hazy, sunny Sundays and long, laughter-filled evenings I share with people who like me for who I am, not who I used to pretend to be.

★

Two years after I started hormones, I was aware of looking subtly different. More feminine. Other people noticed too, not always in a way I was happy about: for example one night as I sat looking at my phone in my local pub, a complete stranger put his arm around me, demanded I put my phone down to have a chat with him and put his head against mine. He ignored my nice requests to piss off and only left me alone when my friend Laura appeared and frightened him off.

More happily, when I was out for my mum's birthday dinner the effervescent waitress included me in her chat; when it was time to pay she ordered me to "put your purse away, woman!"

The taxi ride home was eventful too, the taxi driver looking at me in the mirror before asking a barrage of questions. He seemed surprised that a trans woman could be attracted to women and not men, or that she could have previously been married with children. He thought for a moment and then shared his own story, presumably in an attempt to find common ground.

"One time," he said, "I went to Thailand…"

He looked at me in the mirror, paused, and continued:

"and pumped a ladyboy."

It was the best sex he'd ever had, apparently.

I didn't enquire further, and when the driver dropped me off near my local pub and drove away I cried with laughter for a good 20 minutes. Later that night Laura would have me crying again as she speculated whether the taxi driver had really been the pumper, or if he had in fact been the one being pumped.

My mum called the next day and made me cry in a different way. "You looked really pretty last night," she said.

As Autumn turned to winter, my divorce was finalised and there was some ugly crying. But there was plenty of joy too, especially when I finally got my chance to be Velma from *Scooby-Doo*.

My artist friend Aimee was marrying her lovely boyfriend Colin, and my friends and I were invited to her wedding. This was no ordinary wedding, though. This was a wedding with a fancy dress reception. I did the formal bit in a pretty green dress, changing into you-know-who for the reception. Aimee was a tornado, complete with flying houses. Laura was undead, with actual worms superglued to her face and neck. It was a beautiful wedding and a riotous reception.

I couldn't go to a wedding every weekend, but my friends kept dragging me out of my comfort zone. Angela's club night helped me overcome my lifelong fear of dancing; on one particular night she and Laura conspired to get me onto the dance floor to one of my very favourite songs, Robyn's "Dancing On My Own". Eyes sparkling, Laura grabbed my arm and whirled me around. I told her afterwards that if she decided to strangle me and throw my corpse in a wheelie bin that night, which is very much the kind of thing I can imagine her doing, I'd die a happy woman.

I've come to understand that these highs and lows are going to be the ebb and flow of the rest of my life, a constant mix of affirmation and suspicion, celebration and objectification. The hard bit – which I still haven't learnt – is finding ways to hang on to the good stuff without letting the bad spoil it, because sometimes even the tiniest things try to burst your happiness like a pin through a bubble. For example, a few weeks ago my friend Louise and I went to one of Glasgow's best restaurants, and after many weeks of not really bothering about dressing up I decided to make an effort and glam up a bit with hair, makeup, the works. I felt great. The chat was hilarious. The food was spectacular, the cocktails delicious, the company divine. And when we split the bill and left a far-too-generous tip, the waitress thanked us both and called me sir.

PART SIX

NEW RULES

Music makes the people come together

I've written a lot about not wanting to be noticed, about wanting to blend in, about wanting to lead a quiet life. And that's all true, but sometimes I also want to be carried through cheering crowds in a sedan chair, the lamentations of my enemies barely audible over the roar of the crowd.

So after a fifteen year break I got back into performing live.

I never stopped making music, but I stopped doing it in bands. For fifteen years I either wrote songs solo or remotely with my brother, and while they didn't set the world on fire I loved the process of making them. I taught myself to do all kinds of things, completely losing myself in the details of composing, of recording, of producing. Just as it did in my younger years, music put me into a flow state.

I didn't think much about returning to playing live until many months after I came out, when I realised something really important had changed. I wasn't scared any more.

The old me used to have to stop in lay-bys en route to gigs to be violently ill at the roadside. I'd shake so much I could barely hold the drink I felt I couldn't go on stage without. It was miserable, and while the rush of a good gig could make it all worthwhile there are many gigs that are not good gigs, particularly when like me you're playing to three drunks and a murderer in some dingy basement where the cigarette smoke barely masks smells that are so much worse.

I don't have that stage fright now. I've learnt how to make the butterflies in my stomach fly in formation, to use the pre-show nerves as fuel instead of fear. And that's entirely because I'm trans.

Don't get me wrong. The first time I did it, I was absolutely bricking it. I was at an open mic night at The Ice Box in Glasgow and I took the stage wearing an acoustic guitar and a dress. But I loved every second of it. What I loved about it was that I didn't feel strange, didn't feel defensive about the difference between my outfit and my voice, which was undeniably male. I *liked* that: it meant that straight out of the gate I was messing with people's expectations. You don't expect someone who looks like me to sound like me.

That's profoundly liberating, because instead of keeping my transness secret I can use it as a shield, or maybe a battering ram: if people are going to look at me anyway, it might as well be on my terms and with my chosen soundtrack. It's thrilling in the way an adrenaline-pumping theme park ride is thrilling: for however long I'm on stage I'm feeling waaaaaaagggggghhhhhhh and waving my arms around in glee.

It's made me feel almost fearless, not just in terms of playing but in terms of writing too. If I'm going to go on stage in a dress, then I'm going to take your attention and turn it towards the subjects I want to shout about.

At first I just stuck to open mic nights, but then one of my friends asked if I'd be interested in singing for a rock band. Her partner, who I already knew and liked, was producing some guys down in Kilmarnock and they needed a singer. Was I interested?

I was. There was just one problem, which was the whole being-trans thing. Did the guys in the band really want a singer who was visibly trans, who would present female on stage and who would probably sing about LGBT+ things from time to time?

They did. I had a phone call with Kenny, the band's bass

player, and explained that by trans I meant wearing-dresses-on-stage trans. His response was simple and made me laugh. He told me:

Put on your big girl pants and bring the noise.

Swim till you can't see land

It is very hard to walk into a building when your brain is telling you that you're going to get yelled at.

Despite being specifically invited and turning up to the venue at the appointed time, I nearly didn't attend the launch of the charity I now volunteer for, Scottish Women Inventing Music (SWIM). Every part of me wanted to run away, and I very nearly did.

SWIM is dedicated to achieving equality in music for all women and non-binary people, and it's explicitly trans inclusive – something I checked with the organisers when they invited me along – but even then I was absolutely terrified when I attended its launch event. It was the first women-only event I'd ever attended and I was certain that someone there would loudly object to my presence: I'd spent so long immersed in the anti-trans rhetoric of the newspapers that I fully expected a frosty reception at best and outright hostility at worst. The feeling was compounded by social media – it was International Women's Day and Twitter was a cesspit for trans women as a result – but it's a feeling that I have almost constantly.

Whether it's SWIM or the various women-only music groups I've been invited to join, I tend to keep a low profile for fear of a negative reaction. I'm always waiting for the trans-exclusive shoe to drop. Because it often does: there are multiple outlets I simply won't pitch to because of their clearly anti-trans editorial choices; I also stopped working for one national news organisation after their advertising team worked closely with anti-trans activists to create a particularly appalling cover wrap for their print edition. And there are also some media- and arts-related organisations that could be useful to me professionally, but I won't have any involvement with them because I've seen senior members of those organisations sharing very transphobic things on social media. It is very clear that their definition of women doesn't include women like me.

I hesitated for a long time before going in to the SWIM launch – I was so terrified I was visibly shaking – but I'm glad I didn't turn around and go home. I got to know some really great people, made some new friends and the only time being trans was relevant was when my height enabled me to pass a toilet roll over a cubicle divider to help a fellow delegate in distress. But despite having been a volunteer for several years now, I still worry that when someone hears my voice on the SWIM podcast they'll accuse me of stealing the spotlight from a cisgender woman.

One of the things I hate most about the open transphobia that's flying around right now is that it robs me of things I used to enjoy, particularly music. I have been a fan since my early teens of a particular English, far-left post-punk band, and in the decades since I've gone to see them every time they played Glasgow. But it turns out that the person who designs their record covers and their backdrops and their merchandise, somebody I've met and chatted briefly to in my previous life, somebody whose posters have been on my wall and whose designs I've worn proudly on my chest, turns out to really, really hate people like me and is very vocal and vicious about us online. So a band whose gigs used to feel like sanctuary – a band whose Twitter bio says they welcome everyone without exception – is now a band I can't go and see anymore. Every bit of merch is a reminder of someone who hates me, and may be a sign that the person wearing it shares their views. I'm sure most don't. But it only takes one person to beat you up, and that fear makes it impossible to enjoy the show.

It's not the first time a band I loved has turned out to be problematic. It seems that the nice guys are the ones to watch: the main songwriter of a band famed for their warmth and geniality, a band I used to really love, posts bitter rants about trans women online, while multiple past-their-prime Scots indie musicians famed as much for their affability as for their records have revealed themselves to be as conservative as their music. The guitar player of my very favourite band appears to have fallen down the same rabbit hole. The list of former loves I'll no longer pay to see grows ever longer.

It's as much a practical decision as a moral one. For me, gigs are an important release. They're a source of joy, an opportunity to escape from the stresses and strains and sadness of everyday life. It's impossible to have that transcendence when every time you look at the stage you see someone who doesn't just hate you, but who spends an inordinate amount of their time trying to encourage others to hate you too.

It feels like betrayal. Have you ever discovered that an important friend was talking about you behind your back, sharing your secrets for others to mock? It feels like that, but so much worse: the people whose art helped you survive would actually prefer it if you hadn't; the songs that meant so much to you, it turns out, were never meant for people like you. It's a discovery that sucks all the air from the room and from your lungs, leaving you reeling as one of the few things you could hold onto is ripped from your grasp.

How can art offer escapism when the artist is one of the people you're trying to escape from?

Yesterday, when I was mad

In 2019 I went a bit mad.

Part of my HRT regime involves suppressing my body's testosterone production, and I was doing that with tablets called Spironolactone. But Spiro makes you really crave salt, makes you want to wee every thirty seconds and puts strain on your liver, which is a concern for older trans women like me. So I was switched to twelve-weekly injections of Decapeptyl, also known as Triptorelin, instead.

Decapeptyl is awful for about two weeks, because to stop your body producing testosterone it initially makes your body create too much of it. Overloading a thing, blowing it up and moving onto the next challenge is something I do in video games all the time – but this time I was doing it to my own testicles.

It was a really weird fortnight. At first I thought I was unaffected, and then I realised I'd been shouting at cars. Until the testosterone surge wore off I felt like the kind of person who posts on newspaper comment sections, prone to unspeakable rage at the slightest perceived provocation. It was the most male I'd felt, not just since going on HRT but since *forever*. I really didn't like it and I was very glad when it wore off, but I've been sure I've felt my T levels rising on a few occasions since: I get a bit weird and cranky in the final week of my three-month injection cycle.

My gender clinic doctor told me that I was imagining this, but I've spoken to other trans women on Decapeptyl and they experience the same slump at the same point. This is quite common for trans people: because nobody's done any decent research into many of the things we experience, we're told that we're wrong or that we're making things up by people who don't know any more than we do.

I got my first experience of a TV studio make-up chair a few weeks later, thankfully no longer feeling like The Incredible Hulk, and loved every moment of it. I felt like Beyonce, although because it was TV makeup it's very exaggerated and I couldn't really move my face afterwards; I went to the pub feeling like an Easter Island statue. It was really validating to go in front of TV cameras as me and not feel like a man in a dress, which is why it was all the more upsetting a few days later when I did a remote radio collaboration with an Edinburgh studio and was called a man four times on air by the presenter. I cried after that.

A few weeks later, after meeting friends for a pub quiz and coming home with a beautiful doodle of me in a frock by my glamorous friend Claire, I paused at the digital photo frame in the hallway of my flat. It's packed with family photos, me and the kids, and I was stopped in my tracks by one in particular. It's a picture of me and my youngest, taken about three years previously. We're both laughing; they have long hair and I have a beard, which is how I can date the photo: it's early to mid 2016.

I looked at the photo of the man I used to be. And I looked up, into the mirror.

He wasn't there.

It was more than makeup, more than a nice dress, more than jewellery, more than being a bit pissed on gin, although all of those things were clearly contributing factors. But it was mainly the result of a couple of years of hormones making subtle changes, changes that don't seem like much individually but that make a difference over time, changes that you don't necessarily notice until you really look at a picture of who you used to be.

I looked in the mirror, and I didn't see him. I saw me.

★

The very next evening, my oldest asked me two little questions that were very big questions.

"Dad, do you wish you'd been born a girl?"

"Are you transgender?"

There were a lot of tears (mine, inevitably), some excellent hugs and two hours of questions. He wanted to know *everything*. How long I'd known, how it felt, was I happier, was it why me and their mum had split up, was I on hormones, what did hormones do, how did people react, had I ever got into trouble because of it, did I want surgery… it felt very much like a dam bursting, as if he'd been mulling it all over for a while but was waiting for the right moment to ask. When he was back with his mum the following night Liz texted to let me know they'd had their own big chat about it and everything was positive.

I felt ten stone lighter.

I spoke to my oldest about this recently, and I told him that I'd been amazed by how well-informed he'd been, how empathetic, how he'd put all the pieces together.

"Dad," he said. "I googled you."

Just over a year later, as Liz drove him home from my flat, my youngest would ask what trans meant: was it when two girls loved each other? Liz explained that no, that was what lesbian meant; trans was when someone might be born a boy but grow up and realise they should have been a girl all along. He nodded at this, and asked brightly, "Is Dad trans?" When Liz said yes, he nodded again with satisfaction and changed the subject to something more interesting. His nickname for me has always been "dather", a mix of "dad" and "father"; for a while, he amended it to "Quing of the Dathers". When I asked him why, he said he was mixing King and Queen because "you are a boy who wants to be a girl."

★

When I first came out to Liz we agreed that I wouldn't try to express my femininity on the school run. That agreement ended up causing me problems a few years later when I needed to prove that I was presenting full time as female, but I think it was and is the right decision: I've never felt the need to rock up outside my youngest's school dressed like Dolly Parton. My clothes were all female ones, but I didn't look any different than I did before: I turned up in jeans, trainers and t-shirts just like I did in my previous life and just like most of the school run mums do. There's a time and a place to glam up. 8.50am in a rainy playground isn't it.

That doesn't mean I wasn't noticed or talked about. I was, and I quickly grew tired of the stares. Liz tells me that she encountered some transphobic posts – not specifically about me, but posted by people who knew about me and who knew Liz would read them – on Facebook from some of the school run mums. One mum we considered a friend of the family cut all ties and banned her son from playing with our eldest. A few months later I saw her in the street with her husband and said hello. He smiled and said hello back; she said nothing and turned her back on me.

Liz and I were both worried that other parents would be similarly unpleasant, that news of me being trans would mean fewer invitations to parties or playdates or even result in bullying. As far as we know that didn't happen, but to help minimise the risk I was rarely the parent who picked up or dropped off the kids from social events and the kids' friends were never invited to my flat. I'd still do school runs and sports runs for my half of the days – Liz and I co-parent, with the kids spending equal time with each of us – but on the occasions that I did the party pickups or drop-offs I felt extremely self-conscious and couldn't escape quickly enough. It would take me four years to lose my fear of other kids' parents, let alone talk to any of them at the school gates.

I've since discovered that most, but not all, of my fears were unjustified; having accompanied my kids to parks and other places as me in recent months I've discovered that most people are far too busy looking at their phones or gossiping with their friends to care about anyone who isn't actively trying to kidnap their children. Some people do stare, but when they do I simply pretend that they're doing it because I'm so incredibly attractive they can't keep their eyes off me. Who knows? Maybe at least some of the time it's true.

In April, I travelled to Lanzarote with my children, the first time I'd done so without Liz. I didn't want to present obviously female for fear of trouble, but that raised the prospect of a different kind of trouble: travelling while appearing to be male with female ID and a plane ticket in a female name. I learned three words of Spanish for the check-in on the way back in case I was queried: *yo soy transgenero*, I am transgender. In the end I didn't need to use my spectacular language skills, but on both legs of the trip there was an interminable wait while the check-in staff conferred with each other about me and other holidaymakers' eyes bored into the back of my head.

I boymoded for the whole holiday, keeping myself covered in oversized t-shirts to hide my changing body shape. Far from home with nothing to do but amuse my kids and try to read bits of books, I was able to properly relax for the first time in a long time. My youngest was particularly delighted, because not only was Dather here for a full week uninterrupted, but Dather didn't have to do any work or go on the phone either. We played a lot, ate well, splashed around at the beach and the kids spent most of the time in the swimming pool while I watched them from a nearby lounger.

I was even able to join them, swimming for the first time since I'd come out. I did it stealthily, a heavy metal t-shirt over my swimsuit, and lowered myself into the water when the pool was quiet and I was far from families or their children. I'd forgotten how wonderful it feels to float, to completely lose yourself as you bob on the water with the sound of the world turned down. I didn't stay in for long, though, and I'd left a towel poolside so there'd be no time when my now-wet T-shirt would show other people my shape.

I felt so much joy being in that water and realised how much I'd missed something so simple but so life-enhancing. I tried to recapture that joy a few days later on the beach, but this time I didn't bother with the t-shirt over my plain black swimsuit; three older English women passed me and one barked, "You're not fooling anyone." I honestly don't know if it was directed at me or if it was unfortunate timing, but either way it ruined an otherwise happy, sunny afternoon.

In May, SWIM asked me to lead their working group on activism and advocacy. Thanks to my new policy of saying yes to anything that scares me, I said yes. I still felt like an impostor, but if I was at least I was an impostor making a positive contribution.

There were lots of little moments that felt quite big. I had my first "male fail", which is when you're not really bothering to present female but get gendered as such anyway, in a card shop. I was buying a card for my piano teacher, who was moving house, and when I approached the till the assistant told her colleague to wait a moment while she served "this lady". I burst into tears leaving the shop.

That weekend I went to see the superb singer-songwriter and trans ally Grace Petrie in concert with one of my friends, a butch gay woman. We looked spectacular, me in a black dress and her in a sharp suit. During one of the sad songs my friend put her arm around me (of course, I was crying my eyes out), and I think it's the first time anybody has done that: because I was previously a man it had always been my arm that was the comforter for someone else. It felt really strange. I felt vulnerable and validated. I never used to like other people touching me, but it's something I really love now. Some of my friends are incredibly tactile and that makes me feel really happy and connected to them; I'll be sad when my kids no longer want to have cuddles and hugs.

I went on a week-long sound engineering course and was misgendered constantly by everyone but the tutor, but my skin was growing thicker: I knew there was no malicious intent so I chose not to let it bother me. And once again there were signs that I was starting to lose my stage fright and my previous reticence. When the group needed a singer I was the first to volunteer; singing into a mic while the entire class looked at me through the control room window was no longer intimidating but quite exciting.

The following week I added a mermaid to my tattoo collection. One evening my youngest thought about whose arm the bare-chested beauty was drawn on, started laughing and announced: "Dad! You've got four boobs!"

The summer continued to mix the good and bad.

At a SWIM meeting I forgot I was me and used the gents' toilet, nearly giving some old guy a heart attack when I exited the cubicle in wig, heels and a dress.

I was loudly discussed in the street by a couple of teenage boys in Adidas tracksuits, one of whom said, "That's no a wumman!" His friend paused and then said cheerfully, "Ah'd still stick it with ma willy".

I was sexually harassed by a drunk man and stared at with open disgust by a drunk woman in the same pub on the same night.

And for the first time, both of my children saw me presenting fully female at work. They were on their summer holidays and I had to take them with me to the BBC, so both of them finally saw me as me.

My youngest considered my appearance carefully and delivered their verdict.

"You look funnier," he said. "But not cooler."

We live in a political world

According to many newspapers and broadcasters, a trans person who has an opinion on anything is an "activist" and anybody who really hates trans people is a "feminist". But in late 2019 I actually did two bits of activism. I met Nicola Sturgeon, First Minister of Scotland, to discuss the reality of trans people's lives, and I was also one of the speakers at an event for health providers to raise awareness of the issues LGBT+ people experience in healthcare.

I was asked to meet the FM in a meeting arranged at her request by LGBT Health and Wellbeing, an organisation that supports LGBT+ people in Scotland. I'd known them for a few years: they run the non-binary nights I'd found helpful when I first came out. One of their senior staffers was a constituent of the FM and had spoken to her at her surgery about the increasingly intolerant climate towards trans and non-binary people; the FM asked him if he could arrange for her to meet a range of trans and non-binary people to hear first-hand about their experiences.

The meeting took place because, as in England, the Scottish Government was consulting on how to reform the Gender Recognition Act. The consultation ushered in a period of openly transphobic abuse on social media and carefully worded but still transphobic sentiment in the national and local press. Hate crimes against trans people soared, and the First Minister was concerned enough by this to want to understand what the reality was like for a variety of trans and non-binary people.

The proposed reforms of the GRA were simple and innocuous. The current system, which is horrifically invasive and expensive, would be made slightly less horrifically invasive and slightly less expensive. Every major Scottish political party, even the Tories, included gender recognition reform in their mid-2010s election manifestos without a single squeak of protest from anybody. It was part of Scotland's ongoing drive to be one of the best countries in the world for LGBT+ people.

And then the Scottish and English governments decided to start consultations on GRA reform. Those consultations opened the door to a manufactured culture war.

When the first Scottish consultation's results were announced, the anti-trans groups and their cheerleaders in the Scottish Parliament and the Scottish and English press screamed bloody murder, claiming that a public consultation the anti-trans activists knew about, submitted responses to and encouraged their supporters to respond to had somehow been carried out in secret. They also made it clear that when they had urged people to "listen to women" they didn't mean listening to the majority of women and women's groups who were in favour of gender recognition reform. Their friends in the press amplified their claims, alleging a stitch-up by the Scottish Government in thrall to the press's favourite new bogeyman, the sinister trans lobby.

The First Minister met us in the Govanhill Workspace, a converted church in Glasgow's south side where FM hosts her constituency surgeries. We were ushered into a high-ceilinged meeting room by a faintly harassed aide, and we sat ourselves around the rectangle of tables and made small talk until the First Minister strode in. I was surprised by how calm I was: I'd been more nervous meeting my fellow invitees in the southside café beforehand than I was meeting the FM.

The FM was exactly how I expected her to be: she was pleasant enough but she had the air of someone who doesn't suffer fools gladly. She introduced herself as if we wouldn't know who she was, apologised she couldn't give us more than the allocated time and then listened intently as the LGBT+ Health and Wellbeing members set the scene. She then went around the table asking each of us to describe our experiences of being trans or non-binary, giving each one of us her full attention in turn.

I already knew that many trans people have it worse than I do, but the meeting was still harrowing: the other people in the room hadn't had to seek out their sorrows, and their attempts to talk about extremely vicious treatment at the hands of the people who they should have been able to trust – in particular close family members and healthcare providers – without getting emotional were heartbreaking. The stories of the two youngest guests, a trans man and a non-binary person, were particularly tough to listen to: imagine being cut out of your rightful inheritance by your transphobic family, or lying in a hospital bed and hearing the mocking laughter as your nurse talks about you to a colleague in the most degrading terms.

For my part I made the FM laugh with my description of the so-called sinister trans agenda – "gie us peace" – and spoke more sensibly about how it felt to read constant poison about trans people in the press and online. She nodded as I talked about sometimes being too scared to leave the house or use a public toilet when the entire media was trying to persuade everyone that you were a danger to women and children.

The First Minister was visibly moved by some of the things she was told, and judging by the body language of her aide she let the meeting run longer than it should have; in the end she reluctantly brought the meeting to a close in much the same way my youngest shuts down the PlayStation when they've been called for dinner. The FM thanked us for our time and our honesty, posed for a quick photo and was then rushed into her ministerial Volvo for her next appointment.

The skies opened as we walked back to the café, rain bouncing off the pavements and the streets quickly flooding.

Perhaps we should have taken that as an omen: while I think the FM's concern and her empathy were absolutely genuine and I believe that she is an LGBT+ ally, there is more to a government than its First Minister. Just a few weeks later the Scottish Government announced that it wasn't going to proceed with its proposals for gender recognition reform.

Having already held a consultation during which time the media declared war on trans women, the Scottish Government announced that it would hold another. The anti-trans rhetoric in the press and online was even worse second time around, but the consultation nevertheless still found a large majority in favour of GRA reform.

With GRA reform now the most consulted-upon proposals in Scottish Parliament history, the SNP finally brought the Gender Reform (Recognition) Bill to Holyrood in March 2022, nearly five years after the initial consultation was mooted. In October of the same year, the majority of the Scottish Parliament committee backed the principles of GRA reform, with futher debate as to its legislation due. It's unlikely the Bill will become law before 2023 and MSPs are almost certainly going to propose multiple "wrecking amendments" to try and derail it or render it unworkable before it becomes law.

Writing this book in the midsts of the Bill's process, the pressure groups and the troll armies are into their fifth year of anti-trans scaremongering and outright abuse while the one thing trans people really care about, healthcare, gets worse by the day.

I didn't have much time for politics after the meeting. My youngest started to have mysterious and frequently severe chest pains, and over the next few weeks we had a series of increasingly worried A&E visits that would produce differing diagnoses and treatments. After diagnosing him first with a pulled chest muscle and then acid reflux, the doctors finally worked out what was really wrong. He had bacterial pneumonia, which had become very advanced by the time he was diagnosed, and he was taken into hospital to have chest drains installed.

He made a full recovery, but it was a tough time. The moment Liz and I kissed him goodbye, watched the nurses wheel him into the operating theatre and went into the corridor to cry was one of the most frightening experiences of my life. I've never felt so scared or so powerless.

I think sometimes it takes a scare to make you realise what matters, and what matters most to Liz and I is the health and happiness of our children. Without even discussing it we simply became a team again for the duration of our child's illness and recovery, any rancour over our break-up long gone.

What I remember most about that period is how powerfully protective I felt towards both of my children, how my love and fear overwhelmed everything else. Had there been a way for us to swap places, for me to take the pain away, I'd have done it in a heartbeat. And I know that all the other parents in the ward, some of whose children had much more severe conditions than ours, would have done the same for their own. It's something that comes back to me when I see unaccepting parents of LGBT+ kids and teens on social media. I can't imagine having a heart so cold that I could turn my back on my children because of who they love or who they are.

Burn the witch

It is a truth universally acknowledged that there are no good books about wizards. Witches, on the other hand...

I'm mesmerised by witches and witch trials. I wrote a song recently called *Gallow Green*, named after the place in Paisley's West End where people were executed on charges of witchcraft.

> *Words, they carry no weight when you're pleading the fate of a little-loved, low status girl*
> *It's never women of riches accused of bewitchment and led to the green to be burned*
> *Turn her birthmarks into witches' marks*
> *Give the tattle-tale a stage*
> *This is no safe space when you don't know your place*
> *This is no town for those who won't bow down*
> *Good girls don't go to Gallow Green*
> *Shrewd girls don't go to Gallow Green*

I'm fascinated by the story, partly because it's horrific but also because it happened in a place I know: my brilliant blue-haired friend Becca lives just round the corner, so Gallow Green feels real in a way that, say, Salem doesn't. It gives the story a terrible resonance, reminding me that terrible things can happen all too close to home if you attract the wrong kind of attention.

No matter how many times I read it, the story still makes

my skin crawl. In 1696 Christian Shaw, the eleven-year-old daughter of the Laird of Bargarran, caught her servant Catherine Campbell sneaking a drink of milk. She reported the theft to her mother. Campbell was pissed off by this – then as now, Paisley buddies didn't look kindly on clipes – and told the girl, in front of witnesses, that she wished the Devil would haul her soul through Hell. I'm sure if it were me, I'd have said much worse.

A few days later, Shaw sought her revenge. She began to exhibit similar symptoms to the accusers in the Salem witch trials, news of which had crossed the Atlantic three years earlier: mysterious fits, seizures, convulsions and trance-like states. Doctors found nothing wrong with her and her symptoms became more extreme and bizarre, including pulling feathers and other items out of her mouth and claiming witches' spells had put them there. She may have been at it, or she may have had what we now know as Münchausen syndrome. Whatever the underlying explanation, Shaw said she'd been the victim of witchcraft.

Whether deliberately or accidentally, I think Shaw managed to find the perfect formula: her class privilege meant her accusations carried much more weight than any servant's denials, and she weaponised people's fears, superstition and desire to protect children. The weapon she forged from those base materials claimed multiple lives.

She began with Catherine Campbell but didn't stop there. Shaw then accused Agnes Naismith, a local woman with whom she had no connection. More names were added until more than 28 people stood accused of witchcraft[1]. Seven of those, including Campbell, Naismith and two teenage boys, were tried, found guilty and sentenced to death. One of the accused killed himself in jail the night before his execution; the remaining six were taken to Gallow Green and garrotted. Their bodies were then burned and their ashes taken far away.

As if by magic, Shaw's symptoms stopped. She grew up to become a very successful business owner, a key player in the

Paisley textiles boom of the early 18th Century. As far as I can ascertain, none of the people who survived her allegations were so fortunate.

One of the things I find interesting about witches and witch hunts is the way the facts have been twisted to fit a narrative. In this case, the witch trials have been used to portray women as poor victims of male violence, but the truth is much murkier. While most accused witches were indeed women – 85% of them here in Scotland – and men were judge, jury and executioner, it's well documented that many of the women's accusers were other women.[2] Those women made assertions about their neighbours or romantic rivals, about people they didn't like the look of, about people who didn't know their place, about people who just didn't fit in. Their assertions led to the accused women being tortured and sometimes dying at the hands of men while leaving the accusers' own hands beautifully clean.

There's a term for that: stochastic terrorism. It's when you demonise an individual or a group in such a way that someone else commits an act of violence against them without it being directly attributable to you. And there were many stochastic terrorists in the witch trials. The violence they summoned was patriarchal for sure, but women can benefit from patriarchal violence too when it suits them. That's what these women were doing, using allegations of witchcraft to eliminate their enemies or their rivals and preserve or improve their own status.

One of the worst witch finders in Scotland was a woman, Margaret Aitken: accused of witchcraft, she escaped her sentence by making up a story that she could see the mark of the devil in others. She found a new and murderously successful career as a witch finder and even spawned imitators such as Anne Ewing in Kirkcaldy before she was exposed as a fraud: the witches she identified were brought back the following day in different clothes and she failed to accuse a single one of them. Aitken was tried, sentenced to death and burned at the stake.

Aitken's death toll was well into the hundreds, and other women were responsible for sending many hundreds more to their deaths. So it's galling to see their spiritual heirs, bored straight white women who spend too much time on social media and have taken up bullying as a hobby, claiming to be "the granddaughters of the witches you couldn't burn" and trying to incite stochastic terrorism against inconvenient women like me.

There hasn't been a single day since I came out that I haven't read a newspaper article, a blog post or a social media thread where witch-finders cosplay as victims while waging war on trans women. The problem isn't just the clowns wearing suffragette colours to dance badly in Glasgow's George Square. It's the people who radicalised these goons in the first place, and the people only too happy to give them a microphone.

Since late 2017, the UK and Scottish press have run endless anti-trans stories painting us as dangerous monsters. That was a U-turn: for example in early 2017 *The Herald*[3] urged the Scots government to act against anti-trans bullying in schools while *The Scotsman*[4] defended trans women from what had not yet become a fully-fledged moral panic. But by 2018 both newspapers' star columnists were regularly railing against the invented evils of "trans activists" who were "silencing women", and evangelical groups were being given a platform to describe support for trans and non-binary teens as "child abuse", deliberately and cynically conflating changing gender markers with having "mutilating surgery".[5] The level of coverage was ridiculously one-sided, completely disproportionate for a minor change affecting such a small minority of people, and was an attempt to direct public opinion rather than reflect it: despite the columnists' best efforts, polling from 2017 to 2022 showed a consistent majority of people supported gender recognition reform, with women more likely to be in favour than men. That rarely made it into the papers, who preferred to tell their readers that sinister trans activists were trying to turn their kids trans and must be stopped.

We've heard this all before. When I was younger, there were moral panics over heavy metal records and the board game Dungeons & Dragons; the former allegedly contained backwards messages to worship Satan and/or kill yourself, and the latter was accused of pretty much everything. Similar panics occurred around video games, the Harry Potter books, the urban legend of Killer Clowns and so on.

I've lived through other moral panics too, including the Satanic Panics of the 1980s and 1990s and the attempts by the Keep The Clause campaign and campaigners against equal marriage to persuade people that gay, lesbian and bi people were dangerous predators. And now I'm living through a moral panic of my very own, a panic that means I'm more scared to leave the flat now than when I first came out.

I thought things were getting better for people like me. We'd had the Transgender Tipping Point, a *TIME Magazine* story in 2014 that put the actor Laverne Cox on the cover and talked about the new wave of trans creators. Suddenly people like me were seeing people like me – Paris Lees, Janet Mock, Munroe Bergdorf, Shon Faye, Charlie Craggs, Chaz Bono, Laura Jane Grace, Lana and Lilly Wachowski and many more – in the media, and they weren't the monsters that we'd seen trans people portrayed as for our whole lives: they were there because they were successful writers and models and singers and directors and they were living their best lives. And at the same time, the internet was enabling us to find other people just like us. After years – decades – of being told that we were alone, it became very clear that we were not. Without that tipping point I don't think I'd have come out; if I hadn't come out, I don't think I'd still be here.

What I didn't realise was that that tipping point occurred just as the Christian Right lost its decades-long battle against marriage equality. The UK was implementing the Marriage

(Same Sex Couples Act) and the US Supreme Court heard Obergefell v Hodges, striking down all state bans on same-sex marriage.

Faced with the absolute rejection of its scaremongering and demonisation of gay and lesbian people, the Christian Right found a new target.

Me.

Instead of going after the entire LGBT+ community, the Christian Right decided to focus on trans people. This isn't a conspiracy theory. Multiple Christian Right groups talked openly of their strategy;[6] several, including The Family Research Council, put it in writing on their websites.[7]

The FRC's appalling anti-trans paper is still there now. Its authors claim that trans people and "sexual liberationists" are "targeting children" in order to expose them to "molesters and exhibitionists masquerading as sex educators."[8] As opposed to, say, molesters who are executive directors of FRC Action, the FRC's legislative lobbying group: in 2021 FRC Action's Josh Duggar was convicted of possessing child pornography. A former reality TV star, Duggar's show was cancelled in 2015 after it was discovered that police had investigated him for multiple counts of child molestation of very young girls;[9] Duggar would later also admit to being addicted to pornography and unfaithful to his wife.[10]

The fine, child-protecting people of the FRC wrote in their paper, "Understanding And Responding To The Transgender Movement":

> *While the transgendered are free to dress and act as they choose, to change their names and their bodies, and to be intimate with partners of their choice, many movement activists will not be content until they compel all of society to accept their transgender fantasy.*

It's interesting to contrast that with JK Rowling's infamous tweet of 19 December 2019:[11]

Dress however you please. Call yourself whatever you like. Sleep with any consenting adult who'll have you. Live your best life in peace and security. But force women out of their jobs for stating that sex is real?

Evangelical Republicans used to demand Rowling's "satanic" books be banned.[12] Now they quote her approvingly in their efforts to block LGBT+ people's civil rights.[13]

There is a very organised, very vocal and very well-funded anti-gender movement at work in the US, in the UK and in Europe,[14] and it has significant overlap with QAnon, anti-vaxxers and the far right. It's largely driven by right-wing politicians and religious leaders: in the US, the Christian Right; in the UK, evangelical groups; and in Eastern Europe, the Catholic church. The anti-gender movement isn't just against trans people: it's also against feminism, women's rights, gay rights and women's reproductive freedom – but its media focus is on trans people because the movement sees us as a soft target. Many of its talking points are repeatedly and frequently parroted by UK columnists and broadcasters, or written in books that are given glowing reviews by the authors' friends.

In January 2022, the Council of Europe condemned the whole movement, listing the UK – formerly proud of its record on LGBT+ progress – alongside Russia, Hungary, Poland and Turkey as a place where "the highly prejudicial anti-gender, gender-critical and anti-trans narratives" aim to "deny the very existence of LGBTI people, dehumanise them, and often falsely portray their rights as being in conflict with women's and children' rights or societal and family values in general. All of these are deeply damaging to LGBTI people, while also harming women's and children's rights and social cohesion."[15]

The idea that primarily left-wing, apparently feminist women could be part of promoting such a hateful ideology seems odd, but a now-deleted section of the Hands Across The Aisle website, an evangelical campaign that was created specifically to unite feminist campaigners with anti-LGBT+ groups, listed a number of UK anti-trans groups and left-wing journalists as members[16]. Many high-profile anti-trans figures and almost all the anti-trans groups you read about in the papers or hear on the radio are supporters of and signatories to the Women's Human Rights Campaign's Declaration,[17] which demands the elimination of "transgenderism", the elimination of health care for trans people and the elimination of legal gender recognition. In a formal submission to the UK government Women and Equalities Select Committee in 2021, the WHRC claimed that trans women were created by "sissy hypno" videos on YouTube.[18]

In the UK, the trope that "gender ideology" is being pushed by a conspiracy of Big Pharma and "globalists", a dog-whistle meaning Jewish people, is common, as is the supposed sinister goal of "erasing" women and "sacrificing" vulnerable children. As with antisemitism, transphobia casts its enemies as both high status – a group who have somehow captured the government, the media, the NHS and the entire medical establishment for nefarious purposes – and low status, vermin to be bullied or worse.

The newspapers I see today have the same moral panic stories and rhetoric as the ones I read in the 1980s, but this time it's not just the right-wing press. It's also the organisations you'd expect to be on the side of the victims, not the vicious: the BBC, *The New European*, *The New Statesman*, *The Guardian* and *The Observer* too. *The Guardian*'s US newsroom wrote an open letter[19] condemning the UK edition for their anti-trans editorial stance; meanwhile *The Observer* has become *The Mail on Sunday* for people with arts degrees.

I don't know whether to scream or cry, so sometimes I do both.

If you're not trans you might not appreciate just how overwhelming all of this is. Imagining opening your Sunday newspaper to read three fabricated stories damning people like you and two columns explaining why you're an abomination. Your current affairs magazine has a cover feature portraying you as a threat to free speech. Your light read has cartoons mocking you. You pick up your iPad and relatives have sent you links to online articles spreading misinformation about you and questioning your right to exist. You turn on the radio and you're being discussed as an "issue", a "problem" to be "solved". Some commentators even tried to blame trans people for Vladimir Putin's invasion of Ukraine[20] and trans-inclusive feminists for the US Supreme Court's apparent decision to revoke Roe vs Wade in early 2022.[21][22]

It got so bad that I stopped buying my multiple newspapers and cancelled my many digital subscriptions. But the scaremongering still reached me. Whenever a celebrity shared their ill-considered and ill-informed opinions on trans people, it would take over my news apps and social media for weeks; as various has-beens realised that punching down on trans people guaranteed them column inches for whatever project they were trying to promote, the flood of anti-trans comments became a tsunami. It's become so bad in the UK that when I see a fading star's name trending on Twitter I immediately assume it's because they've said something transphobic or been unmasked as a serial sexual predator. I'm usually right.

A nice day to start again

My wedding day was wonderful. Liz and I got married on the banks of Loch Lomond, a beautiful setting on what turned out to be the hottest day of the year. Liz looked incredible in her gorgeous, hand-made dress, and I looked pretty good in a too-heavy kilt that threatened to kill me with heatstroke long before we got to cut the cake. We got to say our vows in front of the people who mattered most to us, we danced to "We Have All The Time In The World", and at the end of the night everybody jumped around to Runrig's "Loch Lomond" because that's compulsory at Scottish weddings. The following day I took my sore head to the nearby registry office to complete all the paperwork to make our marriage official.

Here's what I didn't have to do before Liz and I were allowed to marry. I didn't have to persuade two psychiatrists that I wasn't insane. I didn't have to gather two years' worth of evidence that I was being called by my name, that I used that name in my work and personal life, and that when I needed to wee I used the appropriate toilets for my gender. And I didn't have to persuade a faceless, faraway panel that I intended to live in the same gender for the rest of my life. Now, though, I do.

The faceless faraway panel is called the Gender Recognition Panel, and they issue a piece of paper called a Gender Recognition Certificate, or GRC for short. Without it, the gender you are when you marry – or when you're buried – is what's on your original birth certificate, even if that turned out to be wrong. So if I were to remarry I'd be a husband, not a wife; if I died, I'd be buried as a man.

The GRC gives trans people some, but not all, of the rights that were stolen from us by a rich Tory and his lawyers in the 1970s.[1] And it's been the subject of countless lies in the press and in broadcast media for over four years now. Unlike the vast majority of people spouting off about GRCs and the Gender Recognition Act that created them, I know exactly what a GRC does and what you have to do to get one. And that's because I got my GRC in 2020.

Getting a GRC was another line I thought I would never cross. But I was already hormonally, socially and to all practical purposes female, so my legal gender was just one more loose end to tie up.

I knew that getting a GRC would not change my life in any significant way. Most trans people don't bother applying for GRCs. There are perhaps 150,000 to 300,000 trans people in the UK but only around 5,000 GRCs have been issued to date. That's partly because many trans people don't see the point (and some refuse on political grounds; why should the state be the final arbiter of who you are?), partly because being on a centrally held database of trans people worries some of us, and partly because it's famous for being expensive and invasive. But it was a loose end that was niggling me.

Most organisations work on the basis of self-ID, where they'll record you as whatever gender you tell them you are, but that doesn't apply to every government department or public sector organisation. While the Passport Office, DVLA and NHS had me in their systems as a woman, Her Majesty's Revenue and Customs and the Department of Work and Pensions considered me male. I wanted to fix that in much the same way that you might (or at least I would) want to fix a crooked picture or a TV that isn't quite centred between two bookcases.

★

According to the anti-trans groups and their helpers in the press, if you get a GRC – which you can do by just saying you're a woman, apparently – you are suddenly able to access single-sex spaces such as women's toilets. The reality is that *you need to use the women's toilets in order to get your GRC*, and you currently have to use them without exception for two years before you can even apply. Then, and only then, can you start the long, expensive and occasionally humiliating application process.

The procedure works like this:

ME: I'm trans!
DOCTOR: Sorry, can't see you now. Come back in *checks watch* three to five to twenty-six years.

(three to five to twenty-six years later)

ME: I'm trans!
DOCTOR: Are you?
ME: Yes!
DOCTOR: Hmmm. Seems a bit early to say one way or another. Come back in *checks watch* two years.

(two years later)

ME: I'm trans!
DOCTOR: Are you?
ME: Yes!
DOCTOR: Well, you've certainly convinced me. You're trans.
ME: Can I have that in writing?
DOCTOR: Yes.
ME: Now?
DOCTOR: Ha ha ha no.

The gender clinic doctor's evidence is based on self-ID: there's no blood test that proves you're trans, no scan that can differentiate between trans and cis, just whether your gender clinic doctor and your GP believe you. The medicalisation of this is unnecessary and dates from the period when being trans, like being gay or being a woman with a sex drive, was considered to be evidence of mental illness and doctors' job was to talk or electro-shock you out of it.

The only bit of the GRA that reforms would change is that unnecessary medicalisation and the £140 admin fee, which has since been reduced. Everything else would remain, including a legally enforceable statutory declaration and the requirement to produce tons of evidence.

I gathered pay slips, contracts, educational certificates, bank slips, identity documents and various other forms of official paperwork. Getting that took a lot of time and sometimes money, and one person can easily throw a spanner in the whole thing. My application was delayed for four months because the gender clinic doctor who I had to get a report from was "a bit busy" to scribble a few sentences and a signature. This is one of several reasons why the GRC system needs reform.

When I sent in my paperwork, the Gender Recognition Panel's admin staff returned my application after a few weeks. My evidence was too concentrated on my coming out and there wasn't enough evidence that I was still living as a woman two years later. If I'd asked for my application to go to the panel anyway, it would have been rejected without refunding the £140 fee and I'd have to wait six months before starting all over again.

I accumulated more evidence and sent my application in again. This time it was returned because it wasn't clear that I had been using the ladies toilets for two years without exception. As a result I had to ask friends and colleagues if they were willing to write witness statements about where I urinate, which was as embarrassing as you might expect.

The panel also queried some unclear language in my initial psychiatric reports, requesting a personal statement that had to go into great detail about various unpleasant life events that I'd really rather not think about. There's something deeply disturbing about having to write about something so very personal when you don't know who will read it.

But eventually, after £240 in fees and postage and lots of trips to the post office, I got my GRC. And do you know what that document does?

Absolutely fuck all.

A GRC isn't an identity document, and you can't ask to see mine. It doesn't give me the right to access spaces, because that's the Equality Act's job. It doesn't change the meaning of the word woman, or erase lesbians, or any of the other lurid claims of the anti-trans movement. It has nothing to do with hormones, or surgery, or NHS treatment.

The only thing my Gender Recognition Certificate enables me to do is to change my birth certificate so it says F instead of M. And even that bit takes forever: it took twenty months between the granting of my GRC and my receipt of an updated birth certificate.

In the UK, trans people have been changing their birth certificates since 2004 without anyone abusing the system; we had an informal system that did much the same from the 1940s to 1971 without any abuse of that either. Gender recognition without the need for medical reports is in place in many other countries – including Ireland, California, Malta, Norway, Argentina, Portugal, Belgium, Denmark, Pakistan and Chile – and the combined populations of countries with self-ID systems for legal gender recognition is over 700 million. The number of cases of self-ID being abused to date is zero.

GRCs aren't a magic key to women's spaces; as I've said, you need to produce evidence that you use women's spaces (if you're a trans woman) in order to get one. What a GRC does is enables you to have a birth certificate that doesn't out you as trans to a potential employer, something that has happened to trans women I know, and it enables you to marry in your correct gender – so if I remarry, we will be wife and wife rather than husband and wife.

There is no reason for somebody who isn't trans to get a GRC. It bestows no everyday benefits, and if you were to get one in order to commit crimes it would be proof of premeditation. The same men who attack women attack trans women too, and the people who are trying to scare you about me are trying to distract you from the simple fact that the vast majority of violence and sexual violence against women and girls is perpetrated by straight cisgender men. Which perhaps explains why so many of the most vocally and vicious members of the so-called Gender Critical movement are misogynistic straight cisgender men. We're the witches they want to burn.

I have very mixed feelings about my GRC. I was worried that if I didn't get my legal gender recognition as soon as possible it might be denied to me in future; there was also the very clear possibility that the government might reframe the GRC as an identity and eligibility document, removing anti-discrimination protections from anyone who did not possess one. In February 2022, leaked documents and whistleblowers' testimonies[2] from inside the Equalities and Human Rights Committee (EHRC), a human rights body whose former chair says is becoming a political instrument of the Conservative government rather than an independent watchdog[3], seemed to confirm that it was indeed heading in that direction.

So in that respect it feels like I've been forced to apply: "Nice human rights you've got there. Shame if anything were to happen to them." I don't think anybody should have to apply to a faceless panel in order to qualify for anti-discrimination protection and other basic human rights, but that appears to be the direction of travel under the Tories.

But my GRC still means something to me. It means something in the same way that my formal diagnosis of gender dysphoria meant something. The Gender Recognition Panel is a branch of the HM Courts & Tribunal Service. Its president is a judge. My application was assessed by a judicial panel consisting solely of legal and medical professionals, and I can promise you that they are very, very thorough and very, very serious.

Hence my mixed feelings. It's a horrible process to go through and it was a weight on my mind for a long time. The resulting certificate is largely useless. But I can't help feeling that it's also a form of validation. It is horrible that I had to produce medical, psychological and documentary evidence of my transness to a faceless, faraway panel of judges and medical experts. But yet again people who specialise in this field looked at all the evidence and agreed that yes, I am who I know I am.

That joke isn't funny any more

I love laughing the way some people love sex. I'm driven by it, spend hours looking for it, and sometimes pay strangers money for it. When I get it, it's a whole-body experience. When I find something really funny, which I do a lot, I lose myself completely and become a shuddering, cackling mascara-streaked mess. I've lost it so many times on live radio it's become a running joke, and my friends frequently see me tear-streaked and howling over something stupid. My best friend says she's never met anybody who laughs so easily or so often.

Comedy is a big deal for me. Which makes it all the more sad that comedy is also where I see the most transphobia. In the last few years it's become the trademark of the "edgy" comedian, typically a middle-aged multi-millionaire who uses their Netflix special to demonise some of the most vulnerable people on Earth before going back to their Malibu mansion to count their cash. And it's also become the go-to for the bottom dwellers, the people whose pub friends told them they were funny and who've spent many years proving those friends wrong.

In early 2020, I played an open mic night for a friend who'd asked my brother and I to be the featured artists amid the usual mix of musicians and comedians. We played a really great set, the audience laughed at my between-song jokes and we took our table with the satisfaction of a job well done. And then the next act, an amateur comedian, got up.

I'd seen him before and thought he was a hack; he was a pensionable peddler of seventies-variety "take my wife, please" jokes with a whiff of misogyny to them. That evening the whiff became a stench. His seemingly interminable five minutes were dedicated to his enjoyment of lap dancing clubs, his horror of women who groom their public hair and, in a piece he was clearly very pleased with, a horrible nightmare in which a beautiful woman turns out to have tricked him because she was "a ladyboy".

I don't think trans jokes are off limits. I had made some during our set and got laughs. But this guy had no unique spin to offer, no unusual and definitely no hilarious take. His entire premise was that he had a dream, there was a sexy woman in it, he was aroused, he discovered she was trans, he was disgusted by her. His expectation was that the room would share his disgust and would give big laughs at the word "ladyboy". But they didn't. Quite the opposite. The room turned very cold and he died on his arse.

I usually hate seeing comics die on stage, no matter how bad they are, but this was thoroughly deserved. I had to sit ten feet away – our table was at the very front – from a man who hoped to mine laughs from sharing his horror of bodies like mine. Imagine how it feels to sit through that, to feel every pair of eyes in the room turn to look at you as it becomes clear what the punchline is going to be. Those feelings linger long after the hack has come off stage.

When I got home from the gig I flopped down on the sofa, went on Twitter and saw a link to a long blog post by another Scottish trans woman, Becca, who was roughly the same age as me. "After six years of being on hormones and presenting completely female, I am still getting misgendered far too frequently and as the years have gone by, the sheer hopelessness of it all has finally sunk in," she wrote. "I would honestly rather be dead than seen as a 'man in a dress'."

It was a scheduled post, timed to go live hours after it had been written. That evening, at roughly the same time as the wannabe comedian was sharing his disgust about trans women, Becca stepped in front of an oncoming train.

I didn't know Becca, but I have been very close to where Becca found herself that night on far too many occasions, and the comedians mining transphobia for money are a big part of the reason for that.

Although it's so frequently used as one, "Trans! Ugh!" isn't a punchline. It's a punch down. The idea of trans people deceiving straight men is so commonly used as an excuse for violence and sexual violence against us that there's a name for it: the trans panic defence. In 2020, at least 350 trans people were murdered and hundreds more attacked, most of them Black or Latinx women;[1] many crimes go unreported or the person is misgendered by the police and press so we never hear about them. I'm writing this in late 2021, which is shaping up to be the most lethal year on record for trans people, particularly in the US.

Many countries have a culture of stigma and shame around trans people and people who are intimate with them, and comedy both reflects and directs that culture.

Remember *Ace Ventura, Pet Detective*? Do you remember the bit where Jim Carrey discovers that the beautiful woman he recently kissed is trans? I do, because I saw it in the cinema, sick to my stomach as the audience howled. Carrey vomits in the toilet, vomits again, uses an entire tube of toothpaste to clean his teeth, takes off all his clothes and burns them before entering the shower to weep. Later in the film, Carrey reveals the woman's trans status by exposing a bulge in her underwear to a crowd of cops. All the men start retching.

Ha!

In *Naked Gun 33⅓*, the third film in a franchise I loved, Leslie Nielsen discovers that his beautiful love interest is trans. Nielsen is so disgusted he vomits into a tuba.

Ha!

In *Dude, Where's My Car?* Ashton Kutcher discovers that Tania, a beautiful stripper, is trans. He retches in horror.

Ha!

Did you notice the word "beautiful" in my descriptions of the trans characters? That's deliberate. In all three examples, the supposedly trans woman is played by a stunning cisgender woman: Sean Young, Anna Nicole Smith and Teressa Tunney respectively. If the transphobic and homophobic gurning shows how comedy treats characters who are the good ones, the pretty ones, the ones who conform to a very narrow idea of white female beauty, imagine the contempt it has for trans women who look like me.

What's said on stage or on screen can end up being screamed in the streets. The comedy trope of trans women as men in dresses does the groundwork for the far right and religious right smear that trans people are not genuine and worthy of respect, let alone human rights. There's precious little distance between the "I'm a laydee" crossdressers of *Little Britain* and the anti-trans groups' claims that trans women are men in drag; I've seen members of the latter gleefully quoting or sending images of the former to trans women online.

I don't think most of the comedians doing trans jokes are bigots, though. I think they're lazy. Supposedly edgy comedians are often going through the comedy equivalent of the mid-life crisis, mediocre men imitating the teen edgelords of Tiktok like pathetic uncles hanging around nightclubs full of people half their age. They were young once, and relevant. And now they're not, so they're going to scream and scream until we're sick.

I'm fascinated by this, because there's such a lack of intellectual curiosity to it. Genuinely clever comedians such as Frankie Boyle, Rosie Jones, Stewart Lee, Josie Long, Kiri Pritchard-McLean, Dylan Moran, Katherine Ryan, Michelle Wolff and Sara Pascoe don't need to punch down because there's so much punching up that needs done, and they do it with precision and power. And at the grassroots level where some of my friends are comedians and/or put on comedy shows, comics just aren't doing it. The people killing it in the clubs aren't ageing private schoolboys or the working men's club comics that Al Murray satirises. They're much younger, much more diverse, much smarter and much funnier.

The problem, though, is that you don't always know which comic has got lazy or if their support act is an arse until you're actually sitting there. And I've been sat in the semi-darkness of comedy clubs many times, feeling the hairs on my neck crawl and ice settle in the pit of my stomach as the man on stage drops the T-word.

It is a very horrible feeling to know that other people are looking at you. And it's even more horrible to hear them laugh.

It's not the same laugh you hear with a normal joke. It's the kind of laugh that Bernard Manning used to get, that Roy Chubby Brown gets, that Dave Chappelle quit his own TV programme because he feared he was getting. Chappelle called it "the wrong laugh", a laugh that "makes you feel shame" because you're hearing the joy of a bigot who thinks you're on their side – an insight Chappelle sadly hasn't applied to his own unapologetically transphobic material, such as the 2021 Netflix special that caused Netflix's own staff to protest outside the company's headquarters.[2]

The wrong laugh is the kind of laugh that stays with you, because it is vocal evidence that to some people you are disgusting, shameful, worthy of nothing but contempt. That keeps us in the closet, and it continues to harm us when we're out of it. When the world keeps telling you you're a monster, part of you believes it.

Sometimes it's a false alarm, Frankie Boyle or Dylan Moran aiming finely honed barbs at lesser talents. But with so much trans stuff in the papers and online, I'm usually frozen in my chair as yet another comic does the Only Trans Joke That Exists, the one where they identify as a monkey or as a one-legged black lesbian but never, ever funny.

You can make trans jokes that are funny. Here's one: Michael Jackson's pronouns were he/hee. Michelle Wolff has a whole routine about trans women in toilets that absolutely slays. Kevin Bridges has a fun one about an angry Glaswegian dad and his trans kid. All you need to do is put in the work, but lots of comedians just don't.

So I sit there and feel the blood turn to ice in my veins. I sit as still as I can, aware of the people nearby surreptitiously looking at me, trying to be as small as I can be so the comedian won't notice me and try to use me as a prop or a human shield. I said earlier that laughter for me is like sex is for other people. So this is the moment when, after some tender foreplay, your partner unexpectedly and violently shits the bed.

There's no way the mood's going to recover from that.

It's the end of the world as we know it

In Spring 2020 the whole world stopped and Scotland went into lockdown. We didn't know it at the time, but Glaswegians would end up spending more time in lockdown than the rest of the UK.

Like many people, I had an awful lockdown, and I don't know if I'd have made it through if I hadn't had my kids to look after and enjoy spending unexpectedly large amounts of time with. As the NHS rightly prioritised COVID-19, the gender clinics closed and all trans-related healthcare – monitoring, referrals, even blood testing – was stopped. The forward momentum that I depended on, the constant progress that was keeping me sane, ground to a halt. All my support stopped too. My social life was locked down, and I wasn't able to see my friends for months.

One result of that was that I stopped paying attention to what I wore: if I hadn't needed to put the bins out occasionally or spend time with my children I'd have stayed in my dressing gown all day. I've heard many women saying that during lockdown they stopped putting as much effort into how they looked: they wore less or no makeup, they didn't bother with bras, their footwear stayed flat. It was the same for me. No sensible person is going to cram themselves into an underwired bra or uncomfortable shoes unless they absolutely have to, and

I absolutely didn't have to. But I felt strangely demoralised. I didn't feel like a liberated woman. I felt like a potato or some other ungendered, sexless thing: a disembodied eyeball in a jar, perhaps, or a balloon with a face drawn on it.

I felt ungendered because gender is partly a feedback loop where you perform a particular role – "man", perhaps, or "woman" – and people respond to you accordingly in both positive and negative ways. In pre-COVID times I went through the world as me, a middle-aged woman, and I spent my days interacting with people who recognised me as and responded to me as a middle-aged woman.

What I didn't fully understand at the time was that those interactions were an important and powerful corrective to the ongoing abuse and demonisation of trans people. Going through the world as me was evidence that the narrative in my own head, that the world is a hateful and dangerous place for people like me, was not true.

COVID took that away, but the negativity never stopped. Lockdown and furlough made the online bullies worse: with more time on their hands they had more time to spend abusing people online. They became bolder and seemed less concerned with maintaining any veneer of respectability, and the real-life interactions that give the lie to their scaremongering were not happening. Not only that, but all LGBT+ support groups had to move online and any life-affirming, battery-recharging events such as Pride were cancelled. Those months were hard.

It didn't help that thanks to various dental mistakes I also had severe, sleep-depriving, painkiller-ignoring toothache for the first five months of the COVID crisis – and to add insult to injury I was in financial trouble too. Most of my employers immediately stopped commissioning freelancers, and I was one of "the excluded", the three million self-employed people who were ineligible for government support. The few savings I had didn't last long.

But apart from the sadness, the pain, the loneliness and the apparent end of my career, it wasn't all bad.

Some of it was quite magical. Few parents get to spend as much time with their children as Liz and I did during the many months of lockdown, and I started inviting Liz over for a weekly family dinner to give the kids some kind of routine; something we've continued to do post-pandemic. I think spending that time together helped heal some of the scars of our break-up: when we separated I don't think either of us imagined we could be friends again, but by the end of the first lockdown that's how we ended up.

Because Liz and I co-parent, my children were only here half of the time. The rest of the time I tried to keep boredom and loneliness at bay by keeping myself busy. I couldn't really concentrate on fiction or films but I wrote a lot of songs; joined an online songwriting group whose weekly deadlines helped me focus; learned some ukulele and rudimentary Spanish; and read a lot of very serious books. It was a good opportunity to try and educate myself. I read all kinds of serious things: detailed histories of the AIDS epidemic; books on intersectional feminism and on racism; books about toxic masculinity; and books about the baleful influence of dark money on politics. This is why I don't get invited to many parties.

I also played a lot of video games, one of my favourite escapes from reality. I played the beautiful and harrowing *The Last Of Us Part II*, an incredibly atmospheric and violent game featuring two female leads and what I believe is the first trans man to be a key character in a big-budget blockbuster. I loved it, cried through quite a lot of it and really wanted to talk about it. And I did, every day, because my friend and BBC colleague Louise is a games journalist and she was playing it too. We'd catch up on Messenger every evening to compare experiences and talk about whatever was on our minds at the time. We already had a great working relationship thanks to our weekly appearances together on Radio Scotland, during which I'd try to make Louise corpse on air, and over the lockdown months we developed a really close, supportive and empowering friendship. Even the end of the world has its upsides.

When I wasn't gaming or sending stupid memes to Louise, I spent a lot of time thinking. And that thinking finally pushed me over my very last and most serious red line. After years of being adamant that I'd never want gender confirmation surgery, I emailed the Sandyford gender clinic asking to be referred for just that.

Surgeries are scary. I've had several, including on my spine, so I'm not the kind of person who seeks out surgical solutions to things if there are alternatives. I'm also a little bit superstitious and fear my luck running out. Liz nearly died both times in childbirth and there was a high risk of complications with my back surgery; part of me feels we've been lucky and shouldn't push it.

My attitudes to surgery were also informed by the fact I'm not attracted to men. What's the point of rearranging the downstairs furniture if you're not going to invite anybody round? As a woman who's attracted to other women, and who fully expected to be single for the rest of her life, I didn't really see the point in changing my bits.

That didn't mean I wasn't open to *any* surgery, though. In 2019 I asked my gender clinic doctor to refer me for a procedure called orchidectomy, which is the surgical removal of the testicles.

I wanted the procedure for purely practical reasons. Every three months I'm injected with Decapeptyl, which is a GnRH agonist: that means it stops my testicles making testosterone. And every three months I feel like death for a week before my top-up – something other trans women tell me they experience too. I start feeling really lethargic and sad, and as a result of that predictable hormone crash I fear not being able to get future injections in time. I'm also aware that it's very expensive medication and that one day my GP may be unwilling or unable to pay for it.

I had another fear, which was that the looming Brexit could affect supplies: my HRT is made in mainland Europe, and at the time the UK was already in the second year of a severe HRT patch shortage, a shortage that began with problems in a single pharmaceutical plant. As I write this there's a second shortage, this time of HRT gel. I don't like my mental health being dependent on such a fragile supply chain; I'm writing this in the period just before all the customs changes kick in and we've already endured months of empty supermarket shelves and odd shortages, and my HRT has proved hard to get on several occasions already.

If I went for an orchidectomy, those potential issues would go away. I'd also be able to reduce the amount of other HRT pills I was taking. At my age there are potential health risks from oral HRT, risks that would be reduced by a lower dose.

Having an orchidectomy was clearly a *sensible* thing to do. But over lockdown I began to ask myself whether it was the *right* thing to do. If I endured a multi-year waiting list for the surgery, lost the weight the surgeons would demand I lose, travelled all the way to the south of England for the procedure and endured the weeks-long recovery period, I'd still have a body that was female above the waist and male below it.

Would I be happy with that? I think the answer would be no.

If after surgery I wished that I'd had Gender Confirmation Surgery (GCS) after all, I'd be back to square one and back on an even longer waiting list. And I'm not getting any younger. If I was referred for GCS in 2020 – a timescale I now realise was hilariously optimistic; as of 2022 I'm still on a waiting list to speak to the consultant who might then put me on the real waiting list – there was a reasonable chance I'd have the procedure in my early fifties, which are no longer so very far away. If I had an orchidectomy first, realised it wasn't enough and then went back into the system, I might not get the surgery until I was well into my sixties. And with my sedentary lifestyle, I might not be around that long.

I think another big part of it was that I was starting to feel much more comfortable in my own skin and in my identity. I still wasn't quite ready to try dating, but I was no longer ruling it out. And that possibility made GCS more relevant.

I know there are open minded people out there who are attracted to people of all genders and of all configurations, but I also know that many of us have very strong preferences about what does and doesn't turn us on. For example, I'm attracted to feminine people of all kinds, but I'm not attracted to cis or trans men: I'm not attracted to masculine people and I find things like facial stubble a turn-off. That's one of the reasons I went for electrolysis: I don't like having it on my own face either.

While I'm sure there are plenty of people who are perfectly open-minded and who, like me, care about hearts rather than parts, I'm also sure that there are plenty of people for whom the shape of my bits is a deal-breaker. The potential dating pool for an overweight, middle-aged, trans woman with children and abandonment issues is already fairly small; it's smaller still if that woman still has her boy bits.

There are other reasons too. I thought that I wouldn't need surgery to feel complete, but after three years of hormones the combination of breasts and male genitals looks odd to me. I didn't have severe body dysphoria, but I wasn't particularly attached to my penis either: it was just there doing nothing in particular, like significant parts of East Kilbride.

If I had an orchidectomy but retained my penis I'd still be unable to wear some kinds of clothes, I'd still be avoidant of open changing rooms and I'd still be considered by some people to be a "mutilated male", not truly trans. I know that shouldn't be a factor, but this stuff does get inside your head.

So I did more research and discovered that there are several kinds of GCS. One of them is considerably less involved and for me, considerably less scary.

★

If you're transitioning from male to female there are two main kinds of gender confirmation surgery. The GCS most people have heard of is called vaginoplasty and creates the external genitalia and a vaginal canal. But there's another option called vulvoplasty that does the former but not the latter. That means it's not as invasive, the recovery period is shorter and there's no need for the post-operative and ongoing dilation which some trans women find difficult. Visually and functionally everything is in its right place, but the depth is much shorter. That's why the procedure is sometimes called cosmetic or zero-depth GCS, although there is some depth; there's just not enough for anybody to stick anything substantial in there. That seemed like the perfect solution for me: the leap from orchidectomy to zero-depth GCS didn't seem so huge.

When I spoke to my closest friends Louise and Laura about it, they agreed that it seemed to be the right decision; Laura promised to throw a post-recovery Happy New Vulva party and told me that no matter which bit of England I ended up getting the operation in, she'd travel down and stay with me as much as the hospital would allow. I was really taken aback by that.

If I get the surgery, I don't know when it will be. COVID shut down all surgical referrals for a long time, leaving a huge backlog, and waiting lists that were already horrific before lockdown are considerably worse now. Getting a second opinion on surgical referral took from November 2019 to June 2021 and the doctor wouldn't speculate about the length of post-COVID waiting lists; I'm writing this bit in May 2022 and haven't heard anything since last June. I won't be looking for a venue for my new-vulva party any time soon.

That's assuming I even get surgery. After all those years of waiting, I may still be refused if I'm considered too fat. It's another example of the little cruelties of trans healthcare: surgeries are off-limits for those of us judged too overweight.

While GCS is life-saving surgery with an exceptionally low surgical regret rate, the NHS still considers it an elective rather than an essential procedure — and elective procedures have a BMI limit. Private hospitals don't, because the BMI is a statistical tool, not a medical one: it's a crude and unscientific formula that has been described as "mathematical snake oil"[1]. But in the NHS it's a useful way to refuse trans people surgery and force the people who can afford it — or more likely, those willing and able to get into serious debt — to pay privately for the same surgeries in the same hospitals with the same surgeons.

At the time of writing I'm still above the BMI limit despite losing almost two stone in a year, and I'm finding further weight loss exceptionally difficult. If I can't get below the limit, I can't have surgery: I simply can't afford the £15,000 to £20,000 the private sector charges when I'm still struggling to find £150 a week for the electrolysis that seems never-ending.

But I'm going to try very hard to meet the criteria because this is the last piece of the jigsaw. I've transitioned socially, professionally, legally and hormonally; all that's left is to do it surgically. Once I've done that, I'll no longer be in transition. I'll just be me.

Skin feeling

It's a warm August evening and I am full of joy over the simplest of things, a summer midi dress with spaghetti straps. I think this is the first time my shoulders have ever been bared in public except for beach holidays, and it feels deliciously, delightfully strange. I can feel air dance across my shoulder blades as people swish past.

This is gender euphoria.

Wearing a strappy summer dress isn't a big deal to some women, I know. But it's a big deal for me because ever since I started being me in public my clothes have been about trying to hide my body completely or to at least draw attention away from the worst bits. The idea that I'd willingly bare anything seemed laughable: if you wanted to see some skin you'd have more luck with an Egyptian mummy.

And yet here I am, bare-shouldered and bare-legged with the bare minimum of makeup, a few mists of Estée Lauder Bronze Goddess and an enormous sense of everything being in its right place. I have a very strong feeling of just being me, of being the person I never thought I'd ever get to be, of being profoundly aware of my body and of being actually ok with it, of being happy in the skin I'm in.

That dress wasn't just a nice dress from the tall section of Dorothy Perkins. It was a marker, a sign of how far I'd come. Wearing something spaghetti-strapped or having legs that aren't hidden inside the thickest, most opaque black tights may not be a big deal for others, but it is quite a big deal for me – especially when it brings compliments from friends rather than snide comments from strangers. It's a sign of growing confidence and of self-acceptance.

It's also a sign of physical progress, because my dress fitted me in a way it wouldn't have before I started transition. There was a euphoria there from having a tangible indication of my progress: when hormones work their magic ever so slowly, sometimes it's nice to notice their efforts. In a fairly short period of time I'd gone from stuffing silicone boobs into my bra to having enough of a chest to carry a sundress without any extra support.

Physically, I was in a pub in Partick. But in my head I was standing in a nice dress like someone in a Taylor Swift song.

Of all the things I missed during lockdowns, I missed that euphoria. Before COVID put the world on pause I was having more and more experiences where instead of being sad about who I was, I felt euphoric.

It sometimes seems that we only get to hear about the sad stuff. I think that's partly because so much of the discussion about us focuses on trauma and tragedy – something that's inevitable if people are trying to talk about legal protections such as protection from hate crimes or the horrifically long waiting times trans people endure for basic healthcare. So when we're trying to improve things then of course we're going to talk about the awful things many trans people experience.

But euphoria is just as much a part of the trans experience as dysphoria. Maybe more so. Perhaps we talk about it less because being happy is less interesting than being sad, or because we worry that our moments of euphoria will seem trivial to you. And, of course, on social media there are always bad actors looking for anything they can take out of context, screenshot and share with their fellow bigots. That makes you very wary of what you post. Band shots aside, I very rarely post photos of me online for the same reason.

And maybe our moments of happiness *are* trivial to others, but some of the greatest joys do come from the tiniest of things. Earlier today I saw my youngest's face light up when they saw me waiting for them after school and my heart felt full to burst.

Many of the things I experience as gender euphoria may seem really trivial. And that's because they often are. They're mundane things. Normal things. Things most people take for granted.

But for me, they're not mundane, not normal, not things I can take for granted. It sometimes feels like I'm an ingenue in the big city, constantly open-mouthed in surprise at the things the locals don't even notice. "You mean you just, like, put on a dress, and go out, and nobody scowls at you? Ever?"

I'm living my wildest dreams.

We walk with steel in our spines

It's four years since I came out and I'm really wishing I hadn't worn an underwired bra.

I'm on a hot stage, I've been waving my heaviest guitar – a huge red Epiphone semi-acoustic – around like a loon for two hours, and I'm paying an uncomfortable and sweaty price for putting style over comfort. This is not a problem I ever imagined having when I started hormones three years ago.

I'm making a video with my band, HAVR. During the same session I'll play a live-streamed solo acoustic performance as part of Queer Fringe, an online concert for Scottish LGBT+ people, and my song *A Moment of Clarity* will make some of the audience cry.

I wouldn't have considered doing either of those things three years ago, but here I am.

I've always considered myself to be terribly shy. That probably seems weird given that for most of my adult life I've been the singer in various bands, but performing or speaking in front of people was always something I felt forced to do, not something I wanted to do. I used to get so scared that I have absolutely no recollection of playing some shows that were a really big deal. I played Glasgow Barrowland once, supporting an NME-famous band. I can't remember any of it, or of any other exciting shows we played. My brain was too busy being terrified.

I had the same stage fright in radio studios even after years of doing shows. A different studio or a different presenter would bring the icy-stomach terror right back, as would the slightest hint of a camera: I'm fairly comfortable in front of a microphone but I'm incredibly camera shy.

Not any more.

In the last couple of weeks I'd been the subject of a professional photo shoot, performed in front of cameras for two live-streamed concerts, played some solo songs for a radio session and made a complete fool of myself in front of multiple cameras as my band was filmed for a live video.

I don't think I'd ever had so much fun.

That's quite odd. You'd think that as a trans person who really hates their body and how they look, the last thing I'd want is to be filmed or photographed. And if I'm honest, I wasn't mad keen on seeing the results of the filming or the photography; I watched what I needed to watch so I could tell the film-maker which edits to make, and I haven't been able to watch it since. But I very much enjoyed being filmed and being photographed while I waved my guitar around like I used to wave a badminton racket. I was right back in my bedroom, pretending I was playing Top of The Pops. It's as if I've spent years pretending to be a recluse like Enya when I was Bono all along.

Incidentally, if you're trans you hear a lot of Enya: she's the soundtrack for many beauty salons so she's been in the background of many treatments and many electrolysis sessions. That's a lot of Enya, and to help me cope I've developed a theory: beneath the layers of reverb that make it hard to work out what she's singing, every single one of her songs is absolute *filth*.

I think a big part of my new-found confidence is that since coming out, I've largely stopped caring what other people think. That's partly a survival mechanism – if I worried about what other people might think of me, I'd never leave the flat – but it's also profoundly liberating. Instead of stage fright I have nervous, puppyish excitement; instead of trying to act cool I'm quite happy to make a complete arse of myself.

Being happy on stage is a very visible demonstration of where my head's at right now. I'm more confident than I was, less fearful and less apologetic.

In one of the songs we filmed, I sing this. And these days I mean it.

I belong right here, I'm a woman on a mission
I'm not looking for approval
and I don't need your permission.

A few months before, I'd got completely lost in the unfamiliar streets of Edinburgh as I tried to drive my friend Laura home from a Kathryn Joseph gig. We'd come to Summerhall to experience an unusual and beautifully intimate concert in what used to be a dissection room, and we were incredibly close to her as she played. Instead of her usual hilarious between-song indiscretions, she played the full show without saying a single word. It's one of the most extraordinary performances I've ever experienced and I don't think I stopped crying from the first note until the last.

In the car afterwards, Laura pretended not to notice that I was driving the wrong way down a one way street and asked me, "Do you ever sit back and think about how far you've come, how amazingly you've done?"

I don't very often, but I did after the video shoot. It's fun to focus on the most obvious journey, the transformation from deeply depressed in-denial drunk to tattooed transgender rock singer. But I think the more telling journey is the one from being in the closet to playing some very personal songs for the Queer Fringe event. I used to be ashamed of who I was, convinced there was nobody like me. Now, I feel very different. As I sang to the online audience:

We walk with heads held high
We walk with steel in our spines
We leave the pain and hurt behind
We walk with joy and pride.

And I *am* proud. I honestly think that knowing what I know now, if somehow I'd been given the choice of becoming a manly man or becoming the openly trans woman I am now, I'd choose trans again. I still wish I'd been born a cisgender girl, but if that's not on the specials menu then I'll happily skip past "man" and order "trans".

There are plenty of negatives, of course. I wish I'd known who I was decades before, because I've hurt others and been hurt in return. I grieve the adolescence and young adulthood I spent in the wrong gender, the experiences I never got to have, the possibilities I didn't know existed, the painful procedures I now have to undergo to try and undo some of the damage testosterone did to me. There are times I feel so sad I can barely breathe, and the isolation from the return of COVID restrictions in late 2020 brought me to the brink of suicide. I've had to learn a lot of lessons in very hard ways. I've made a huge arse of myself on far too many occasions. And there are whole chapters of my life I dearly wish I could rewrite.

But there are new chapters being written too.

My relationship with my children is more joyous, more emotional and so much funnier than I could ever have hoped, and the fact that I'm trans doesn't faze them in the slightest; the other evening I overheard my eldest telling one of his friends not to worry if they overheard weird noises because "it's just my dad. She's playing a video game." When my youngest told Liz recently that I "wasn't like any of the other dads", the reasons were nothing to do with my gender: he said I "play *a lot* of video games", used bad words and told dad jokes that were much, much worse than any other dads' dad jokes.

Liz is happily married, and she and I are friends.

I have found friends who I love more than I could ever have imagined, and who I know love me.

I have a dog who – and I've checked this – turns out to be not just a good girl, but the very best girl.

And while I didn't like the old me very much, I sometimes think this me is pretty great.

I can't change the past, but I can try to be a better person going forward.

Now that I'm me, I've lost a lot of hang-ups and gained a lot of confidence. I smile more, laugh more, hug more, listen more, cry more, feel more. When I smile in photos, it reaches my eyes. I'm more engaged with the world around me, more sympathetic and empathetic. More sociable. More cheerful. More open. More fun.

It's had an effect on my work and on my creativity too. When I write, I use a wider emotional palette, a more vivid vocabulary. When I make music I'm no longer scared of doing something that people might mock, so I experiment more and take more risks; it's still to an audience of about eight people, but I'm enjoying it so much more. And as I've discovered, stage fright doesn't stand a chance when you've walked down Glasgow's Sauchiehall Street looking like a man in a dress.

Accepting and embracing being trans saved my life and my sanity, and I think it's made me a better human too. I try not to judge people, to make assumptions. My circle of friends is wider, more diverse and more vibrant than ever before. I try to be kinder and more respectful to others, to hope for the best in people rather than fear the worst, to empathise rather than criticise.

Here's what I hope you'll take away from this book.

I want you to see yourself in me. I want you to understand that just like you, trans, non-binary and gender non-conforming people don't want to be *tolerated*. We want to be *celebrated*, defined not by our pain or our struggles but by our love and our laughter.

I want you to see and share our joy.

Because if you do, then the Carries of the future, their families and their friends will understand that being trans offers possibility and pleasure, not pain or punishment.

To help make that happen, we need to hear more voices from across the trans and non-binary community.

In the US, there are more people who claim to have seen a ghost (60%)[1] than know any trans people (11% to 20%). The 60% is from a survey of Fox News viewers. It's 18% for the wider population. The discrepancy makes sense: you're much more likely to be visited by an apparition from beyond the grave than see any positive representation of trans people on a platform Rupert Murdoch controls.

Trans people are in a very similar situation to the one gay, lesbian and bisexual people found themselves in during the 1980s and 1990s. Then, as with trans people now, people didn't think they knew any gay, lesbian or bi people. Then, as now, media contrarians, bigots and hate groups took advantage of that lack of familiarity and painted perfectly nice, ordinary people as monsters. Then, as now, people were dehumanised and demonised to fit a particular political agenda.

But eventually, love wins. As the gay rights movement helped make the world safer for gay and lesbian people, more gay and lesbian people felt safe to come out. That visibility changed everything: it's hard to hate people you know, to believe that your friends and family members are members of a sinister lobby or a terrifying threat, when you know that they're just putting out the bins, worrying about the rent and wondering what's for dinner, just like everybody else.

Chances are you know somebody who's trans or non-binary too, but they might not have come out to you or to anybody else yet. But we were always here, and as more of us become visible, more of us will feel safe to be ourselves. Trans and non-binary people are not a fad or a phase, a lobby or an ideology, a cult or a conspiracy. We're your sons and your daughters, your sisters and your brothers, your friends and your colleagues.

We're technicolour people forced to live in black and white, rainbows told to choose between pink or blue.

Epilogue

It's a Sunday afternoon and I'm visiting Category Is Books, the wonderful LGBT+ bookshop on Glasgow's South side and one of only two LGBT+ bookshops in Scotland. It's one of my very favourite places, run by two of my very favourite people. It's much more than just a great bookshop; it's a hub for the LGBT+ community. I've enjoyed book launches there, taken part in a fanzine launch there and I visit frequently to keep my ever-growing collection of queer-themed pin badges current.

It's the kind of place where you bump into people you know, and my visit was no exception. I was delighted to see a few friends there, so what was supposed to be a five-minute visit turned into an hour of chatting with my friends and other customers. One of them was a young woman who really reminded me of one of my children. She was fiery, funny and fast-talking with that tweenage thing where your brain is moving too fast and your mouth is struggling to keep up with all the things you have to say. Like my kid, she's confident in a way I never was, a firework in human form.

One of the things she talked about was her school. She laughed as she talked about being known as "the gay kid" in her class, something she's visibly proud of. The school has an LGBT Club, where she's made friends with other gay kids (and straight kids who just come along for the chat), and LGBT Champions, of which she's one. She's clearly thriving there, happy in her own skin.

"Your school sounds amazing!" I said. "What one is it you go to?"

"Garnock," she replied.

Garnock was my school too.

My old school is gone, bulldozed and replaced by a shiny new campus on the other side of town. But it's not just the buildings that have gone. The attitudes that kept LGBT+ kids, students and teachers in the closet, that taught us to be ashamed of and to hide who we are, are gone too.

Garnock Academy was where I learned to hate and hide who I was.

Garnock Campus's LGBT+ Club follows me on Twitter.

The kids are all right.

Acknowledgements

My name may be on the cover, but of course any good book is a team effort. And I have the A-Team on my side crafting tanks from toilet rolls, pitying fools and refusing to go on any planes.

Heather McDaid and Laura Jones at 404 Ink are an absolute dream to write for. I've wanted to be with 404 Ink since I read *Nasty Women* way back in 2017, so to be part of the same family as so many incredible writers makes me very happy.

My wise, patient and brilliant editor Kirstyn Smith is the Professor X to my Ex-Man, and without her inspiration, encouragement and threats this book would be twice as long and half as funny.

Thanks to Ludovica Credendino for the title, which is so much better than anything I came up with, and to Wolf for creating such a stunning cover.

I am very grateful for my close family, my music family and my rainbow family: the friends who gave me a safe space when the rest of the world didn't feel safe at all; the colleagues and peers who've been so supportive; and the LGBT+ elders, authors, fellow travellers and allies who have taught me so much, and from whom I still have so much to learn.

I'd particularly like to thank two hilarious, kind and beautiful humans who I absolutely adore. Louise and Laura are the best friends, role models and bad influences anyone could have.

And I'd like to thank Liz. I'm glad we're still friends and wish her all the joy in the world.

And I wish you joy too. Thank you so much for reading.

C x

Endnotes

Sharp dressed man

1. "These are the stories The Sun want you to forget" Jim Felton, *The London Economic*, 21 October 2020. thelondoneconomic.com/news/these-are-the-stories-the-sun-want-you-to-forget-206515/. Accessed 17 May 2022.

2. "'Gay plague': The vile, horrific and inhumane way the media reported the AIDS crisis" Ella Braidwood, *Pink News*, 30 November 2018. pinknews.co.uk/2018/11/30/world-aids-day-1980s-headlines-tabloids/. Accessed 17 May 2022.

3. "British Paper and Science Journal Clash on AIDS", William E. Schmidt, *The New York Times*, 10 December 1993. nytimes.com/1993/12/10/world/british-paper-and-science-journal-clash-on-aids.html. Accessed 17 May 2022.

4. "PIERS MORGAN: Enough! When even world leaders are cowed into supine silence by cancel culture, it's time to stand up to the howling woke mob and tell them we're not playing by their stupid intolerant rules anymore" Piers Morgan, *Daily Mail*, 12 May 2021. dailymail.co.uk/news/article-9570947/PIERS-MORGAN-time-stand-howling-woke-mob.html. Accessed 17 May 2022.

5. "Piers Morgan identifies as penguin and demands to live in aquarium in furious rant" Kyle O'Sullivan, *Mirror*, 11 September 2019. mirror.co.uk/tv/tv-news/piers-morgan-identifies-penguin-demands-20005622. Accessed 17 May 2022.

6. "You may notice a familiar name wrote the story "SCRAP EASTBENDERS" when Eastenders featured their first gay kiss." @JimMFelton. *Twitter*, 24 February 2022, 9:46AM, twitter.com/JimMFelton/status/1231878024406163457. Accessed 17 May 2022.

7. "TEN SHAMEFUL MOMENTS FROM THE SUN'S PAST", *Tabloid Corrections*, 23 November 2017. tabloidcorrections.wordpress.com/2017/11/23/ten-shameful-moments-from-the-suns-past/. Accessed 17 May 2022.

8. "It's getting better" *The Economist*, 3 March 2012. economist.com/node/21548961. Accessed 17 May 2022.

Been caught stealing

1. "Life Story: Marsha P. Johnson (1945-1992)" *Women & The American Story*. wams.nyhistory.org/growth-and-turmoil/growing-tensions/marsha-p-johnson/. Accessed 17 May 2022.

2. "National LGBT Survey: Research report" *gov.uk*, 3 July 2018. gov.uk/government/publications/national-lgbt-survey-summary-report. Accessed 17 May 2022.

Girl afraid

1. "Eddie Izzard to use the pronouns 'she' and 'her'" Lucy Campbell, *The Irish Times*, 22 December 2020. irishtimes.com/culture/stage/eddie-izzard-to-use-the-pronouns-she-and-her-1.4443791. Accessed 17 May 2022.

I've got the power

1. "New report tells us how public actually feel about trans people" Nancy Kelley, *Stonewall*, 11 August 2020. stonewall.org.uk/about-us/news/new-report-tells-us-how-public-actually-feel-about-trans-people. Accessed 17 May 2022.

Cherry Lips

1. "BBC backs non-binary poet facing 'hate from around world'" Marc Horne, *The Times*, 21 February 2020. thetimes.co.uk/article/bbc-backs-queer-poet-facing-hate-from-around-the-world-68tm2vhch. Accessed 17 May 2022.

2. "Whitehawk FC's Sophie Cook: 'I had to change my life or end it'" *The Guardian*, 31 August 2020. theguardian.com/football/2020/aug/31/sophie-cook-whitehawk-fc-transgender-bournemouth. Accessed 17 May 2022.

3. "Dress Like a Woman? What Does That Mean?" *The New York Times*, 3 February 2017. nytimes.com/2017/02/03/style/trump-women-dress-code-white-house.html. Accessed 17 May 2022.

4. "#DressLikeAWoman: Twitter backlash over reports of dress code for Trump staff" Elena Cresci, *The Guardian*, 3 February 2017. theguardian.com/us-news/2017/feb/03/dresslikeawoman-backlash-over-reports-of-dress-code-for-trump-staff. Accessed 17 May 2022.

Love and pride

1. "Five arrested at Pride Glasgow", *The Glasgow Guardian*, 22 August 2017. glasgowguardian.co.uk/2017/08/22/five-arrested-at-pride-glasgow/. Accessed 17 May 2022.

Sexy! No no no

1. "New Research Shows a Vast Majority of Cis People Won't Date Trans People" Zhana Vrangalova, *them*, 20 June 2018. them.us/story/cis-trans-dating. Accessed 17 May 2022.

Flip your wig

1. "Doctor who runs online gender clinic for trans kids 'competent to give treatment', tribunal rules" Maggie Baska, *Pink News*, 26 April 2022. pinknews.co.uk/2022/04/26/doctor-helen-webberley-trans-healthcare-gendergp-tribunal/. Accessed 17 May 2022.

Shake it off

1. "Bono Quotes?" *U2 Interference*, 18 June 2002. u2interference.com/forums/f288/bono-quotes-58474.html. Accessed 17 May 2022.

Call me

1. "Revealed: the transgender email" Sian Griffiths, Josh McStay, *The Times*, 18 March 2018. thetimes.co.uk/article/revealed-the-transgender-email-573sblsnb. Accessed 17 May 2022.

2. "Pronouns are rohypnol: important article by @HairyLeggdHarpy @UGMediaLtd https://uncommongroundmedia.com/banned-from-medium-pronouns-are-rohypnol/ Sure, sometimes preferred pronouns are polite, and we can be polite when we chose. Bu every women has learnt from experience that politeness is exploitable & can put us in danger." @MForstater, *Twitter*, 3 June 2019, 2:35PM. twitter.com/mforstater/status/1135540452499828736?lang=en-GB. Accessed 17 May 2022.

3. "Pronouns are Rohypnol" Fair Play for Women, 4 June 2019. fairplayforwomen.com/pronouns/. Accessed 17 May 2022.

It's just history repeating

1. Christine Burns, *Trans Britain: Our Journey From The Shadows*. Unbound, 2018.

2. "Lesbian Stereotypes" O'Brien, Jodi, ed. *Encyclopedia of gender and society*, Vol. 1, Sage, 2009, p492.

It's different for girls

1. "Transgender Suicide Attempt Rates Are Staggering" Luke Malone, *vocativ*, 5 March 2015. www.vocativ.com/culture/lgbt/transgender-suicide/. Accessed 17 May 2022.;

   "Transgender people face alarmingly high risk of suicide" Laura Ungar, *USAToday*. usatoday.com/story/news/nation/2015/08/16/transgender-individuals-face-high-rates--suicide-attempts/31626633/. Accessed 17 May 2022.

2. "Cultural sexism in the world is very real when you've lived on both sides of the coin" Charlotte Alter, *Time*. time.com/transgender-men-sexism/. Accessed 17 May 2022.

Burn the witch

1. "Katherine Campbell (10/6/1697)" *Survey of Scottish Witchcraft Database*. witches.shca.ed.ac.uk/index.cfm?fuseaction=home.caserecord&caseref=C%2FEGD%2F1778&search_type=searchaccused&search_string=lastname. Accessed 17 May 2022.

2. "Introduction to Scottish witchcraft" *The Survey of Scottish Witchcraft*. shca.ed.ac.uk/Research/witches/introduction.html. Accessed 17 May 2022.

3. "Editorial: Transgender bullying must be tackled" *The Herald*, 30 July 2017. heraldscotland.com/news/15442395.editorial-transgender-bullying-must-tackled/. Accessed 17 May 2022.

4. "Insight: Arguments over gender definition deflect from real issue" *The Scotsman*, 12 March 2017. scotsman.com/news/people/insight-arguments-over-gender-definition-deflect-real-issue-1454199. Accessed 17 May 2022.

5. "SNP plans to allow under 16s to change sex branded '"child abuse"'" *The Scotsman*, 9 November 2017. scotsman.com/news/politics/snp-plans-allow-under-16s-change-sex-branded-child-abuse-1436976. Accessed 17 May 2022.

6. "Christian Right tips to fight transgender rights: separate the T from the LGB" Hélène Barthélemy, *Southern Poverty Law Center*, 23 October 2017. splcenter.org/hatewatch/2017/10/23/christian-right-tips-fight-transgender-rights-separate-t-lgb. Accessed 17 May 2022.

7. "Understanding and Responding to the Transgender Movement" Dale O'Leary, Peter Sprigg, *Family Research Council*, June 2015. frc.org/transgender. Accessed 17 May 2022.

8. "The Christian Right's Love Affair with Anti-Trans Feminists" Cole Parke, *Political Research Associates*, 11 August 2016. politicalresearch.org/2016/08/11/the-christian-rights-love-affair-with-anti-trans-feminists. Accessed 17 May 2022.

9. "Court documents detail how Josh Duggar molestation allegations first came to light" Michelle Mark, *Insider*, 11 February 2022. insider.com/court-documents-detail-how-josh-duggar-molestation-allegations-were-revealed-2022-2. Accessed 17 May 2022.

10. "Josh Duggar Admits Porn Addiction, Being 'Unfaithful' in the Wake of Ashley Madison Data Dump" Michael Rothman, *ABC News*, 20 August 2015. abcnews.go.com/Entertainment/josh-duggar-admits-porn-addiction-unfaithful-wake-ashley/story?id=33210211. Accessed 17 May 2022.

11. "Dress however you please.
    Call yourself whatever you like.
    Sleep with any consenting adult who'll have you.
    Live your best life in peace and security.
    But force women out of their jobs for stating that sex is real?
    #IStandWithMaya #ThisIsNotADrill" @jk_rowling, *Twitter*, 19 December 2019, 12:57PM. twitter.com/jk_rowling/status/1207646162813100033?s=20&t=FK_gddLUU-TaKlcBK0Kd-A. Accessed 17 May 2022.

12. "Is JK Rowling in league with the Devil? A history of Harry Potter-inspired 'satanic panic'" *The Telegraph*, 2 September 2019. telegraph.co.uk/books/news/jk-rowling-league-devil-history-harry-potter-inspired-satanic/. Accessed 17 May 2022.

13. "GOP senator quotes J.K. Rowling while blocking vote on LGBTQ

bill" Tim Fitzsimons, *NBC News*, 19 June 2022. web.archive.org/web/20200619231227/https://www.nbcnews.com/feature/nbc-out/gop-senator-quotes-j-k-rowling-while-blocking-vote-lgbtq-n1231569. Accessed 17 May 2022.

14. "Anti-gender research" *European Parliamentary Forum*. epfweb.org/node/551. Accessed 17 May 2022.

15. "Council Of Europe Criticises UK's Treatment Of Transgender People" Hannah Shewan Stevens, *Each Other*, 29 September 2021. eachother.org.uk/council-of-europe-criticises-uks-treatment-of-transgender-people/. Accessed 17 May 2022.

16. "Who We Are" *Hand Across the Isle*. web.archive.org/web/20171-003085955/https://handsacrosstheaislewomen.com/home/. Accessed 17 May 2022.

17. "Declaration Signatories" *Women's Declaration*. https://www.womens-declaration.com/en/signatures/. Accessed 17 May 2022.

18. "Submission to Women and Equalities Committee on Reform of the Gender Recognition Act", *Women's Human Rights Campaign (WHRC) UK*, 27 November 2020. committees.parliament.uk/writtenevidence/17510/pdf/. Accessed 17 May 2022.

19. "Why we take issue with the Guardian's stance on trans rights in the UK" Sam Levin, Mona Chalabi, Sabrina Siddiqui, *The Guardian*, 2 November 2018. theguardian.com/commentisfree/2018/nov/02/guardian-editorial-response-transgender-rights-uk. Accessed 17 May 2022.

20. "Right-wing media is blaming trans rights and Pride flags for Russia's invasion of Ukraine" Lily Wakefield, *Pink News*, 26 February 2022. pinknews.co.uk/2022/02/26/ukraine-us-trans-rights-pride-tucker-carlson-matt-walsh/. Accessed 17 May 2022.

21. "UK anti-trans campaigner Julie Bindel blames feminists' focus on trans women for Roe v Wade's overturn.
    In the last year she has tweeted TWICE about abortion, one of which was an attack on trans men.
    Here's how many times she's tweeted about trans people: (h/t @MiaGingerich)"
    @AriDrennen, *Twitter*, 5 May 2022, 4:03PM. twitter.com/AriDrennen/status/1522230559270834176. Accessed 17 May 2022.

22. "American feminism has turned its back on women" Hadley Freeman, *UnHerd*, 4 May 2022. unherd.com/2022/05/american-feminism-has-turned-its-back-on-abortion/. Accessed 17 May 2022.

A nice day to start again

1. "Corbett v. Corbett (otherwise Ashley)" pfc.org.uk/caselaw/Corbett%20v%20Corbett.pdf. Accessed 17 May 2022.
2. "Leaked EHRC Guidance Reveals Plans to Exclude Most Trans People From Bathrooms" Ben Hunte, *Vice*, 10 February 2022. vice.com/en/article/3ab5my/leaked-ehrc-guidance-trans-people-gender-recognition-certificates. Accessed 17 May 2022.
3. "The EHRC is becoming a political instrument, former Chair says" *Institute of Employment Rights*, 22 January 2021. ier.org.uk/news/the-ehrc-is-becoming-a-political-instrument-former-chair-says/. Accessed 17 May 2022.

That joke isn't funny anymore

1. "Murdered, Suffocated And Burned Alive – 350 Transgender People Killed In 2020" Jamie Wareham, *Forbes*, 11 November 2020. forbes.com/sites/jamiewareham/2020/11/11/350-transgender-people-have-been-murdered-in-2020-transgender-day-of-remembrance-list/. Accessed 17 May 2022.
2. "Netflix staff protest against 'transphobic' Dave Chappelle show" *BBC News*, 21 October 2021. bbc.co.uk/news/world-us-canada-58990325. Accessed 17 May 2022.

It's the end of the world as we know it

1. "Top 10 Reasons Why The BMI Is Bogus" Keith Devlin, *NPR*, 4 July 2009. npr.org/templates/story/story.php?storyId=106268439. Accessed 17 May 2022.

About the author

Photo: Eoin Carey

CARRIE MARSHALL is a writer, broadcaster and musician from Glasgow. She's the singer in Glaswegian rock band HAVR, a familiar voice on BBC Radio Scotland and has been a regular contributor to all kinds of magazines, newspapers and websites for more than two decades. She has written, ghost-written or co-written more than a dozen non-fiction books, a radio documentary series, and more.